The Caste War of Yucatan

Nelson Reed

The Caste War of Yucatan

Stanford University Press
Stanford, California

Acknowledgments for photographic illustrations:
nos. 2, 3, 4, 12, and 13 courtesy of Antonio
Canto López; no. 5 courtesy of Alfredo Barrera
Vásquez; nos. 6, 9, and 10 courtesy of the
Carnegie Institution of Washington.

Stanford University Press
Stanford, California
© 1964 by the Board of Trustees of the
Leland Stanford Junior University
Printed in the United States of America
Cloth ISBN 0-8047-0164-4
Paper ISBN 0-8047-0165-2
Original edition 1964
Last figure below indicates year of this printing:
80   79   78   77   76

To Juliette

Foreword

THE WAR OF THE CASTES in Yucatan is one of the least known but most colorful episodes in Mexican history. Indeed, if told offhand that as recently as 1848 the descendants of the ancient Maya, after centuries of subjugation, fought their way across the peninsula of Yucatan and came within a hair's breadth of driving their white masters into the sea, one might suspect a literary hoax. But this is what happened. The military campaigns of the Caste War subsided after seven years, but not because the rebel Maya had been decisively conquered. Yucatecan patriots, Mexican generals, and even American mercenaries, facing what we now call guerrilla tactics, simply gave up hope of winning a total victory. Despite huge losses in action, recurrent famine, and the ravages of cholera, the rebels held control of the jungles of eastern Yucatan for the rest of the century. Occasional raids brought them food, guns, alcohol, and prisoners—white men and women who ended their days as slaves in Maya villages. And, beginning with the cult of the Speaking Cross, which sprang up in the darkest days of the war, the Maya developed their own society, a new synthesis of the Spanish colonial and ancient Maya cultures.

Mr. Reed is not a professional historian, and he might have used this sort of material to write either a narrow military history or a swashbuckling historical novel. Fortunately, his ambitions lay elsewhere. He has put the complicated details of the war into coherent order; he has used contemporary newspapers, letters, and memoirs to make men and events come alive; and he has placed the war and its repercussions in the context of the whole history of Yucatan in the nineteenth century.

For scholars, the main contribution of this book lies in the information it presents on the existence of various independent Maya states after 1855, and on what a contemporary source called "the mummeries of the Talking Cross." Until now, very little has been written on these matters, chiefly because contemporary Yucatecans, their pride hurt by the success of the rebels, ignored them as best they could. Mr. Reed's quest for information thus led him to unexploited British, German, and Yucatecan sources, and finally into the jungles of Quintana Roo, where he talked with Indians whose grandfathers fought in the Caste War. Few of our historians of Mexico, including the Mexican ones, have been willing to stray on a mule that far from the comforts of archives and libraries.

Perhaps a word about annotation will forestall unwarranted suspicions among professional historians. When I first saw the manuscript, it was devoid of all scholarly apparatus, and no source citations were appended to it. Mr. Reed, acting on outside advice, eventually supplied me with a bibliography and a considerable number of source notes. But having checked my own sources at some length, I was already convinced of the accuracy of his work, and his efforts only strengthened my conviction. Thus I found myself in an odd position; I had to tell him that the source citations, at least, seemed undesirable and should be abandoned. Scholars, I said, would be able to see that he had followed the ground rules of their craft, and many of them might find the annotation an annoying and unnecessary display of technique; and general readers and scholars alike would doubtless find copious footnotes an annoying drag on the brisk pace of his narrative. This, I soon learned, had been his own feeling from the beginning, and I am certain that he accepted my recommendation with a certain satisfying sense of irony.

And so, after many months of systematic harassment from his friendly critics and editors, Mr. Reed has at last been allowed to write the kind of book he wanted to write—which is a privilege more rare than might be supposed. For my part, I think he has earned it, and I am happy to have had a share in arranging the publication of his work. I am also pleased that I can put aside my old notion of writing a comprehensive history of the Caste War. Mr. Reed has written that book for me, and he has done it very well indeed.

HOWARD F. CLINE

Library of Congress
November 1963

Preface

THE IDEA OF THIS BOOK first came to me when I visited Bacalar in 1948. Knowing nothing about the place, I was surprised to find the overgrown ruins of a Spanish colonial town, including a church and a moated fortress picturesquely situated on a hill above a lake. A few people lived there, and a missionary priest had partially repaired the church, but street after street of roofless stone buildings stood as evidence of its past. In answer to my questions, I was told that the place had been destroyed by Indians in something called the War of the Castes.

On returning home from that trip, I looked into the literature on the subject, particularly Alfonso Villa's *The Maya of East Central Quintana Roo*; I was fascinated with his sketch of how the Maya Indians had revolted against their masters, almost taken the peninsula of Yucatan, and then withdrawn to the deep forests of Quintana Roo to establish an independent society and to worship a "Speaking Cross." Included in Villa's work was Howard F. Cline's "Remarks on a Selected Bibliography of the Caste War and Allied Topics," a blueprint of a book begging to be written. My studies had been in archeology rather than anthropology or history, and I thought in passing that Cline would probably publish the results of his research. Years passed, and from time to time the Caste War came up in my reading, and each time the thought of Cline's bibliography was at the back of my mind. Then I read Serapio Baqueiro's *Ensayo histórico sobre las revoluciones de Yucatán*, which gave further details on the early years of the revolt, and I was caught: I decided that if no one else was going to write the book Cline had outlined, I would have to do it myself.

Then came a year of tracking down Cline's sources, finding the work which has come out since his, searching through libraries and archives in Mérida, and going through the government archives in British Honduras. I had traveled through much of the area before, but now I made specific trips, returning to Bacalar, to the east coast of Quintana Roo, into the forest, and finally to the former shrine-capital of the Maya, Chan Santa Cruz. It was an enjoyable time, with all the pleasures of research: finding the detail that corrects a misunderstood situation, discovering the fact that lights up a particularly dark corner of history.

There should be enough battles in this book for anyone's taste, but the reader must be warned that the shooting doesn't start until Chapter Three. Without intending to write a history of Yucatan or a cultural study of the Maya, I felt that some background information on these subjects was necessary to an understanding of the Caste War, and I have tried to give the essentials in the first two chapters. I have also included, in the later chapters, a certain amount of political and economic history, to explain or give perspective to post–Caste War developments among the Maya.

My sincere thanks go out to Howard F. Cline, for his many suggestions and recommendations; to J. G. Bell, for his warm support in the face of considerable odds; and to Gene Tanke, for his most intelligent assistance in the editing of the manuscript.

NELSON REED

St. Louis, Missouri
November 1963

Contents

Line Illustrations

Eight pages of photographic illustrations
follow page 244

Part One

The Two Worlds of Yucatan

One

The Ladino World

THE DEATH AND DEPOSIT at the bottom of a warm, shallow sea of billions of Tertiary and Holocene creatures; their formation into one great limestone bed; the eventual rising of that mass above water to become the peninsula of Yucatan—these remote events helped to shape the troubles of 1847.

Despite a heavy annual rainfall, water was a major problem for the inhabitants of Yucatan. Rainwater seeped through fifty to one hundred feet of limestone down to the water table, where it was carried off by an underground drainage system, then beyond the reach of man. A dependable supply of water could be found only in caves, or where erosion had broken the limestone down to the water table, or where the roof of a cave had collapsed to form a *cenote*, or open sinkhole.* Water could also be found in a very few rivers and lakes, in swampy low places called *aguadas*, and—such was the need—even in small hollows of rock after a rain. But these sources failed in the dry season, and then, to live, the people had to cluster around the cenotes. Whoever controlled the water controlled the country.

Geology enforced other limitations. It was impossible to plow in soil that was never more than a few inches deep, and this prevented the planting of wheat and other crops that had to be sown on well-cultivated earth. The only practical tool under such conditions was the planting stick, and the only successful plants were those that gave

---

* Common nouns in Spanish or Maya are italicized only at their first occurrence; these and many proper nouns are listed in the Glossary, pp. 283–86.

a large yield to the individual seed, such as corn, beans, and squash. Because the soil was thin, it was quickly exhausted; every third year the farmer was forced to seek new land. To be near his corn patch, he lived in hamlets and villages rather than in cities, and this isolated settlement pattern encouraged in him considerable independence and resistance to change.

The natural vegetation that could survive on this rocky foundation varied with the rainfall. Both rain and vegetation were lightest in the northwest corner of the peninsula, and there the dry bush was seldom over thirty feet tall. Then, spreading in rough arcs toward the east coast and the south, the dry bush gave way to dry forest and then to a dense rain forest, where immense mahogany, sapodilla, and ceiba trees, jammed together and festooned with lianas and parasitic air plants, reached over a hundred feet high in search of the sun. This forest ran in a belt some forty miles wide along the east coast, cut across the base of the peninsula, and then merged with the vast, continuous wilderness of the Petén. The monotonously flat plain of northern Yucatan was broken by a range of hills, the Puuc, which was not over three hundred feet high but impressive by contrast. The hills lay in an inverted V, with one arm on the Gulf of Mexico at Champoton, the northern point at the town of Maxcanu, and the other arm ending near the Bay of Chetumal. Their elevation made water difficult to reach; their valleys, particularly in the southeast, formed swamps and shallow lakes.

For these reasons, the bulk of the population clustered in the relatively more favored northwest. The eastern forest and the land south of the Puuc was almost completely uninhabited; there were no roads to neighboring countries, and the island quality of this near-island was strongly accented. The disaster that was to threaten Yucatan in 1847 would have to be met initially with resources from within this isolated state.

Yucatan was conquered by the Spanish in 1546, after nineteen years of struggle. Then came a series of revolts, quickly and brutally suppressed; starvation, caused by the dislocations of war; and plague, spread by new germs attacking the unprotected blood of the native Maya Indian. Finally, a numb peace came to the sadly diminished land. Even this was disturbed as foreign priests hunted among the ruins, sniffing after brimstone and the old gods, whipping heresy from the survivors. Time solved that problem — time, Franciscan schools, a growing Spanish tolerance, and partial acceptance by the Maya of an obviously successful God. The foreign invaders replaced the shattered class of native nobles and priests, organized the country on European lines, and adapted to local conditions. This state of affairs lasted for over three centuries, and by the time Europe had moved through the Renaissance and the Enlightenment into industrial society, Yucatan was a social fossil.

But the colonial sleep was a time to recover strength. Fewer than 300,000 Mayas survived the Spanish conquest, and this number was more than cut in half by 1700—some indication of the power of smallpox and social disorganization. With peace and readjustment, however, the population of Yucatan began to climb with slowly accelerating force. From 130,000, the count of Mayas, Mestizos, and Spaniards rose to 358,000 in 1800 and to 580,000 in 1845. More people meant the need for more food, and thus a struggle for land began. The Maya saw new villages spring up to share his forest, watched the white man's ranchos and haciendas crowd around him, and he worried. To the shopkeeper, more people meant a larger market, and a merchant class began to develop. The politician found more scope for his activities, more rewards for office, and office became a prize to fight over. A look at the population figures and some simple multiplication suggested that Yucatan would soon have a population of several millions, and provincial *Ladinos* began to toy with thoughts of independence.*

To the uneducated Maya and his half-educated master, life was still a series of cycles: one was born, one died, and on earth nothing changed, or could change. Social structure, agricultural methods, religion—none of these could be altered, for Providence guided the world. To the farmer, a lost crop meant that a personal God (or gods) was angry with him and that only prayer could bring food to his hungry family. There was nothing a reformer could do with people who believed that all debts would be squared in heaven, that the whipped serf would ascend to Glory while his master would pay

---

* *Ladinos* were all those of Spanish or half-Spanish descent who considered themselves "white" and lived, dressed, and thought according to a European heritage; they lived apart from the native Maya, or *Indios*.

below. The ambitious found their outlets in the Church, social position, political office, and scholarship, all of them accepting the changeless state of the world.

Nevertheless, the European ideas of reason, the perfectibility of man, and human progress—applied by English colonists to their business problems in the New World, accelerating as they recrossed the ocean to level the Bastille, and carried by an army of citizens across the face of Europe—reached distant Yucatan in faint and ebbing waves. In Campeche, a French monk talked of the Encyclopedists; a priest questioned dogma at the Seminary of San Ildefonso in Mérida; his students, absorbing his doubts, formed discussion groups, read forbidden books, and dreamed of a truly new world. And if those young colonial aristocrats worried about the extension of their new-found ideas to Yucatan, and wondered whether liberty must mean equality even for the Indios, they could find reassurance in the careers of Patrick Henry and Thomas Jefferson, gentleman patriots of the new school who were also slave owners.

A second wave of ideas, and a stronger one, also crossed the Atlantic. Spain, briefly free of both Napoleon and Ferdinand VII, formed a congress that passed revolutionary laws for Spain and her empire: freedom of the press, local elections, no forced labor, no tribute to the Crown, no Church tax; and with each decree came a mighty howl from the threatened vested interests. In Yucatan, the Maya paid the royal tribute and the Church tax, together with the heavy cost of collection; and from pulpit and collector's office came the warning that the natives wouldn't work unless forced to, and that unless they were forced, the provincial economy would collapse. Their concern was premature. Napoleon fell, Ferdinand returned, and the laws were vetoed; and as the King's portrait was carried in solemn procession by local aristocracy to the Mérida cathedral, the more prominent liberals found themselves on their way to San Juan Ulúa, a fortress prison off Veracruz, and liberal churchmen were driven from classrooms to restricted lives in monastic cells. All over Mexico, conservatives consolidated their position; after crushing Hidalgo's social revolution, they turned and won their own reactionary independence from Spain in 1821. The Spanish governor of Yucatan resigned without a fight, and in spite of a separatist tradition, the peninsula joined the Mexican Union.

For liberals of the Independence generation the struggle was against the Church and the Crown, against the Middle Ages. Spain had suppressed Yucatan's monasteries, thirty of them in the last year of its rule, and this suppression was allowed to stand by the new ruling class, which had inherited the extensive monastic fields. The two hundred monks were secularized. The local Church never recovered from this blow, and from that time on had only a small role in Yucatecan politics. Aristocracy was virtually voted out of existence with abolition of the *fuero militar*, a status giving special privileges and immunities and the obligation to fight the King's enemies—almost the New World equivalent of the knight. The enemies were few, for the title had never meant more than prestige, and most of its thousand-odd inheritors were interested in a very different future. Enthusiasts erected scaffolding to chisel away the Royal coat of arms that decorated the cathedral façade and even mutilated the *escudos* of their own homes. Another ancient custom, the entail of land, ended for the Casa Montejo, home of the conquistador of Yucatan and the most important private residence in the state; for the first time in its 283 years, after sixteen generations, it was sold. To the traditional gentleman, nothing could be more important than his coat of arms, and nothing lower than trade; yet the aristocratic homes around the plazas of Mérida and Campeche began to be altered to accommodate shops, offices, and *cantinas*. The commercial age was on with legal recognition of the corporation, which was first used for a *henequen* plantation, and then for a coach line, a paper mill, a gunpowder factory, and a cotton mill. The sons of the patriots of 1821 accepted their fathers' victories over the past and made their own revolution, the creation of a mercantile society.

There was a feeling of excitement in this second generation, a belief the Yucatan had a brilliant future. And yet in fact they had little to work with. Under the rigid control of Spain, the peninsula had exported small amounts of hides, beef, and tallow to Havana; some beeswax, woven cotton, salt, and handicrafts to Mexico; and dyewood to Europe. With the loss of Spanish protection, Argentine cattle supplied the Cuban market; beeswax and woven cotton, which had come from the tribute of the Maya, failed when the tribute was suppressed. Dyewood, cut mainly in the south along the waterways that fed the Laguna de Términos, was collected at the port of Isla

Carmen and shipped to Europe. While dyewood was by far the most valuable export, the industry was on the decline: competition from Belize had driven prices down, wasteful cutting had ruined the best stands of timber, and labor was hard to get.

With the traditional money crops failing, Yucatecans were forced to experiment. Henequen, a special type of cactus raised for the fiber taken from its leaves, had always been grown in a small way by the Maya, and was developed as a source for rope that could be sold to the Spanish merchant marine. An overseas market was gradually developed, and in 1833 the first commercial plantation was founded; its eighty acres of land were cleared and laid out with row on row of henequen plants, in contrast to the traditional small clusters in gardens and orchards. Incorporation was necessary for this project, because it took eight years for the plant to mature for harvest and few men could afford the cost of development. The experiment was a success, and the *hacendados* (landowners) gradually began converting their rural estates to the new crop. This was done slowly, without displacing the customary raising of corn and cattle, so there was little dislocation or change for the Maya workers. By 1846 the crop stood second in value of export, employed more labor than any other industry, had created a need for seven separating mills in Mérida, and was still growing fast. The port of Sisal, which for the rest of the world became the name of this green gold, was developed primarily to handle overseas shipment of the fiber.

Sugar cane had a very different history. Introduced and grown from early colonial times, it had been consistently banned by the Crown, which wanted neither alcoholic peons nor competition for Spanish wines. Independence ended the ban, and with encouragement from the state government, plantations were started in 1823. Although it required much better soil than henequen, sugar cane was a far more lucrative investment; the harvest of the second year usually paid all costs, and profits after that often ran to 700 per cent annually.

With these developments the forest became important to the enterprising Ladinos. To a government run by merchants, land was Yucatan's most available asset. Except for the small amount owned by hacendados or by villagers, all land had formerly been part of the *monte del Rey*, the King's forest. Under the Republic it was called *terreno baldío*, or uncultivated land. As monte del Rey it had belonged to all—which meant both the cattle-raising hacendados, who paid a token grazing fee, and the native Maya, who raised corn unmolested by theories of property rights. As terreno baldío it was public land that should be cultivated and could be sold. This was against the interests of the Maya and the older class of hacendados, who had never bothered to purchase more than the grounds that their buildings actually stood on; but neither group could resist the pressures of the new age and the sevenfold profit of sugar cane. State land became the major asset of a continually bankrupt state treasury. Nothing was simpler than to escape impossible debts by dispensing grants of land valued at a very low price; and if the creditor had no choice in the matter, it now became his concern to develop the land to recover his money. Frontier land was later to become the only reward that could attract recruits for the various revolutions.

The Indio had little experience with the individual ownership of land. He was accustomed to hold it communally by lineage or by village, with each member free to use what he needed, to own the planted crop and the harvest but not the land. This had been legally recognized by the Crown in a type of village holding called *ejido*. To the Ladino legislator, however, the ejido was as much a product of the past as the fuero militar, and he did all he could to convert common lands into private property. Various laws limited and attacked the ejido. The burden of proving the ownership of land was placed on the villager rather than on the Ladino buyer. Carrying this principle further was a decree that the presence of small settlements need not prevent the sale of land. Private rental was allowed within the ejido, which was in effect private rental of common ground. As a final blow, in 1845 the Indios were forced to pay taxes to cultivate their own land. Reaction to this measure was so strong that it was quickly repealed.

Throughout the 1830's the all-important water rights had been protected. But in 1841 this protection was removed, and a cenote that had served an area from time immemorial suddenly became private property to be exploited for private gain. The digging of wells, the construction of rain-catching water tanks, or the restora-

tion of ancient tanks abandoned since the Conquest were more creative ways of developing the arid forest, but the seizure of land
involved stirred up bitter feelings.

Because of the population increase, new and larger Indio villages
joined in the competition for water. Between the hacendados and
the expanded villages, all terrenos baldíos of the settled areas were
claimed, and a migration began into the sparsely populated forest
of the south and the east, a migration by men of both color. New
names appeared on the map, strange names for that country: Dzitnup,
Put, and Cholul became Barbachano, Moreno, and Libre Unión;
Nojacab, Dzibinocao, and Kokobchen became Progreso, Iturbide,
and Závala. Once only the names Mérida and Valladolid had recalled Spain, and they were used only by those who spoke Spanish.
Iturbide rose from an Indian hamlet to a bustling village in a few
years; John Stephens, an American traveler and author who visited
there in 1843, was told that since the land had belonged only to the
natives, it had been considered free to all comers. The villages of Hopolchen, Bolonchenticul, Tihosuco, and Peto all grew to have popula-
tions of around five thousand; the frontier grew from 120,000 to 200,-
000, and climbed from one-fifth to one-third of the state's population.

More than land was needed for the sugar plantations. Harvest
time put the planters "at the mercy of an irresponsible population."
Unfortunately, according to white belief, the Indio was lazy. In six
months he was able to raise the necessary thirty bushels of corn for
himself and his family, and thirty more to trade for salt, cotton, and
gunpowder; and with this he was content. Clearly, this was an attitude that stood in the way of progress; someone had to give the extra
sweat needed to raise Yucatan to the level of the other nations of the
world, and it was obviously not going to be the Creoles. Besides,
they were the planners.

And so they planned. In the more settled areas around Mérida
where henequen plantations were being developed, there were
established practices to fall back upon. These ancient colonial
haciendas had been served by a class of natives who were serfs in
the true sense of the word: they came with the property, whether
inherited or through purchase, and couldn't leave or marry without
the master's consent. In the days of subsistence farming, this Indio's

duties hadn't been heavy—tending an extra cornfield for his Señor, putting in an occasional day's work around the big house. He was called a *lunero* because usually he owed a day's work every Monday (*lunes*).

At the time of Independence, the Maya were declared free along with all other citizens, but it was intended that "the custom of the land"—the relationship between master and servant—would be maintained. Custom is hard to change, particularly when it is comfortable for those in charge. It was then said that the natives worked for the hacendado in exchange for the personal use they made of his land and his water. But old customs didn't satisfy the new requirements. Borrowing from the logwood contractors, the sugar and henequen planters organized a self-perpetuating system of debt peonage. Workers were given advances on their wages in the form of *aguardiente* (usually rum), corn seed, or a cheap shotgun, and the advance would be entered in a book as the *chichan cuenta* (the little bill, in a Maya-Spanish corruption). The amount being small, the native would forget it, thinking that one day he would perhaps repay it. He could never repay. If he thought of leaving his master, he was faced with the *nohoch cuenta* (the big bill), and would find that the sum of many small loans was hopelessly beyond his reach. Not only was juggling the accounts common; many hacendados kept no books at all. No native could be hired without a release from his former master or without his debt being assumed by his new employer; a native without a release paper was fined as a vagrant, and the fine would be sold to a labor-short planter. It was a tidy system.

Nor were villagers who avoided the apparently generous "gifts" and loans exempt from exploitation. As citizens, they were liable to taxes assessed by the *jefe político,* a white local official of the hacendado class; failure to pay meant debt servitude. Orphans were considered the state's responsibility, but prey would be a better word: they were collected by the local authorities—even when they had uncles, older brothers, or other close relatives able to support them— and sold for twenty-five pesos to townsmen or hacendados as servants. Any property of a deceased villager was attachable for debt, which reduced his survivors to a compliant attitude about accepting loans; and the debt itself was legally inherited by the sons. And if all else failed, there were the famines, conveniently spaced every few years, when at the expense of a little surplus corn a lifetime servant could be bought.

Thus white-written and white-administered laws guaranteed that the expanding sugar and henequen fields would not be "at the mercy of an irresponsible population." These lawmakers were liberal democrats. As they gradually tightened their economic grip on the Indio, they gave him the vote, and saw no contradiction. The theory behind the land and debt laws was that the Maya must become participating citizens of the state. It was a conscious plan to destroy the old ways of the self-sustaining villages and replace them with the rules of economic cooperation and progress. When philosophy and greed combine, their strength is hard to contest.*

The importance of cash crop farming must not be overestimated. Ninety-five per cent of the laboring force was still engaged in corn farming, but the new industries affected many aspects of Yucatecan life. Transportation now became important, and most of the roads in existence by 1847 had been built since the time of Independence. Wagons could haul goods more economically than pack animals, so the sugar planter demanded wagon roads. The construction was accomplished by drawing on an ancient custom called *fagina*, which obliged every citizen to work from four to six days each year on some public project or pay the equivalent in money; the money payment of one *real* (twelve and a half cents) per day was so small that only the brown citizens were forced to give actual labor. Personal travel was encouraged by these roads; a scheduled stage line was organized between Mérida, Sisal, and Campeche, and two-wheeled carts carried passengers through the back country. Travel helped break up the isolated groups of the past, the *patrias chicas* (little homelands), the local districts and neighborhoods that claimed a man's first and

* The new work contracts did give the Maya laborer some protection; they guaranteed minimal food and clothing, medical care and burial expenses, and forbade the separation of families by work assignments. But the wages were low, even by nineteenth-century standards. A worker could make from 12 to 36 pesos a year as compared to 600 for a teacher and 1,200 for a jefe político; the Bishop received a base salary of 8,000 pesos annually, and priests were known to have collected as much as 14,000 in parish fees. At this time, ninety pounds of corn or a Maya woman's dress cost about half a peso.

View of the Plaza de Armas, Mérida

strongest loyalties. When travel had been difficult and uncertain, people had stayed home. Before there was a market for surplus goods, they had limited themselves to subsistence farming. Villagers in the neighborhood of Tekax considered that place their capital and never went to Mérida or Campeche, and the same had been true of a dozen sleepy back-country towns.

In the Yucatan of 1847, there were four definable areas—four patrias chicas—with distinct economic, political, and social problems. They were Mérida and the northwest, Campeche and the south, the frontier, and Valladolid.

Mérida was the center of the Yucatecan Ladino world. It had been the residence of the Captain General under the Crown, the seat of the Governor during the union with Mexico, and later the capital of the independent state—the home of the legislature, the high courts, and the ruling Bishop. The center of Mérida was the Plaza de Armas. This square—vast and undeveloped, dusty in dry times, muddy in the rain, glaring white beneath a tropical sun—was crowded with herds of mules, wagons and carts, and trade goods during the busy hours. It was surrounded by the most important buildings in the city. To the east stood the cathedral of San Ildefonso, completed in 1571, with its flat, plain façade, two faintly dissimilar towers, bells so long cracked and out of pitch that only strangers noticed, and an interior claimed to be the finest in Central America. Adjoining it to the south was the Bishop's Palace, a bare two-story building marked by a wooden cross that stood before a door large enough to admit carriages to the central courtyard. The Palacio Municipal, of Moorish style and topped with a clock tower, was to the west; and the Governor's Palace was part of the long arcaded block that ran along the northern side of the plaza.

These arcades or galleries, an architectural feature inherited through Spain from the Grecian *stoa*, bordered the plaza of every Yucatecan town that aspired to urban civilization. Although Mérida's principal market was elsewhere, vendors set up their stands and in the cool shade of those arches laid out mats displaying their wares: pumpkin seeds and tamales for the hungry; sashes, scarves, coral necklaces, and cheap hand mirrors for the vain; and for the lucky, the cry "para hoy, para hoy" and a ticket that could bring riches in the daily lottery. Behind the arcade were rows of more formal shops, plus the barber shop, the billiard hall, the cantina, and the card room. A crowd of dark-eyed Indian boys waited for those who wore boots and might need them polished one more time, while their fathers looked for the odd job or begged. Here a man could meet his friends, arrange a business deal, smile at the latest scandal or at a pretty half-caste, complain about the government, or simply watch the people and the hours go by. The galleries were the living heart of Mérida.

Facing on the plaza and scattered throughout the nearby streets were the homes of the *gente decente*—the "decent people," the leaders of provincial society. These houses were much alike from the outside. Their ornamentation was limited to carved details around the huge doors and the tall projecting windows; the walls were thick, the ceilings high, the windows shuttered against the heat; family life turned in toward the patio and garden. Undoubtedly the finest of these houses was the Casa Montejo, built by the conquistador and Yucatan's first provincial governor, Francisco de Montejo, and owned in 1847 by the wealthy Peón family. Its doorway was flanked by carved panels. Corinthian columns, together with a male caryatid said to represent the architect, supported a *putti*-encrusted balcony. Above, on either side of the Montejo crest, were two armored pikemen standing in Gothic pride with each foot on a wailing Indio.

Mérida was a city of light, of open sky, of white stone buildings, flat roofs, and square blocks. Breaking the skyline were thirteen churches, two monasteries, and the largest building after the cathedral, the fortress of San Benito. San Benito had five bastions and walls forty feet high and eight feet thick, walls raised on the foundation of what had been the major temple pyramid of the ancient Maya city of T-ho. The fortress, the object of the many coups d'état staged in the city, lay four blocks east of the plaza. Beyond the center of the city, the domain of the Creole aristocracy, the houses became less pretentious: first they lost the decorative touches that gave charm to blank walls, and as one walked farther, flat beam and lime cement roof construction gave way to the thatch roof of the indigenous *choza* —a rectangular hut with rounded corners and walls of stone or wattle, the most common form of dwelling in the peninsula.

There were over 48,000 people living in Mérida in 1847. The city dominated the old colonial country of the northwest, including the towns of Maxcanu, Ticul, Sotuta, Izamal, and Motul. At the beginning of the century, half of the state's population lived in this area; by mid-century, it was closer to one-third, and Mérida's traditional position of authority was threatened. Her trade via Sisal was primarily with Cuba and the United States, while Campeche's business was with Mexico. This would cause trouble when the state was faced with war and blockade and by a choice of enemies. Merchants in the capital felt one way about taxes and import-export duties on rum; sugar planters felt quite another way. Liberals in Mérida could write laws for the protection of the Indios, but these would be ignored by hacendados on the frontier. The day had passed when the rest of Yucatan would patiently accept instructions and commands from Mérida.

Campeche, the second city of the peninsula and the only port until the development of Sisal, was in a slow decline. It was famous for its walls, which had been built against the pirate attacks of an earlier time and which proved of value in the recurring civil wars; the walls had never been carried by storm and earned for the city the title "New Troy." The slim-towered cathedral of the Immaculate Conception, ornately worked in the baroque style, its stone walls turned to an ochre tint by time and the sea wind, was considered the handsomest church in Yucatan. It stood on the north side of the main plaza, while to the west were the palaces of the government and municipality and the custom house—all with arcaded galleries on two levels and backed up against the sea wall.

Campeche had a population of twenty-one thousand, many churches and monasteries, a poorhouse, a hospital, a Naval School, and a theater. Its streets were narrow and cramped within the walls; a smell of fish and of the sea hung in the sultry air; vultures grew fat on the fishermen's leavings along the rocky beach, and there were mosquitoes. The suburbs were more attractive, with orchards and gardens and palms, but they were for the inferior classes. A wharf projected 140 yards out into the Bay of Campeche, which was of little use to ships of any size because it stood dry at low tide and gave no protection when the wind was from the north or northwest. Campeche was inhabited by a restless, vital people, active in politics and trade; as the traditional port of entry, it had a higher percentage of white citizens than any other city in the state.

To the decline of Campeche's income from logwood was added the collapse of her shipyards and merchant marine. The special rebates on duties that had existed under the Crown to assist Yucatan and protect Mexican shipping were lost in the years following Independence, and this was a heavy blow to the port city: whereas more than two thousand of her citizens had been sailors or shipwrights in 1811, only 470 were thus employed in 1845. The increased duties stimulated smuggling, particularly of English goods through Bacalar, and contraband quickly exceeded the value of legal imports.*

Sisal was developed in 1811 as a port for Mérida and quickly grew into a serious competitor for Campeche, for it had the advantage of being closer to the most densely inhabited area of the state

---

* In 1841 the English ship *True Blue* was seized unloading contraband on the north coast of Yucatan. Several days later an English corvette dropped anchor off Sisal and demanded the value of the ship and its cargo under threat of bombardment. The Yucatecan authorities paid, thus setting a precedent for English smugglers.

View of the waterfront at Campeche

and was served by a better network of roads. Neither location had
much to recommend it as as a port; tenders were necessary for ocean-
going ships and there was no protection against the dreaded *norte,*
the seasonal windstorm from the north. But the need was there,
and by 1845 Sisal was shipping cargoes worth twice those shipped
by Campeche and absorbing the market of the northwest. Sisal never
grew beyond one long street crowded with wagons, oxen, mules,
whorehouses, and cantinas, and ending at the wharf and customs
house, with a little fort for protection—all of this built on a sand bar
and surrounded by marshes. The profits made in Sisal were controlled and collected in Mérida, and the struggle between Mérida
and Campeche was eventually to grow from arguments in the counting houses into civil war.

The frontier, which spread in a radius averaging 80 miles from
Mérida, could be divided into three main sectors: the dry Chenes
country; the area along and to the south of the *camino real* that ran
through Tekax and Peto to Tihosuco and the district of Tizimin.
Two other pockets of civilization were important for the frontier.
One, isolated in the middle of the frontier, was Valladolid, long settled and with a very different outlook; the other was Bacalar, which
could be reached from the civilized parts of Yucatan only by a six-
to eight-day journey on a pack trail through the uninhabited forest
from the Peto road.

Bacalar stood on the west shore of the river-like lake of the same
name, opposite the mouth of a small stream, the Chaak, which led to

the Rio Hondo and thence to the Caribbean sea. It had been built as an outpost against the English at Belize and it had a moated stone fortress called San Felipe. Queen Elizabeth, good Protestant and businesswoman that she was, had seen no reason to condone the gift of half the world by the Roman Bishop to the King of Spain, and had felt that unoccupied territory in the New World was free to all comers. In the fifty years following her reign, English settlements were made at Carmen, in the Laguna de Términos, along the Honduras coast, and in the bay area known as Belize.* Of these, only Belize survived the continuous hostile efforts of the Spanish; it was relatively isolated on a difficult lee coast, and fortunes could be made there in dyewood. These early Englishmen had been part-time buccaneers, or irregular members of the British Navy, depending upon whose view one took (and the Spaniards and later Yucatecans took the darker one, long after the reality had passed). There were never very many of them— about a thousand whites with five thousand Negro slaves and free Mulattoes, plus a scattering of Carib Indians. Forbidden by a compromise treaty between England and Spain to raise more than subsistence crops, they followed the jungle rivers searching for good stands of dyewood, and, later, mahogany. By 1847, the ancient antagonism with Bacalar had settled down to a peaceful distrust, and Bacalar, with a population of 5,000, took on new importance as a receiving center for the English trade goods, mostly contraband, that flooded Yucatan.

The frontier was considered Yucatan's hope for the future. In thirty years its population had grown from a fifth to a third of the state's total; it raised two-thirds of the corn crop and over ninety per cent of the sugar. All along the frontier new towns were springing up, and old ones were booming. There were a number of market towns for the area: Tekax, Peto, Tihosuco, Bacalar, and Tizimin, each with a normal population of about four or five thousand. While the white settlers in these towns had similar goals—free land, debtor's

---

* There were pirate bases at Cozumel and Rio Lagartos in 1599, a colony on the Bay Islands in 1642, and settlements at Belize and on the Mosquito Coast by 1662. There are still international disputes over the ownership of Belize and British Honduras.

laws, and low taxes on sugar—they were too isolated from each other to make common cause. They also lacked the rigid class structure of the more settled areas, mixing more easily with the Indios, but this did not prevent their ambitions from bringing them into direct conflict with the other race.

The one pocket of resistance to the frontier movement and point of view was Valladolid. Its citizens, thinking too much on their past, considered themselves the elite of the state. They called their city "The Sultaness of the East," and on the principal streets were mansions with Castilian coats of arms above their doorways, most of them roofless and abandoned. In this city of the Hidalgo (from *hijo de algo*, the son of someone important), the citizens were preoccupied with racial purity and excluded not only the Indio but the Mestizo from the center of town and from positions of authority. These gentlemen still looked down upon work, except the gentleman's occupation of cattle-raising, as socially degrading, and so sugar plantations weren't developed near the city. The camino real to Mérida was little used, and the products of neighboring Espita and Tizimin were shipped out by sea or hauled west on a branch road. There was no school, no doctor, no druggist, no cobbler, nor any builder in stone in this city of fifteen thousand. Yet they had seen what progress could mean: outside interests had established a steam-driven cotton mill there, possibly the first in all of Mexico, with looms, a steam engine, and even engineers from the United States. The mill employed 117 workers, produced 400 yards of cloth daily, and created a market for the local cotton planters, yet it was allowed to fail on the death of its founder.

As Yucatan moved away from its colonial traditions, the Creole leaders of Valladolid found themselves more and more out of step. Their social privileges were questioned by the other classes; and the Mestizo, aware of the advancement of his group in other parts, became particularly rebellious. In response, the social privileges were more rigidly enforced. While sugar cultivation by-passed the city to the north and the south, some of this new drive was reflected in the Valladolid area by the extension of cattle ranches onto land bought or expropriated from the Indios. The proximity of cattle forced the natives to fence their cornfields, a heavy extra labor for them, and there was much bad feeling about the straying of cattle. Very few white men lived outside the city; there were seven Indios to every white man in the Valladolid district, the highest ratio in Yucatan.

Mérida, Campeche, the frontier, and Valladolid—these were the four little homelands within Yucatan. Sharing much, but with conflicting interests, each would someday find itself ready to take up arms against the rest. These conflicting interests that defined the patrias chicas, these flaws in the Yucatecan Ladino society, explain a great deal of the later talk about patriotism and sacred ideals. Just as Yucatecan Ladinos separated themselves from Mexico, so within Yucatan itself they would break up into petty quasi-republics, creating anarchy within their own world and an opportunity for their long-suffering Indio enemy.

Progress brought a changing class relationship. Under the Crown, Yucatecan society had been dominated by men of Spanish birth. The royal Captain General, his lieutenant, and the Bishops always came from the mother country—along with most of the high judges, officials, and army officers. After them in status came the Creoles, people of supposedly pure white blood who had been born in the New World. Next stood the Mestizos, far down the ladder, of mixed white and Indian blood; a few Mulattoes of white and Negro blood; and the Pardos, of Negro and Indian blood. (This African line, which came from several hundred ex-slaves who migrated from neighboring Tabasco, was never important in numbers and was eventually absorbed.) At the bottom of the ladder were the Indios. Independence discredited or expelled the Spaniards, and their position was inherited by that part of the white population known as the gente decente, or upper class.

This upper class dressed according to contemporary European fashion, if a few years behind it: the women with off-the-shoulder, pinched-waist, full-skirted dresses, using perhaps more color, more lace and frills than were considered stylish elsewhere, but pleasing by all accounts; the men with black swallow-tailed coats, loose white pants, vests, and top hats. Town life was the only existence they knew or could tolerate, and when not abroad they could be found in Mérida, Campeche, or perhaps in Valladolid. Owning haciendas which they seldom saw, they considered Mérida their true home, the center of all that made life worth living.

In Mérida fiesta followed fiesta, all building up to the day of Corpus Christi, when the part-time militia officers could strut before fan-hidden glances, strut in all their shakoed, epauletted, tightly buttoned glory. There were the religious processions that filed through the streets beneath floral arches to the solemn music of a half-Moorish Spain, the gaudily dressed images on litters—a gruesomely suffering Christ, a doll-like Virgin—rocking over the heads of the faithful. The processions continued through the day and by torchlight far into the night. Bands played hymns and the latest Italian opera, played them for a people who enjoyed their religion. The bands played concerts in the plaza; they played in the uniquely Yucatecan bull rings, temporary scaffoldings of poles lashed together, for a provincial imitation of the Fiesta Brava; and they played, with more enthusiasm than skill, quadrilles, contredanses, gallopades, and waltzes for the balls that climaxed each fiesta and each change or attempted change of government. And always there was gambling, the passion of both sexes, of all ages and all classes: the choice ran from lotteries, raffles, dice, and the cock pit to the glories of a political coup. In Mérida it was even possible to watch the distinguished aeronaut, José M. Flores, ascend seven thousand feet into the heavens in his gaily decorated balloon.

The Mestizo was in the typically uncomfortable position of the half-caste, looked down upon by the white man and despised by the Indio. When skin and features ran to the mother's side, a Spanish family name was often the only distinguishing mark; when the father was favored, local attitude was decisive. Mestizos were excluded from various churches, fiestas, and *barrios* (semi-autonomous suburbs) of the towns. Denied European dress in colonial times, they had developed their own fashions to set themselves off from the natives, and these fashions continued long after the legal occasion for them vanished. As the old caste lines began to weaken, their privileges and restrictions became highly complicated and varied from one place to the next. Since there was more Indian blood around than the upper class was willing to admit, particularly in the older families, the outward symbols of status had a high emotional value. Occasionally a particularly attractive Mestiza could move up to the Creole group, but a Mestizo almost never made it.

Increased economic activity added to the traditional Mestizo roles —carpenter, builder, tailor, herdsman, and manual laborer. Most new haciendas needed an overseer, a position that offered considerable authority and the chance to make a small fortune far from the owner's control. There were also openings as soldiers, wagoneers, shopowners, and traveling peddlers; but the most revolutionary possibility for the Mestizo was to become a hacendado in the new lands, with indebted labor of his own. These prospects made Mestizos increasingly aware of restrictions they had previously accepted; change made them uncertain, and dissatisfaction made them ready for the promises of revolutionaries. Together with the Creoles, they formed the Ladino society, approximately one-fourth of Yucatan's population.

The Indio was considered naturally stupid by most of the first two classes, little better than an animal—able to work long hours in the sun under conditions that would kill a white man, but lazy unless watched. He had the exasperating habit of never giving a direct answer, always adding "maybe" or "perhaps." He had forgotten his own word for yes, said no very easily, and said "good" with an expression that meant "not bad." He was thought to be highly superstitious and deeply religious; he would spend a year's earnings on religious fiestas, but had no fear of dying in a state of mortal sin. The Ladino, of course, was not notable for his fear of sin, especially of the venal variety. Like his medieval European protoytpe, the hacendado was said to enjoy the right of first night with a native bride—Creoles even claimed that insult would be taken if it were not exploited—and many white men kept a little brown *amiga* available. In a novel of the Caste War, *Cecilio Chi,* written by a Ladino of the period, the Maya heroine marries a Creole and leaves Yucatan with him to live in Europe. It was said that the Indio could hear only through his back, so the whip was kept handy and used frequently. A good Indio was known for his honesty, his hatred of military life, and his humility; above all, he was docile. But sometimes the Creoles wondered, and there were repeated whisperings of a general rebellion. Beneath these convenient misconceptions and ideas of racial superiority ran a deep current of fear.

The Church had played a major role in the life of Yucatan, and its loss of power, prestige, and morale had a far-reaching effect on all classes. With Independence, the monasteries had been suppressed and their land had come under civil control. The secular Church had been largely supported by tribute, an unpopular word after Independence and therefore renamed "obvention"; this made little difference to the Indios who had to pay it, on the theory that they had the greatest need for a Christian education and should therefore bear the expense. Hacendados were assessed for their men, and officials and soldiers were used to collect from the free natives. Tithe was what the white men were to pay, but there is no record of a forced payment, and it was abolished in 1843. The obventions, too, were lowered by politicians; first women were exempted, then the men's rates were reduced, and finally they were canceled at the same time as the tithes, the state undertaking to collect a uniform tax on everyone, granting the church one hundred thousand pesos in place of its lost income. This was a serious cut for the priests, some of whom had received up to fourteen thousand pesos annually from the larger Indio parishes, and they did their best to recoup the loss by raising the fees for marriage and baptism as high as the market would bear. In their revolutionary demands, the Indios later asked that the price be reduced to the equivalent of ten days' labor for a marriage and three for a baptism.

Another source of income was land cultivated by religious brotherhoods of Indios known as *cofradías* to support the local priest and to raise money for the village fiesta. These fiestas were a religious duty, and a matter of pride for the natives, and they spared no labor or expense to make them as elaborate as possible; they were outraged when laws were passed forcing the sale of this land. This break with tradition reflected poorly on the Church. Legal immunity of the priesthood was lost, along with the Bishop's right to assign parishes, as liberal politicians chipped away at what they considered a relic of the past. The Bishop of that time, José María Guerra, the first Yucatecan to hold the post, was in no position to resist. He had backed the wrong side in politics and had been exiled and reinstated by force, and was haunted by an anti-bishop, a man consecrated for the same job in Venezuela with liberal backing and always ready to move into his seat. The seduction of nuns and the use of champagne for sacramental wine were among the more picturesque charges that flew back and forth between these rivals, but Guerra had possession and held the post until his death.

There was a general decadence among the Yucatecan priesthood. Most of the priests lived quite openly with their housekeepers, who were not necessarily of the lower classes, and had children without scandal; indeed, this was so common that parishioners were said to distrust the cleric who had not settled down with one woman. Justo Sierra O'Reilly, son-in-law of the governor, and envoy to Washington; his brother the curate of Valladolid; and two sisters who became nuns, were all born of such a union and it had no ill effect on their careers. There were limits, however. The curate of Tizimin was driven from his church for refusing to give up his harem of Indias, and there was a priest who drunkenly acted out his feelings for his parishioners by saddling an Indio and then mounting and driving his spurs into the man's body. It was said that the clergy preached only in Lent, Holy Week, and on the Saint's day of their village, and then poorly; they were absent from their parishes so often that it was necessary to pass a law against excessive absence. They dissipated the traditional respect of the natives by seizing cofradía and ejido lands.

There were exceptions, of course. The curates Vela, Sierra, and Carrillo proved by their lives that they had a true vocation for the priesthood; that there were so few like them bespoke the moral collapse of the Church. Once the only career open to bright younger sons, the priesthood could no longer attract the best men. Only one church was built in Yucatan in the nineteenth century, and people were surprised that such a thing would still be done. Yucatan lacked the violent anticlericalism of Mexico, for the Church was but a feeble antagonist. Its drive, prestige, and spirit were gone, and the social structure of Yucatan lost another element of stability.

Education and printing had brought great changes to Yucatan. Under the Crown there had been four or five schools shared between Mérida and Campeche, and these were primarily for the clergy; the rest of the state depended on local curates to teach reading, writing, and simple arithmetic. The first constitution recognized the need, and by 1841 there were 67 schools on the peninsula. At the Seminario de San Ildefonso in Mérida such subjects as Latin, ethics, philosophy, and dogmatic and moral theology began to be neglected in favor of law, literature, and medicine. The movement was led by liberal priests, assisted by a slowly increasing number of educated laymen. Outside influences were important. A doctor came from Guatemala, an exiled priest from Spain; the sons of the wealthy traveled to Europe, the United States, and Mexico, all returning to add to the sum of new ideas and new enthusiasms. A Marine Academy, the first in Latin America, was founded in Campeche; education for girls became possible, even if it remained unlikely; scholarships were offered to deserving students. The Congress voted a pension to send Gabriel Gahona, a promising young artist, to Italy. The funds were well spent; Gahona's woodcuts, which began to appear on his return in 1847, were skillful caricatures of the manners and morals of the local scene and anticipated the style of the better known Mexican, Posada. The Lancastrian system of teaching was adopted: advanced students taught beginners, and these beginners, supervised by the few teachers, would go on to teach others. From Mérida and Campeche this method spread to the towns and then to the villages.

There was, of course, resistance to the spread of education. The Indios considered reading and writing almost sacred arts, the exclusive property of priests and scribes. Their traditional suspicion of the white man, added to their need for the labor of their children, made them hesitant to join the program. Hacendados saw no reason for their servants to learn such things as addition, which would only make them uppity and lead to arguments over debts, and they resisted the program. There was never enough money for teachers and school buildings. Education made slow progress in the back country.

With a relatively larger base of literacy, and free from the censorship of Spain, white Yucatecans burst into print. The first printing press was imported in 1812 to publish state proclamations, and it was quickly followed by others that fell into private hands. The effect was explosive. Yucatan had been an isolated colonial province in which few could read, books were rare, and news traveled only by word of mouth or an occasional slow-traveling letter; now, within a few short years, it was flung into the modern world, and a large part of its inhabitants (the white ones, at least) could learn what had happened in the capital or overseas within a few days of the time

the facts were known in Mérida. Sudden political action became possible; people could form opinions on major issues; special interest
groups recognized themselves and organized for action. The first act
of every revolutionary was to print several hundred copies of his
"plan" telling what he was for and what he was against and inviting
all of like mind to join in his movement. In the beginning, the newspapers were of a political nature, largely given over to comments on
the morals and ancestry of the opposition, but gradually articles began to appear on science, biography, and history.

Intellectual curiosity was stimulated, and some discovered that the
Indio had not always been stupid and brutish. The curate Carrillo
of Ticul amused himself hunting out the ruins so plentifully scattered
through the forest of his parish, ruins that had always been known
but always ignored. Juan Pío Pérez, while serving as a state interpreter, became fascinated with the old Maya documents in his charge,
and when political fortunes turned him out of office, he used his
leisure to study and translate them, to write articles on the past glories
of the Indian race. The travelers Stephens and Catherwood, Yucatan's first tourists, went wandering into the forest to see sights that
no one realized were sights; their interest and later their magnificent
books helped make Yucatecans aware of their own history. Cogolludo's seventeenth-century *Historia de Yucatán* was republished to
satisfy this new interest. (Creoles were amused that an Indian, the
chief Jacinto Pat, should have the eighteen pesos and the presumption
necessary to buy a copy.) Newspapers printed poetry and the woodcuts of Gahona, plays were written and produced in Mérida, and
there were novels on local and contemporary subjects by Justo Sierra
O'Reilly. Suddenly, Yucatan had an intellectual life of its own.

This was the country, the background, the social order in which
the Ladinos lived and breathed and which they set about to change.
Although Yucatan was isolated, her history makes little sense without
a knowledge of what went on around her, particularly in Mexico. All
of the problems of the Mexican Republic, the power struggles and
class rivalries, were worked out or reflected on a smaller scale in the
peninsula, usually to its disadvantage. At the time of Independence,
Yucatan chose the federalist, as opposed to the centralist philosophy
of government, a choice based on her tradition of a separate ad-

ministration under the Crown. Federalism became synonymous with liberalism and opposed to centralist-conservatism. López de Santa Anna, a liberal hero and at first a federalist favoring state's rights, changed sides after a term as president of Mexico had made him impatient of criticism; in 1835 his national congress voted away the hard-won liberties that the people could not yet understand or defend. Under his centralist regime, states were made administrative departments, state governors were appointed rather than elected, and the remaining elective offices were limited to the very rich.

This was an affront to the principles of the ruling class in Yucatan, who were accustomed to exercising local rule, and they watched helplessly as the new regime rode roughshod over local interests in an effort to create a uniform nation. Protective tariffs were lost, ruining Campeche's shipping and threatening the sugar industry. National troops were sent to garrison Yucatan but paid with state money. Yucatecans were sent overseas to fight rebellious Texas liberals—a serious matter for the soldiers involved, for there was no provision for their return upon discharge.

In May of 1838, Santiago Iman, a captain in the state militia, raised the banner of revolt against centralism at Tizimin in northeastern Yucatan. Though defeated in the first skirmish, he was able to maintain himself in the forest. Reinforcements came to him when men of his old battalion seized the ship that was taking them to the Texas war and forced the captain to put them ashore. But this wasn't enough to turn the trick, and after a second minor battle with the authorities Iman was again forced into hiding. In his despair, a truly revolutionary idea occurred to him. The Indios, long forbidden to bear arms, had recently been forced to serve in the army: many of them owned shotguns, all of them carried machetes, and their numbers were unlimited. Iman spread the word that he fought against the overseas use of state troops (particularly dreaded by prospective Indio conscripts) and promised that if the Indios joined him he would suppress the Church obventions they were forced to pay. The response was overwhelming. With a mob of thousands he took Valladolid, and, encouraged by this success, the whole state rose to his assistance and drove the Mexican troops from their last stronghold of Campeche in June 1840. Until Mexico returned to the federal system, the rebels declared, Yucatan would remain independent. Yucatecan liberals, once more in control of their own destiny, began the reformation of the state by the election of new officers.

Santiago Méndez was made Governor. He was a tall, thin man in his fifties, a merchant of Campeche, devoted to the ideals of progress and particularly the progress of his native city. As his pince-nez and restrained manner suggested, he was not the *caudillo* type but a practical businessman and a good administrator. Miguel Barbachano, the new Vice Governor, was only thirty-four that year; an orator with the fine manners and presence gained from a Spanish education, he was not fond of administrative details, overly willing to delegate authority, and of a gambling nature. He was also born in Campeche but came to be associated with Mérida.

A victorious Yucatecan commission was organized to revise the Constitution of 1825, but on finding so many faults in that document the delegates decided to start afresh with a new constitution. All Yucatecans were declared citizens, including the native majority. The first state bicameral legislature was formed, with the first direct election of senators, deputies, and governor. After what they had seen of the dictatorial powers of Santa Anna, the commission was very much concerned with institutional checks and controls. They developed the judicial principle of *amparo* (later adopted in Mexico), which gave the courts power to interpose against laws or decrees they felt might be unconstitutional; essentially, this was designed to protect the citizen from abuse by the administrative or legal authority of the government. To this they added religious freedom, the suppression of special privileges, and the principle that all powers not specifically delegated to the government remained vested in the people.

There was in this extremely liberal constitution of 1841 the Spanish love of principle and disdain for pragmatic compromise, a reflection of the cast of mind that had produced great saints and grand inquisitors, pious churchgoers and church-burners, Don Quixote and Sancho Panza. This bent for abstract idealism, combined with the code of absolute personal loyalty to a leader, stands behind the hero-villain nature of many nineteenth-century Latin American politicians. In spite of the new constitution, the governor of Yucatan continued to be very much the head of his party, ruling by decree under the special powers given to him in states of emergency (which were perpetual) or through an executive council. Beneath him in the all-important executive line were the superior political chiefs of the five departments and the subaltern political chiefs of the many districts. These men were the governor's appointees, responsible to him and not to the local citizens. Towns of any size elected a mayor, an alderman, and an attorney general to work under these political

Governor Santiago Méndez

chiefs. Subordinate to the town officials was the traditional Indian village government, called the Republic of the Natives, which continued to operate in spite of legal suppression.

The centralist authorities in Mexico did not take this constitution-making lightly, but, surrounded by anarchy, they had to content themselves with declaring Yucatecan ships outside the law and closing mainland Mexican ports against them. In answer to this, the Yucatecans hired a fleet of three ships from the new Texas navy, and these patrolled the sea lanes between Veracruz and the peninsula for several months before they were discharged. The Yucatecans went further. A new flag was raised above the Palacio Municipal of Mérida, a flag with two horizontal red stripes flanking one white one, and five stars on a green field: five stars for the five departments, the flag for the "sovereign nation" of Yucatan. The young Vice Governor was most enthusiastic about this symbolic act, thinking of the title of Vice President or better, but Governor Méndez hesitated before reality: with the Mexican market closed, Yucatan would be reduced to a subsistence level. Méndez wavered between the dream and the economic reality for two years.

The problem was solved in 1843 when Santa Anna, returning to power after his San Jacinto defeat and capture at the hands of the

Texans, sent a commission, an ultimatum, and an expeditionary army to Yucatan. Glad to abandon the sordid details of trade for the more congenial glories of a war against tyranny, Yucatecan patriots flocked to arms. The Mexicans dallied through the summer, content with the occupation of Carmen; this gave Yucatan time to raise and arm a force of 6,000 men—enlisted, after the manner of Iman, primarily among the Indios—who were promised land and, for the second time, a reduction in their church tax. Méndez resigned in favor of his Vice Governor, and went down to prepare the defenses of Campeche. One of Governor Barbachano's first printed orders declared that in answer to the military challenge, "Quién vive?" the countersign was to be "Yucatán!"

The officer caste, the usual partner to the Church in Latin American reaction, had been crushed by the liberal victory. The whole spirit of militant caudillismo, or rule by military bosses, was discredited; Yucatan was to be run by civilians. General Iman returned to the obscurity from which he had come. Command of the state army was given to an exiled Mexican officer of federalist persuasion, Pedro Lemus.

General Lemus had a small body of regulars to depend upon: the Light Battalion, with six companies of 100 men each, normally garrisoned in the fortress of San Benito at Mérida, and a company of cavalry. He also had some 200 artillerymen for the defense of Campeche and a detached infantry company at Isla Carmen, which had surrendered to overwhelming odds. His main reserve was the National Guard, composed of citizen soldiers expected to drill once a week; these men, who followed liberal principles by electing their own officers up to the rank of captain, were organized by companies of not more than 150 men according to towns and then joined in battalions.

On paper, this was an army of 1,000 regulars and 6,000 reserves. But the battalions varied widely in equipment and training. They were a ragged band, at least to foreign eyes. The enlisted men, usually Indios or Mestizos, wore their normal dress: flat straw hats and sandals; white cotton pants reaching halfway from knee to ankle; a blouse hanging to the hip, belted for the machetes and crisscrossed with bandoleers; some sort of gun, a water gourd, and whatever personal equipment each man wanted to pack along. For those who could afford such things, and for the regulars, there were tightly buttoned uniform cotton jackets, long pants, and hats with shako or visor; most did without these trappings.

The officers (almost all Creoles, in spite of the elections) went in for dark blue jackets with tails, high-collared, tight-fitting, and splendid with gold buttons and epaulets, with white pants and high boots, if possible. They armed themselves with pistols and swords, swords that would be the last defense against the universal machete. These Creole officers were often very young; there were cadets of twelve, lieutenants of fifteen, and many teenage captains. There were occasional breaks in the caste line when the need for leadership outweighed tradition; Mestizos, Mulattoes, and even an occasional Indio captain appeared in the backwoods companies.

In November of 1842 the Mexicans finally got around to what they had come for; they landed 5,000 men at Champoton and marched north, defeating Yucatecan forces in several skirmishes. This cost General Lemus his command on suspicion of treason, although he was exonerated by a court-martial that lacked definite proof. His post went to a *Meridano*, Colonel Sebastián López de Llergo.

Colonel Llergo, with the heavy artillery of the city wall behind him, fought the invaders to a dead stop in the suburbs of Campeche. There matters rested for three and a half months, until the impatient Santa Anna sent reinforcements under his bastard son, Jose López de Santa Anna, with orders to take the high road for Mérida. This was unrealistic, but the Mexican general had to make some move, so he tried the sea, re-embarking most of his soldiers and sailing north. In self-defense the Yucatecans again hired the services of the Texas navy for 5,000 pesos per month.

The Mexican maneuver was poorly organized. Several canoes were lost in a storm; the troops ran out of water and grounded a steamship when they landed to take on a fresh supply; and the fleet was under observation most of the time. The makeshift expedition finally reached its objective, a fishing village above Mérida, and landed some 1,300 troops. As the Mexicans wandered uncertainly toward the capital, Llergo finished the placement of his men. There was a day-long skirmish within sight of Mérida's towers, but the assault never came; unprepared for anything but a walkover, the Mexicans had exhausted their supplies and were constrained to end the farce by surrendering. The captured gunpowder was used for salvos and fireworks celebrating the victory of Llergo (now a general) and federalism.

Unfortunately, the economic facts remained intractable. In spite of their military success, Yucatecan leaders came to realize that "national" independence was not practical, and a commission was sent to arrange matters in Mexico City. Having proved that they could defend their rights, they now won the guarantees previously denied them: control of state affairs, a state militia with no foreign service for the soldiers, special import-export duties, and free passage for the products of Yucatan to all ports of the Republic of Mexico. In exchange, the Yucatecan commissioners accepted a centralist regime; Yucatan would become a department, with no control over national affairs. This was a face-saving formula, and Yucatan, with her own troops and the barrier of the Gulf of Mexico as guarantees, had most of the advantages in the negotiations.

Her leaders had less success with another problem—what to do about the land promised to the Indio volunteers; so many of them had enlisted that it was considered impossible to reward them all. Consideration of the problem was simply postponed—an act that put a heavy mortgage on the future.

His Serene Highness López de Santa Anna had signed the treaty of reincorporation in December of 1843. But the treaty terms and the defeat of his army still galled him, and two months later he reneged, issuing a decree banning the entry of all products of Yucatan to Mexican ports. Next, in accordance with centralist doctrine, he appointed a governor for the state. Yucatan was losing by decree what she had won by force of arms. Several unsuccessful protests were followed with a declaration of independence by the Mérida garrison, the renunciation of national ties by the state assembly, and the election of Miguel Barbachano as provisional governor, all in December of 1845.

Yucatan would once more stand aside until Mexico returned to sanity and federalism. And as it happened, that came quickly. The Mexican-American war began in 1846, and the mercurial Santa Anna, overthrown and exiled in that year, was smuggled back into Mexico by American agents, supposedly to end the war by losing a mock battle and accepting the American terms. The agents should have known better. Santa Anna had championed all shades of political philosophy during his turbulent career, and had betrayed them all in turn; he was theatrical and vain, a supreme egotist with an unshakable belief in his own glory. But in spite of all this he also believed in Mexico. The "mock battle" was Buena Vista and was not mock at all. In fact, he almost won it, and afterward he had no idea of quitting. Needing whatever assistance he could get, he promised Yucatan her full rights as listed in the treaty of 1843, and in a more dramatic reversal he ordered a return to the original federal constitution of 1824. This was all Governor Barbachano needed. With the Mexican nation threatened by a foreign enemy and with his own federalist principles victorious, he accepted the gesture and declared that Yucatan was once more Mexican.

But the government in Mérida had ignored something of vital concern to Campeche: the American war fleet. Involved in the landings at Tampico and Veracruz, it had not yet appeared in Yucatecan waters; but Yucatan's reunification with Mexico could bring it down on Campeche with disastrous results. The sidewheel steamers *Mississippi* and *Missouri*, swift and powerful, had cannons that fired the new explosive shells instead of solid shot; these cannons, which far outranged the city's guns, could easily level her antiquated wall, gut the center of town, and sink her merchant marine. Patriotism was all well and good, the *Campechanos* thought, but reunification was poorly timed, or, as their manifesto said, "inopportune." Campeche revolted against Mexico.

For once a revolution was truly popular. When ex-Governor Méndez refused to go along with their first attempt, the local revolutionaries chose Domingo Barret, declaring for the independent constitution and state of Yucatan, which is to say for neutrality. The Light Battalion was won over, and together with the Sixteenth of Campeche, it marched north toward Mérida. The Fifteenth Battalion (of Maxcanu) embarked in a small flotilla to take Sisal, the half-formed Seventeenth headed through the Puuc, and envoys were sent to rally the Indios with old promises and new guns. Barbachano hastily mobilized his forces and sent them south to meet the rebels, asking his fellow citizens in a proclamation if they wanted to be considered "perfidious, nefarious, without honor in the eyes of Mexico and of the civilized world." Under the circumstances, the answer was Yes. Lacking the determination of the southern battalions, the government troops were defeated and driven back on the capital.

The sugar country along the Tekax-Tihosuco road had contacts with both Mérida and Campeche, adherents to both causes, and a dissatisfied population ready to accept any promises of tax reduction. In January 1847, Antonio Trujeque, the subaltern political chief of Peto, raised a native battalion at Tihosuco, and Lieutenant Colonel Pacheco did the same at Yaxcaba; after assisting at the capture of Tekax and taking Peto, they marched against Valladolid, some 3,000 strong, and stormed the city. Indio troops got out of hand, looted cantinas, and ran amok, shouting "Kill those who have shirts!" Oppressed Mestizos in the city arose to avenge old wrongs, and Valla-
ᴊolid began to pay for its aristocratic pretensions. The captured Colonel was dragged from the house in which he was held prisoner and hacked to death; a paralyzed curate was macheted in his hammock; girls of the most aristocratic families were stripped and raped before their helpless relatives, then tied spread-eagle to the grillwork of windows and repeatedly stabbed and mutilated. And it was said that after the Indios had carried bodies through the streets in a triumphal procession, they ate human flesh to prove their brutality. Violent emotion clouds the facts of that day, but it is reported that the sack continued for six days and that at least eighty-five civilians were murdered. With this news, a wave of dread rolled across the state. Barbachano, cornered in Mérida and facing what he considered a race war, surrendered.

Two

The Mazehual World

FOR THE MAZEHUAL of Yucatan, the silent forest was not empty;
it was alive with spirits, the owners and protectors of the wild places.*
Before clearing his cornfield, the Mazehual would call out to them,
asking permission to use their property; after stating how much land
he would need and offering payment in the form of specially prepared
corn gruel, he would seal the bargain by erecting a small cross—because, after all, he was Christian. At planting time there were the
guardians of the cornfield to be considered—four of them, one at each
corner of the field. They protected the young plants from animals
and thieves, and without their help the corn would never ripen; and
again, the farmer offered corn gruel as part payment to these spirits
and promised more at harvest time. To fail in these acts would
threaten one's *Tamen* or state of harmony with heaven, and a breach
in this harmony could ruin a crop and bring starvation. The burnt-
over, rocky clearing was a holy place and the act of raising corn a
holy duty, for corn was the divine food, the sustenance of man and the
gods.

In a cyclical view of life, the seasons and the years progress in
an orderly pattern, and the past is the key to the future. Most of the
Mazehualob had neither the time nor the intelligence to acquire the

---

* *Mazehual,* the Nahuatl word for "common person," apparently came into
the Maya language about 900 A.D. with the Mexican conquest; combined with
the Maya plural suffix *-ob,* it meant "common people" or "peasants"—all those
between the nobles and the slaves. By 1847 the word had lost any derogatory
meaning for the Maya, and they used it in speaking of themselves. This attitude
still prevails in Quintana Roo, but the Yucatecan Maya now uses the word to
describe a social inferior.

learning necessary for prediction, and so they consulted an *H-men* (literally, "he who knows"). The H-men could find lost articles, cure sickness with his herbs and prayers, and read the future by looking into his sacred stones or by counting grains of corn; but his first responsibility and preoccupation was to assist in assuring a successful harvest.

The first step in corn growing was to clear a field; between August and January, whenever the Mazehual found time, he cut a stand of trees and left them to dry in the sun. (Since the thin soil of each field became unproductive after three years' use, this was a continual labor.) Sometime during the spring the cut wood had to be burned, and choosing the time was important. If the wood was too green, the burn would be incomplete and the sun wouldn't reach the planted corn; but if the Mazehual waited too long, the rainy season would catch him and it wouldn't burn at all—which happened occasionally and meant famine. For this decision the farmer consulted his local H-men, who turned to his *Xoc-kin*, the count of days. As all life is a cycle, so there are little cycles within big ones, and by knowing the rules it was possible to predict the future. If it rained on January 4, for instance, April, the fourth month, would be rainy. This was Spanish peasant magic, long since naturalized in Yucatan. Xoc-kin was infallible, but the H-men, unconsciously or otherwise, kept an eye cocked on certain birds, watched for the swarming of flying ants, and listened to the croaking of frogs before giving the word to burn, sometime in April.

Around the beginning of May would come a great rumbling of thunder, a signal for the *Chaakob*, the rain gods, to leave their cenotes and assemble in the heavens, thence to ride forth on horseback, each with his sacred water-filled calabash, sweeping the country from east to west with life-giving rain. Sultry heat then gave way to a moist coolness, trees put out fresh foliage, and the villages were deserted as the Mazehualob set about planting.

A planting stick was used in the thin rocky soil, in the pockets of red earth or the most fertile black earth. If the Chaakob were beneficent, if the rains fell well at the right time, weeding was necessary from the middle of June through July. If not, worry over drought or excessive rain (causing rot) grew instead, and it was time to see the

H-men. His first inquiry would be whether the ceremonial "feast of the cornfield" had been observed. This was the last part of the vow made by each farmer to the spirits and gods, to reward with food and prayers their efforts in making harvest possible; it was supposed to be done when the crop was in, but was frequently let slide until the forcible reminder of drought or sickness warned a man that his Tamen was threatened. Failure to perform the ceremony was held to be the most common cause of disease, and its celebration the normal therapy. By restoring harmony with the gods, this rite could restore men to health, crops to fruitfulness, and ensure these benefits for the future. Men were continent before the ceremony, and women were never present. A crude altar was built in the cornfield, food and drink were placed on it, and after much prayer, after the gods had taken the essence of the offerings, the devout had a feast on the merely physical but very satisfying remains.

If August passed and the rains continued poor, worry changed to fear and the farmer faced his most serious crisis. Again, the H-men was ready with an answer, a last resort when other means had failed, the rain-bringing ceremony. All the men of the village would spend several days hunting the wild game necessary for the meat offerings while the H-men went through the preliminary rites. On the third day after the rites had begun, a presentation was made at an altar built under a ceiba tree. The rain gods were summoned, with great care that none should be omitted, in a ritual invitation to the god of every cenote in the area. As they gathered from their watery homes, called by prayer and lured by offerings of food and incense, boys crouched under the altar croaking as frogs do before the rain, branches of the tree were pulled back and forth as if lashed by a windstorm, and a dancer impersonated *Kunu-chaak,* the chief rain god, with his lightning wand and sacred calabash.

After these hints, the Chaakob always sent rain, sometimes even before the ceremony was over—unless some prayer had been incorrectly made or some man had failed to remain celibate for the necessary three days. The first harvest came in September, and if there had been the right amount of rain, no locusts, and no hurricane, then it was a happy time of feasting, the end of worry for another year. The main harvest began in mid-November and continued, for some types of corn, until the following March, the clearing of new fields going forward at the same time. A man could raise all he needed to support himself and his family in six months of labor, but he was bound by the timing of the seasons: when the rains came he had to be ready for planting, and he would let nothing stand in his way.

Deer were important to the Mazehual; they were necessary for his religious feasts and were his primary source of meat. Either in groups or by himself he would spend several weeks of the year in hunting. In the more remote and backward villages, bows and arrows were still used occasionally, but by the 1840's most men had shotguns. Hunting, like clearing a new field, was a trespass on the domain of the forest spirits, who had to be propitiated or tricked by various spells. The lonely forest had its share of demons, like the *Boob* (half horse, half puma) or the *X-tabai*, a beautiful woman but one whose male pursuers were never seen again. Most common among the spirits were the *Aluxob*—dwarfs and tricksters who caused many of the unexplained accidents of life and were usually encountered in the shape of clay idols among the ruins of the Ancient Ones. In this form they could be brought to life by burning incense before them for nine days and nights. When it was known that a particular Alux was causing trouble, an H-men would go to his home in one of the overgrown pyramids and make peace with offerings of food and drink.*

Various stories were told about these ruins. It was said that the men who had built them had worked in darkness and were turned into stone when daylight came, which explained the statues and the carvings. Others said that there had been a "good time" when rocks were soft and could be moved by whistling, when there was no labor to the clearing of a cornfield, and when a single grain of corn would feed an entire family. This was the time of the Red People and the old Itzá kings. Because of pride, or loss of magic power, or the losing of a horse race between the King and a foreigner at Chichén Itzá, the good times ended and the present bad times began. The old king went down into a cenote, or into a tunnel which led from Tulum

---

* Members of the Lacandon tribe still offer incense in ruined temples. In seeking out a god reported by the archeologist Tozzer (in 1907) to be living at Temple 33 of Yaxchilan, the author was told by a Lacandón that the god had moved to Lacanha, because too many foreigners had disturbed his peace.

eastward under the sea, or to an island in a lake in the southern jungle, and the foreigner, the *Dzul*, took power. The grandfathers told of an old woman who lived in a cave near Uxmal and would give water to the thirsty in exchange for babies, which she fed to a giant snake. A king at Chichén Itzá also kept such a snake and demanded human tribute until both snake and king were killed by a young hero. Many of the villages had books written by the prophet Chilam Balam which told of these things.* At some of the ruins strange music could be heard on Good Friday; these were avoided, but others were repaired and lived in.

As the farmer's field was protected by four spirits, so his village was guarded by a second set of four, one to each of the crosses erected at the edge of the village. The Mazehualob recognized five directions; the fifth was the center and was marked in every village with a cross and usually with a ceiba tree. The fifth direction was under the care of the village patron saint, who controlled the well-being of the entire community. His favor was gained by dedicating a fiesta to him. Normally held in April or May, this fiesta was organized and paid for by the members of one of the cofradías (lay brotherhoods), who raised a crop on land set aside to meet expenses. The man in charge, the *cargador*, who made a large personal contribution, was particularly responsible for the success of the celebration, and he accepted his post as a necessary step in social advancement within the village hierarchy.

A good fiesta called for large quantities of aguardiente, food, fireworks, musicians, and perhaps an amateur bullfight, all of which could easily cost the cargador a year's income. Like the "feast of the cornfield," it was a religious duty, an annual contract to secure the protection of the village saint. To fail in performance would be to risk disaster, and to be stingy with the funds would invite similar treatment from above.

* These books, written in Maya using the Spanish alphabet, are collections of history, prophecy, ritual, and customs. Although they date from the years following the Spanish conquest, they are in part copies of the pre-conquest hieroglyphic books and are named after the Maya priest Chilam Balam, who prophesied the coming of the white man. Copies have been kept to this day by the Maya in Quintana Roo, where they are called both books and bibles, having served both functions.

The image of the saint was brought out from the church to enjoy the dancing of the fiesta—the Jaraña, the Vasquería, the Spanish-American folk dances. There were other dances, from which women were excluded. These were performed by the *X-Tol* brotherhood, in masks, feathered headdresses, and crowns. The wooden gong, turtle-shell rattle, and clay flute replaced the violin and horn. This was a local form of the "conquest dance" common to all Central America, a dramatization of the struggle between Christian and Moor (with the Indio as Moor), a mask of European carnival laid over a native past. Use of the *tunkul,* a drum-like wooden gong made of a hollow log with a narrow slit cut lengthwise in the top, was often banned by the white Dzulob. Its resonant boom, which carried for miles through the forest, made them uneasy.

Besides the guardian of his field and village, each man had his individual guardian. The Mazehual could seldom afford an image, and the cross was a ready substitute. Each family had its personal cross, inherited by the eldest son and kept in a separate hut, an *oratorio,* because it was too holy to be defiled by domestic life. Each was dedicated to a saint or simply to the "Holy Cross," but each contained inherent powers and different crosses of the same name were not necessarily of equal sanctity. A priest was necessary to bless them, but, once blessed, the crosses rather than the saints became the object of worship. (When possible, cheap figurines or holy pictures were used to represent saints, but because these were rare a cross itself could also represent a saint.) God, *El Gran Dios,* was of little importance because he had no cross of his own. Various lineage crosses gained special reputations as they were handed down through the generations of a successful family and were treated accordingly, becoming in time the primary crosses of certain villages. The Old People had worshiped their gods in exactly the same way, and the few remaining pagan Lacandones retain this custom in the deep forests of Chiapas, collecting and inheriting incense pots that represent their various deities and keeping them apart in a house of idols.

The Christian Mazehual shared a large part of his religious beliefs with these Lacandones; their rituals and their gods were the same, or variations of the same concepts. The difference was that the Christian God moved in at the top of their pantheon, and Christian saints had infiltrated the lower levels. *Nohochaakyum,* the "Great Father Chaak," was replaced by El Gran Dios, and the Chaakob or rain gods came under the rule of San Miguel Arcángel, on the sixth or penultimate level of heaven. On the fifth level were the *Kuilob Kaaxob,* the lords of the wild places; on the fourth, the guardians of the animals and their leader San Gabriel; on the third, the evil spirits. Wind gods lived on the second level; and on the first, just above the earth, hovered the *Balamob,* guarding the village crosses and the cornfields. Below in hell was *Kisin,* the earthquake god, identical with the Devil.

The Mazehual of Yucatan prayed much as all Catholics pray; he counted the beads of his rosary, said the Hail Mary and the Our Father, and he knew the Apostles' Creed and the hymns. He was led in worship by the *Maestro Cantor,* a native layman who had memorized by rote a stock of necessary prayers in Spanish and Latin and was able to chant them for over an hour without repetition—and often without understanding. The Maestro Cantor, made necessary by the scarcity of priests, was highly respected. The Mazehual was like all other Christians except that when his prayers failed, when in spite of the promised novena crops continued poor or sickness persisted, he could seek help from his H-men and the gods and spirits of the forest. He would pray first to his saint, then to the Balamob. He knew that the priests disapproved of these other rites, and that white men laughed and sneered at them, and so he celebrated them secretly, out of sight somewhere in the woods. Naturally enough, he despised the white man as an incomplete Christian.

Village life was almost completely self-sufficient. Land was held in common and there were many cooperative projects, such as building a house, clearing a field, or joining in a group hunt. Everyone belonged to a family, each person stood in a definite relationship with all others, and all looked with suspicion and distrust on the outsider. The village leader was elected for an indefinite period, though not for life. He was usually from the class known as *Almehenob,* "those who had fathers and mothers," and thus a relic of the old native aristocracy, however poor he might be. Called governor or chief when the King had ruled, and *Alcalde* since Independence was announced by the white men, he was known as *Batab* (lord) to his own people, who were required to support him.* Although more serious crimes were referred to higher authority, he was responsible for keeping the peace, and he enforced his decisions with the whip and forced labor. Under him were his lieutenant, a council of elders, and the *Alcalde Col*, who administered village land; there was also the *Alcalde Mesón*, in charge of a building kept ready for any traveling white man. The young men of the village were required to serve occasional duty as litter bearers, servants, or guides for white travelers and as errand-boys for the council of elders. All men were liable for fagina, usually six days of labor annually, maintaining public roads and buildings.

The council met in a building called the *audiencia*, which was often the only stone structure in the village, a court house and town hall in one. This was the special domain of the *Escribano*, the scribe or secretary, one of the few literate men in the back country. He was supposedly elected, but usually held his job for life and then passed it on to his son. In his care were all the village documents—genealogies, copies of proclamations, and most important of all, the papers dealing with the land. The circular, hand-painted maps made by the Old People, the land treaties going back three hundred years, the vital royal grant of common land, and the involved bills of sale and wills were all kept in a locked chest and carefully guarded as the village's only proof of ownership.

When the white Dzul had first arrived in Yucatan and pacified the country, he had forced the scattered villagers to congregate in towns, and titles to sections of land were given to those who lived on them. This struck hard at basic Mazehual tradition, at the idea that land belonged to all within the community. The villages began buying back their original holdings, which, as the men of Ebtun said, "were formerly the same as the forest of the town." Some began immediately, some only after a lapse of a hundred years, patiently collecting money, patiently waiting for an heir who was willing to sell.

But once established, private property survived alongside the communal holdings, maintained by white example and ordinary greed.

---

* The *Batabob* were considered noble by the Spanish Crown and were granted immunity from the taxes and services owed by the common natives; the rank and the immunity survived Independence.

This was the land that could be sold in time of famine, or to help meet the cost of a fiesta, or to pay for death masses and burial. In colonial times, the Royal Protector of the Indians had frequently stopped illegal sales; but that office was abolished with Independence, and in the years that followed the white man took land by fraud or simple expropriation. The titles had a way of disappearing when submitted as evidence to a Dzul court. The farmer knew his village land; he could count off the stone cairns, the crosses, and the individual trees that marked its boundaries. But in spite of his saint and his protecting Balamob, those boundaries were no longer inviolate.

Only in the most distant settlements were the Mazehualob free to work out their own destiny. These backwoods Maya people were called Huits (loincloths), after the short, rolled-up pants they wore. Isolated in families or small community clusters, they lacked priestly care and knew more of the native gods than of the holy saints. The men let their hair grow to their shoulders, and the women went bare-breasted. Their numbers were estimated at six to twenty thousand, but to count them was like counting the birds of the forest.

For the majority of the Mazehualob the white man was always more or less there, for his power ranged far beyond his physical presence. It was felt in little ways: the uneasy feeling when questioned by a Dzul, the petty services that could be demanded, the inherited sense of inferiority. And there were the big things. They saw their sacred corn trampled and smashed by unfenced cattle, their very land stolen away. They had no recourse when their women were raped or seduced, when their families were broken by labor laws, or when they found themselves bound for life on a hacienda in debt servitude.

The Mazehual had not always been docile in the face of such treatment. He had fought, first against the original invader and then in a series of hopeless colonial rebellions, until he was powerless to do more. The most recent rising had come in 1761 at Quisteil. A merchant was killed during a fiesta, and the local priest fled to Sotuta with the cry of rebellion. The twenty men sent to arrest the murderers lost half their number in ambush, including the military commander of the area, and what had probably begun as a drunken riot was made to seem a revolt in earnest. Committed by this act, the Batab of Quisteil fortified his village, and calling on neighboring chieftains, raised a mob of 1,500 men in a few days. He then changed his name to Canek, after the pagan ruler of the Itzá nation, which had been conquered only sixty-four years earlier. The Itzá, living in isolation in the jungles of Guatemala, had avoided Spanish domination for almost two centuries, and during that time they had provided sanctuary for fugitives from Yucatan. The Books of Chilam Balam had prophesied that a King of the Itzá, of that line which had once ruled all Yucatan from Chichén Itzá, would one day return and drive the foreigners into the sea.

To the name Canek, Jacinto added the title of king; he was crowned in Quisteil church, offering himself as the fulfillment of the legend. His reign was brief. Two thousand well-armed Dzulob converged on Quisteil within a week, took the place by assault, and slaughtered 500 Mazehualob. Canek escaped that day but was captured soon after and marched up to Mérida with the other prisoners. The vengeance was brutal. He was drawn and quartered in the main plaza, his bloody fragments burned, and his ashes scattered to the wind. Eight others were garroted, two hundred received two hundred lashes and had an ear cut off to mark them as rebels. This was the end of Jacinto Canek and his kingdom, but not the end of memory; the story of his dead heroes, passed on through the generations, was still remembered in 1847.[*]

The Mazehual had finally accepted what he could not prevent. In some ways, life under the white man was not very different from what he had always known. The hacienda was organized on the lines of the village, with petty officials to assign the cornfields and the community work projects, and an official to use the whip on delinquents. A *mayordomo* or manager assumed the Batab's authority to rule the people and collect taxes. But there was a difference. The manager was not usually a Mazehual, but a *Kaz-Dzul* (Mestizo), and his position encouraged him to sweat the people and keep false accounts, to build a private fortune. Set apart from the traditional system of religious and moral prestige, his motivation was economic

[*] In the early days of the Caste War, the name Jacinto Canek was written on house walls as a revolutionary slogan.

—and there was no check on it. The master, the hacendado, was seldom seen. He lived far away in the city, and his rare visits were like a descent from another world, a holiday when the peasants, excused from work, dressed in their best and lined up to kiss his hand. The town Mazehualob actually lived in what amounted to separate villages of their own, the barrios. They grew corn, since the fields were never very far away, and worked as servants, laborers, government employees; the women worked as cooks and maids. It was a more sophisticated, varied life than in the villages, and a more difficult one. There were more and better churches, where a boy could learn the prayers necessary to become a Maestro Cantor, or learn to read and write. There were also more laws, more jails, and more sergeants looking for volunteers. The villager, of course, also loved the town fiestas and the large markets like those at Izamal and Halacho, where it was possible to buy all manner of things—new hats, brightly colored scarves, coral jewelry for the wife, perhaps a gun for himself—but he wasn't really comfortable until he was on the trail home. The town Mazehual, on the other hand, was accustomed to the life, knew the complicated rules for getting along with the white man, and looked down on his country cousin. He had his own chief, his council of elders, his church, his H-men, his X-tol brotherhood, and all the rest. The main difference, when it existed, was his separation from the land, which meant inability to raise corn and a loss of contact with the forest gods. One new element was witchcraft, the special inheritance of the Mestizo; in towns, the H-menob spent much of their time warding off curses.

Village life, the life of the vast majority of the people, had been a closed affair. The village was the little homeland. But the new roads that allowed white men and their customs to penetrate the back country began to break up this isolation. As porters, mule drivers, and field hands, the Mazehualob began to travel for the first time. Stopping at villages along the road, gossiping with strangers of their own blood and language, they discovered a larger world of people like themselves, people with the same troubles and the same desires. The newly indentured Huit found similarities to his condition among the Cupuls, in the villages around Valladolid, down among the Chenes, and on the sugar plantations of Peto. This knowledge was greatly increased when the Dzulob called on the people to fight against other foreigners called Mexicans, and men of the eastern villages crossed the entire country to the siege of Campeche. That had been a great experience in other ways. Before Independence the Mazehualob had been forbidden to serve in the army or to own military weapons, and lack of tradition plus family and village ties had made them reluctant to enlist, particularly if there was a chance of being sent overseas. Fighting in Yucatan under their own leaders and for their own objectives was another matter, and they learned to like the sound of bugle and drum, the excitement of battle, the pride of victory won. The white man's newspapers praised them; Governor Barbachano called them "valiant sons of Nachi Cocom and Tutul Xiu" (two former Maya rulers), and their church tax was reduced. They were called a second time with promises of land; they won that victory, but found that the Dzul had lied about the land.

Then the army men came a third time to recruit with new promises, and this time the enemies were the men of Mérida and their leader, Barbachano. Now the Mazehualob were more experienced. A company of them led by the Batab Cecilio Chi set an ambush near Peto and routed the Mérida men—all without the advice of Dzul officers. Then they marched north to Valladolid, the city of the masters, and they took it by storm. Alcohol brings a man closer to God, the Mazehual believed, and helps him see more clearly; there was a great deal of aguardiente in Valladolid, and the victorious people saw most clearly. At last they recognized their power and discovered their real enemy. For the robbery of the land, for imposed slavery, for whippings, for impiety to God and the forest spirits; yes, and for Jacinto Canek and the severed ears of their grandfathers, for each of these sins there was a debt to pay, and it was paid with the machete. They committed violent acts in an orgy of release, and, when it was over, they knew shame and fear and a terrible hangover. Each man made for his village to hide from the inevitable punishment, to be purified of evil winds by his H-men.

The punishment never came. All were equally guilty, and their leaders were protected by the new jefe político, who didn't want to punish the men who made the revolt possible. The people lay low for a time, until it was clear that there would be no reckoning, and then they began to think of the rape of Valladolid in a different light; remembering how easily their victory had been won, remembering the aguardiente and the loot, they sat in their huts until late at night, talking of the war, and wondering what to do with their new power.

We must pause now between the overture at Valladolid and the opening scene—the dark streets of Tepich village sometime before dawn of July 30, 1847—to ask why the Caste War came to Yucatan. We know that the country was divided by race; but even more, it was split by opposing conceptions of a common world. Corn, a mere commodity to the white man, was sacred to the Maya; for the white man uncultivated land was simply wasted land, but for the Maya it was the rightful home of the forest gods.

Why did these two antagonistic societies in Yucatan come into open warfare in 1847, after living together for over three hundred years? The most obvious answer would be that the coming of independence to Central America created an unstable political situation. There had been many rebellions during the period of Spanish rule, but the Crown always had enough central authority in the colonies to suppress them. Independence, however, brought with it disunity among the colonies, civil war, and anarchy; the inherited resources of the central authority were squandered, and when the need came, there were no reserves.

Independence from Spain also made the social situation more explosive. The Creoles, formerly content to enjoy feudal rights under a monarchy that afforded some protection to the native population, became interested in a fuller use of their human resources. The Church, tribal organization, anything that blocked the drive toward progress, was swept aside. But native groups, subjected to greater pressure than ever before, were also more inclined to resist. Enlisted by the Creoles in the cause of revolution, they were awakened by it. They learned something of the military arts, and developed a taste for warfare; their knowledge of social injustice grew as they saw the Creoles break their revolutionary promises; and from small victories at arms, they formed an exaggerated idea of their own strength.

This process of political and social fragmentation was spreading throughout Latin America in the mid-nineteenth century. The Quiche Maya of Guatemala were suspected of planning rebellion in 1843, and the Tzotzil Maya of the Mexican state of Chiapas did revolt in 1868, almost taking the capital of San Cristóbal de las Casas. To the north, the Yaquis of Sonora fought a full-scale war in 1845–46, and the Pueblo Indians of New Mexico mounted an uprising more racial than political in character. Each of these rebellions occurred in a remote area, where the people were still living under a quasi-tribal organization; everywhere, the spirit of revolt was strongest where white authority had been only recently imposed.

This was the case in Yucatan. The Caste War was initiated and maintained by the Maya of the frontier—by the Huits, and those who had only recently left that category. The field hands of western Yucatan, long familiar with the whipping post and peonage, not only failed to rise but actually joined the white man against their own race; they had reached an adjustment to the Ladino way of life, had transferred their loyalty from the village to the hacienda or town. What was dangerous was not long oppression but sudden acculturation, the forced march from one world to another.

The last serious Maya rebellion had come in 1761 at Quisteil— which was then a frontier village. Eighty-six years later, and fifty miles to the east, a similar threat faced another generation of Maze-hualob; and it was not only the threat of physical enslavement, but an attack on their religious and moral standards, on the only way of life they knew or could accept. In the words of Manuel Antonio Ay and Hyacinth Canek, the Maya put forth their case:

> We poor Indians are aware of what the whites are doing to injure us, of how many evils they commit against us, even to our children and harmless women. So much injury without basis seems to us a crime. Indeed, therefore, if the Indians revolt, it is because the whites gave them reason; because the whites say they do not believe in Jesus Christ, because they have burned the cornfield. They have given just cause for the reprisals of the Indians, whom they themselves have killed. . . . But even these things, now that they have begun, will not discourage us even if they last twelve years and always go against us, for we are God's sacrifices. They will have to say whether God gave them permission to slaughter us all, and that we have no will in the matter. . . . Therefore if we die at the hands of the whites, patience. The whites think

that these things are all ended, but never. It is so written in the book of Chilam Balam, and so even has said Jesus Christ, our Lord on earth and beyond, that if the whites will become peaceful, so shall we become peaceful.

This was their voice: confused, frightened, determined, and horrified by Ladino blasphemy, by the sacrilegious destruction of growing corn. Few men can question the survival of their own culture; individuals may die, but the world one has embraced with one's own mind and heart must live on. The Maya in Yucatan, finding resistance possible, took up arms in defense of his world.

Part Two

The Caste War

Three

Revolt
1847–1848

THE H-MEN'S FINGERS moved rapidly as he counted the grains of corn, twelve grains for the first twelve days of the new year and for the twelve months to follow. One, two, three yielded death, war, and destruction in the land, the events of each day forecasting the manner of its month. A second twelve grains were counted with the days meeting their months in reverse order; January 24 matched the month of January, reinforcing the sign of January 1, and all the omens were bad—destruction in the land, war, and death, in each of the four directions, and under God the Son, God the Father, and God the Holy Ghost. Thus the H-men counted his Xoc-kin to the uneasy Maya, who knew the predictions were true.

There was fear among the white men, too. Governor Barret decreed that the Carnival of 1847 would not be celebrated in Mérida that year, against the possibility that the disbanded northern militia might re-form behind masks. The same fear had kept him from transferring his government to Mérida and made him pick Campeche men to garrison the city's fortress of San Benito. These efforts accomplished little. The revolt came on a Sunday afternoon in late February during a band concert in front of San Benito; the predominantly male audience came to life at a signal, rifles and pistols were brandished, and the fortress was taken in a bloodless coup. Freshly printed manifestos blossomed on city walls and were sent off in bundles to the towns and villages; the militia was re-formed (with more enthusiasm among the officers than the men), and patriotic celebrations and balls were given. In spite of all this, the citizens of Mérida simply didn't care. The men of Campeche did. Their

Seventeenth Battalion hurried over the mountains, their garrison at Valladolid made forced marches west, a fleet landed troops at Sisal, and the revolt collapsed. Colonel Cetina, a man we shall hear a good deal of, was sent to join his chief, Barbachano, in Cuban exile, and most people gave a sigh of relief.

But this minor, almost bloodless revolt was not what the H-menob had prophesied. The people of Valladolid, remembering the horrible fifteenth of January, counted the months forward to twelve, then backward three: October was the month to watch. Bonifacio Novelo, who had come to symbolize the Valladolid massacre, was still at large, supposedly terrorizing the villages of the northeast but in fact supported by them. The guns that the Campeche men had distributed to the Maya volunteers couldn't be collected; they were being kept as advance payment on promised rewards. Signs were in the air, but the politicians, who didn't count grains of corn, thought they could change the future. The most prominent men of the Méndez party came from all parts of the country to a conference at the neutral town of Ticul, where the problems that threatened anarchy were to be resolved. There were debates on reorganizing the government, the army, and the tax system; but buried beneath the verbiage of justice and liberty were two questions that no one could answer: how to break the deadly cycle of revolution upon revolution, and what to do about the Maya. These questions were simply tabled, everyone agreeing that they had better be considered sometime after the regular elections. The conference adjourned and Barret's government moved to Mérida on the twenty-third of June. A lost last chance.

Rain had come while the politicians talked at Ticul, and the Maya had been busy with their planting, seemingly indifferent to the fact that they were being cheated again; they finished their cornfields by the date of adjournment. More than corn had been planted. Colonel Cetina was back, having landed secretly on the north coast, conspiring at Tizimin to cast his opposition vote. He had come from Havana with money, weapons, and the nerve to fish in troubled waters. Tizimin was the town from which Santiago Iman had proclaimed against the Mexican government of Santa Anna nine years before. It was a sleepy place, ready for the rattle of drums and the call of the bugle, far from the eye of the government and with the woods close by in case of failure. Cetina first gathered some 300 Mestizos indifferently armed; then for the necessary battalions he turned, as had Iman and all leaders since, to the Maya.

Envoys fanned out along the back trails with the usual promises of tax reduction and land. These men avoided white settlements, left no mark of their passage, kept no records, and later would have good reason to forget what they had done; it is impossible now to trace their movements and the alliances they thought they made. One of them was seen at Chichimila, a village five miles south of Valladolid, collecting money for the cause, and the chief there, Manuel Antonio Ay, was definitely enlisted. So was Jacinto Pat, the cacique of Tihosuco, known as a Barbachanista with much influence in the area; his ranch, Culumpich, was chosen as depot and assembly point. Besides Pat there was Cecilio Chi of nearby Ichmul, and, less certainly, Bonifacio Novelo, the outlawed Mestizo assassin of Valladolid.

The original intentions of these men are not known, but there is good evidence that they held their own councils and discussed a program quite different from the one being planned by Cetina. They had fought the Dzul's battles before and been swindled, and we can only guess how far their talk went. It was later reported that Pat wished to replace the Ladino government, that Ay was for driving the white men from the land, and that Chi was simply for killing them, down to the last woman and child. We can't know, and perhaps they didn't either; at any rate, their destiny was shaped more by events than by ideas. Their first move was to send Novelo south, with all the money they could raise, to buy arms from the English at Belize.

Colonel Cetina, then, in preparing a Barbachanista revolution against the government, had an uncertain alliance with various Mestizo and Maya leaders south of Valladolid, who were themselves preparing for a purpose that might or might not coincide with his. All of these towns south of Valladolid—Chichimila, Ichmul, Tihosuco —were on the frontier; and to a large extent, the Maya involved were the half-civilized Huits, with their long hair, their loincloths, and their experience of recent outrage.*

The intended day of assault is unknown, but after the planting the Maya began to move; supplies were being assembled at Culumpich in early July. One of the few Ladino settlers in this forest country was alerted by long columns of natives passing his hacienda of Acambalam, and learning of the conspiracy through a trusted servant, he rode into Valladolid and warned the commandant, Colonel Eulogio Rosado. With the January massacre in mind, the Colonel wasted no time; he immediately sent an order of arrest to Trujeque, now jefe político of the Peto district, naming Cecilio Chi and Jacinto Pat. It took several days for this message to reach Peto, and several more for the uneasy Trujeque to prepare a small force to seize the men he had led in battle only six months before. On arriving at Pat's ranch of Culumpich, he found no trace of the guns alleged to be there; deciding that the report was false and a plot to destroy the caciques involved in the Valladolid massacre, the men of his own party, he spent the day visiting with his old friend. However, he did send a certain Captain Beitia with a small troop to the nearby town of Tihosuco, to look for Cecilio Chi.

Meanwhile, new evidence was uncovered. A suspicious cantinero in the village of Chichimila had taken a letter from the hat of Manuel Antonio Ay while serving him in his tavern; finding the ambiguous contents incriminating, he had informed Colonel Rosado. A patrol quickly seized Manuel Antonio and several others, along with further correspondence. An immediate trial revealed how a revolution was to be headed by Ay, Chi, Pat, and Novelo, all fighting for the reduction of taxes on the Maya; a Mestizo, named treasurer by the rebel group, informed to save his neck. For Manuel Antonio Ay there was no escape. The January atrocities called for revenge, and a stern example was to be set. He was taken to the Chapel of Santa Ana, in a barrio of Valladolid, and on the next day, July 26, he was led out to face a firing squad.

* The American traveler John L. Stephens, writing in 1841, describes Huit tribesmen he saw north of Valladolid: "Naked, armed with long guns and with deer and wild boars slung on their backs, their aspect was the most truculent of any people we had seen. They were some of the Indians who had risen with General Iman, and they seemed ready at any moment for battle."

There was no weakness in him, a small brown figure in white cotton pants and shirt, barefoot, hatless, guarded by an escort of infantry and cavalry. His people had come from the many surrounding villages to see him die, filing into the city since early morning, blocking the streets with their numbers. The entire garrison was under arms, with loaded cannons placed at important intersections. Trouble was expected, but the Maya humbly obeyed orders and stared at the preparations in their usual silent manner. "Preparen las armas! Apunten! Fuego!" and as the volley echoed across the plaza, sending flocks of vultures into the air, Manuel Antonio slumped against a bullet-pocked wall. This was the beginning of the prophecy of death.

The execution did a number of things. First, it set a precedent; up to this time revolutionary prisoners had not been shot in Yucatan. Cetina, for example, whose three attempts against the government helped to make the Caste War possible, was punished with nothing worse than exile. But he was white, and Manuel Antonio's fate was a stern warning that the natives would not be treated by white men's rules.

The warning worked, but not in the way it was intended to. It showed Cecilio Chi and Jacinto Pat what to expect if captured and committed them to a war to the death. It isolated Cetina from whatever Maya allies he had, thus dividing revolutionaries along the lines of race. Ladino fears turned a political, then a social, revolution into a racial one, thus evoking sadism and savagery on both sides.

Colonel Cetina made his declaration on the day of the execution. He had undoubtedly learned of the initial security leak, probably heard of Ay's capture, and come to realize that further delay would be fatal; so with his 300 men he marched south to the suburbs of Valladolid and demanded the city's surrender. In response, Rosado sent envoys who told of the execution, explained the racial threat, and insisted that this was a time for white men to stand together. Cetina must have had his own doubts, but despite whatever commitments he had made, he yielded to this argument and entered the city peacefully, adding his troops to the garrison. Rosado soon sent these dubious reinforcements to hold the town of Tixcacalcupul, in order to avoid a possible clash within the city. Cetina hadn't given up yet, but

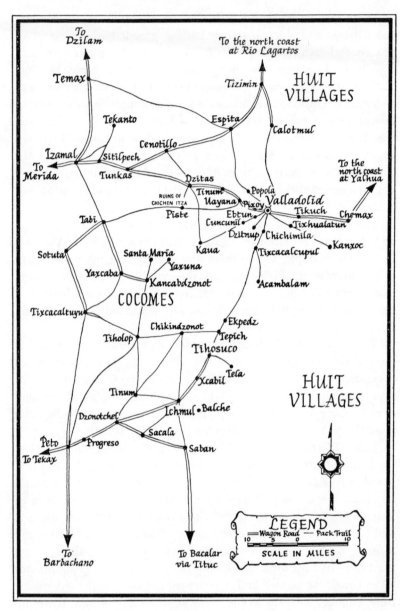

Valladolid and the frontier, 1847–48

by postponing his decision he lost any hope for control of the Maya.

There is conflicting testimony as to whether Cecilio Chi had heard of his comrade's execution by the time Captain Beitia found him, drinking alone in a Tihosuco cantina. It was eleven at night, the town dark and silent, and the captain had left his soldiers behind. One version has it that Chi seemed perfectly innocent and Beitia saw no reason for an arrest. The other has it that Chi was drunk and furious about the execution, that he angrily promised to report to Ichmul to face charges in person the next day, and that the captain was afraid to seize him. At any event, Trujeque found more convincing proof the following day, but by that time Chi and Pat were gone. This proof, an intercepted letter, called for the neighboring villages to join in an attack on Tihosuco. Startled out of his former doubt, the jefe político hurried to the threatened town. Finding neither hostile natives nor the missing leaders, he led his militia on to Tepich and Chi's nearby ranch. Again the conspirators had evaded them, and the soldiers expressed their irritation by looting and burning the ranch, with a white officer raping a twelve-year-old Indian girl for good measure—the first sack, the first rape of the Caste War.

The Ladinos of Tepich were given some guns for self-defense, but they didn't feel sufficiently threatened to return with the troops to Tihosuco. The next day a patrol was sent to another settlement, where five Mayas were arrested and brought in. In the early hours of July 30, 1847, Cecilio Chi struck back. Surprising Tepich, he slaughtered the twenty or thirty Ladino families—men, women, and children without distinction, sparing only some of the girls for rape—less out of lust than of hatred, it was said. A survivor escaped to Tihosuco with the news; the Caste War was on in earnest.

Tihosuco was thrown into panic. Outlying houses were abandoned, everyone congregating in a little plaza at the southern edge of town where barricades were hastily thrown up while messengers raced off for reinforcements. Retaliation was taken on the available prisoners, men who obviously hadn't been involved in the massacre: they were lined up against a wall and shot that afternoon. The night was spent in fear and trembling, with false alarms and sporadic volleys from nervous sentries imagining movement or noises in the dark. Morning brought confidence with a company of militia from Ichmul, and two *guerrillas* were organized to attack Tepich. Guerrillas were groups of soldiers, from platoon to regimental size, that acted independently on the narrow trails, often without hope of relief if they found more than they could handle; they were much like modern commando units. Fighting in the rain forest, in the lower bush of the west, was like fighting under water. Sergeant or general, no one could maintain control past the range of a bugle, past the next bend in the path. Everything depended on tactics; strategy seldom existed.

Captain Beitia led his guerrilla, some two hundred men, into an ambush. He fled from the scene, leaving his wounded to be mutilated, and with them, his career as an officer. The second guerrilla, of equal size, made contact with the enemy in what became the normal manner, by receiving a volley from men hidden behind a stone barricade. Yucatan is a vast limestone plain, with at best a thin layer of soil, and the terrain had an abundance of loose rock; the rocks had been used to build walls for livestock, for they could be quickly thrown up and laid without mortar—a technique easily adapted to the needs of war. At first the barricades simply blocked the trails, but, as the Ladino soldiers learned to their sorrow, they were capable of many refinements—flanking walls for enfilade, carefully masked strong points, support lines, and pitfalls bristling with pointed stakes.

This first barricade was easily carried, and the second guerrilla reached Tepich. They returned there the next day to find what was left of Beitia's wounded. What they found enraged them. They put the village to the torch, shot the Indians who ran out of the flames, desecrated the church and the shrine huts, and filled the village well with stones. Tepich had ceased to exist. All this was watched by Maya from the surrounding forest; too weak to resist, unable to save their families, they stood by and learned how the white men made war.

Meanwhile couriers raced to the west, to Peto, Tekax, Ticul, and into the capital, spreading fear like the carriers of a plague. No one seems to have paused or questioned; no one wondered any more if the expression "Caste War" might be only political propaganda. The horror of Valladolid was too recent, burned too deep in memory. The

Creoles had busied themselves with political conferences, carnivals, and rebellions, but they acted as if they had always known that this moment would come. Instant harmony was created by proclamation, just as revolutionary principles had been, and it was just as lasting. Excited crowds gathered before the houses of Barbachano and Méndez, the latter recently elected to succeed Barret as Governor in September. Bands played in the streets, rockets fizzed skyward, church bells rang. It was the fifth of August, 1847. As after all fiestas, there would be second thoughts and regrets in the morning, but now all was enthusiasm for "the holy cause of order, humanity, and civilization."

Printers labored far into the night turning out the new proclamations. On August 6, it was ruled that all men from sixteen to sixty were to report for military duty (only white or half-whites need apply; that lesson had been learned) and to list whatever guns they owned. Of course there was no organization capable of enlisting, much less equipping, a large-scale army. This was no petty revolt, fought by the lowest caste and by those who liked that sort of thing while the "better" class of people remained neutral. Now the lowest caste, the vast majority, was the enemy.

The first units to march east from Mérida would be organized and at least partially trained militia; but without their former Indio ranks, they needed replacements by the thousands, and would need thousands more when decimated in battle. This was to become total war: approximately 17 per cent of the Ladino population would be under arms before it was done, as compared with about 2 per cent of Americans in the American Revolution, and 10 per cent in the Second World War. So the recruits were sworn in and drilled awkwardly in the Plaza de Armas and all the little plazas across the country. Gahona's woodcuts show them without uniforms, often without rifles, confusing the orders of the newly created officers, who themselves knew little more. They spent their nights poring over the manual of arms. They learned, or at least heard, that the flintlock rifle is loaded in eleven movements, all according to the book; those who didn't learn to load and fire quickly, instinctively, under all types of conditions, with a hand that didn't tremble from fear or exhaustion, would be paid for their clumsiness by an Indio machete. The use of that indispensable tool and weapon couldn't be taught; it was simply a matter of slashing before you were slashed, with no nonsense about parry and thrust.

Men warmed again to the sounds of the soldiering trade. There were the bugle calls, tuneless and caterwauling to unfamiliar ears, inherited from the old King's army, which had taken them over during the holy war from the Caliphs of Granada and Seville: barbaric invocations, Christianized now by long usage, music no soldier can hear without emotion. *La Diana*, in the clear early dawn; *Oración*, to end the day, or a life above the open grave; *Ataque*, which meant just that; and *Degüello*, attack without quarter (heard that last day at the Alamo)—quick, demanding, orchestrated by the whining of bullets. These memories would stay with the aging veterans, to lift their hearts and straighten their backs on patriotic holidays far in the future.

For the present, the bugle, together with popular ballads adapted to march time for flute and drum, would help them along the weary trail, because there was more to soldiering than heroics. They had to learn how to march ten or twenty miles, down rocky, winding, jungle paths, with shoes or sandals that could take the wear, with feet that didn't blister. They had to learn to conserve water; not to drink when thirst was strong and sweat it all away, but to rest a time in the shade and then rinse the dust from the mouth. They had to learn to cook and eat the miserable food, to sleep on the hard ground wrapped in a blanket and still be able to move the next day. These details meant little to the frontiersmen and nothing to the Maya, who knew no other way of life; but the city men of the west suffered, and it would be weeks before they were worth the equipment they carried. Still, they marched.

If the politicians had once been hesitant and cautious about implementing their liberal principles, they now abandoned them with conviction. On August 6, the constitution, Rejón's beautiful constitution of 1841, was amended. The Indios were stripped of a half-won citizenship, reduced to wards of the state without legal rights, their leaders to be appointed Ladinos rather than elected natives. They were to be brought in from their settlements and put under the close supervision of town authorities—an atavistic attempt for Creoles whose ancestors had been trying to do just that since the Conquest. Idleness and drunkenness—a nuisance to drunken, usually idle masters—was to be stopped. Punishment was to be by "customary but prudent means," and stone masons set to work replacing the *picotas,* the whipping posts once torn down in revolutionary enthusiasm. Much of this simply restored legal sanction to practices that had never stopped, particularly in the back country. The colonial laws were to be imposed on all Maya, not just those under arms in an alleged racial war—a war that the congress had first heard of two days before and about which they had little accurate information. Did these congressmen feel rushed, did they wonder if all of this was somewhat premature? Apparently not. Theirs was the conviction born of fear.

The inevitable witch hunt began. Masters saw rebellion in the eyes of their servants, in a strange look, in an unusual laugh. A night patrol in the capital was insulted by some drunken natives, who reportedly shouted the names of their ancient kings. Such incidents won credence for the story that Cecilio Chi intended to enter Mérida on midnight of August 15, to be crowned after the massacre of the entire white population. The city became a hysterical armed camp. Heavy mounted patrols arrested Indians until San Benito could hold no more. At sunset on the fifteenth, bonfires were lit in the streets of the city to prevent a surprise attack. Strong points and outposts had been established, and citizens stood ready in their doorways with ancient muskets, sabers, and pikes while the womenfolk tended jars of boiling water, which could be thrown from the rooftops. It was a sleepless night, but the attack never came.

Still, fear and suspicion mounted. Francisco Uc, the cacique of of nearby Uman and a wealthy, educated man, was suddenly found to have brown skin. He was arrested on the evidence of letters that were never shown in court and on the testimony of his adopted son, who would inherit on his death; he was defended by influential white friends, but only until the lynch mob began shouting for their blood, too; and so he was condemned, joined before the firing squad by various other caciques and notables of his race. Over one hundred petty leaders were sent to the Presidio in Campeche and forty were dispatched to the fortress of San Juan de Ulúa off Veracruz. Trusted Ladinos were appointed in their places.

Maya who had led peaceful lives now paid for rebel atrocities and successes. They found themselves dragged to the picotas, or suspended by their ears, whipped until they confessed to a plot they knew nothing about. Rumor and official reports told of savagery on the frontier, of how the Maya had killed a boy in front of his mother and sisters, cutting out his heart and drinking his blood before they raped the women and left them half dead beside the mutilated body.

Each such account, whether true or not, triggered new acts of vengeance. Pressure was put to the native population in more formal ways: an edict demanded the seizure of their guns, the guns that provided them with the only meat they ever tasted; confiscated weapons soon filled public buildings and became the objects of a brisk black-market trade. Little settlements of two or three huts built close to a cornfield were burned and the people driven into the towns like prisoners of war or slaves. The men then had to walk all day to reach their cornfields; their women and children stayed behind as hostages. And yet these people, the servants and workers of the old haciendas in the northwestern corner of the peninsula, were not involved in the rebellion, and they even looked down on their less civilized eastern brothers. Francisco Uc might have been in correspondence with the rebel caciques, but so was Miguel Barbachano. The "plot" of August 15 simply didn't exist.

Stern punishment cowed house-servants, but it goaded free men to action. While the ashes of Tepich were still warm, with the cries of those who had been burned alive ringing in their ears, Cecilio Chi, Jacinto Pat, and several other leaders met at Culumpich to declare a war of total extermination, a war without quarter against the white race. Cecilio assembled men at a ranch in the forest, held it against the guerrillas until they became battalions, and then scattered his men with orders to reassemble at a designated point. Guerrillas hit Jacinto Pat at Xcanul, and he made them pay with sniping and ambush before he broke off and scattered. He lost some dead and ten prisoners, including two of his cousins, who were thrown to the ground with their hands tied behind them to be shot and left for the vultures. White reinforcements, eight hundred strong, had come marching into Tihosuco, and after dividing into guerrillas they hunted up and down the jungle trails, looking for the enemy, scattering his forces when they could find him. But the enemy could be found only when he was ready and waiting.

As this went on, the Maya built up a war chest by picking off isolated haciendas, sometimes collecting as much as two thousand pesos plus jewelry at one place, amusing themselves with any white or half-white men stupid enough to have stayed on. At Acambalam, where their plans had been betrayed by a brother of the race, the Maya servants were slaughtered with the rest as "plate-lickers" and "white men's dogs." With the looted valuables, Bonifacio Novelo headed south to Belize for a second time, to buy guns and ammunition on a small but vital scale. The native leaders had apparently been forced to move before they were ready, before all preparations and alliances were complete, and their major task now was simply to survive, to prove that revolt was possible. A few more adherents had come in, notably Florentino Chan of Dzitnup, near Valladolid. Cocom chieftains from the Yaxcaba-Sotuta region sent encouraging answers, but the vast majority of their race was holding back to see what the future would bring. For this reason, fighting was limited to a few necessary skirmishes while the leaders waited for the Belize supply column to return.

Colonel Cetina studied these developments unhappily, puzzling over the Maya intentions, unsure whether they were bloodthirsty savages or Barbachanistas and allies. Rosado sent him north to his home ground of Tizimin, where he neglected to report the disposition of his troops and the acquisition of new reserves of powder and shot from the port of Rio Lagartos. When deserters from Cetina's ranks reported open talk of revolution, Rosado sent a battalion and two cannons to question the truth of this. Not liking Cetina's answer, the battalion took his camp and smashed his force on the twenty-seventh of September. This convinced Colonel Cetina, and nine days later, after secretly crossing the state with a corporal's guard of survivors, he seized the fortress of San Benito in Mérida and declared the Barbachano government restored. Mérida accepted this desperate gesture, transforming it from a fantastic gamble into a political reality.

The countermove was prompt. Forgetting their talk of a sacred struggle against savages, the Méndez faction coolly drained the frontier to meet what they considered the more serious threat. Colonel Bolio left the Tihosuco camp with his men and marched through Peto and Tekax, collecting the forces that had gathered to fight the Maya and ordering them in the opposite direction. Colonel Oliver headed west from Valladolid with all the Campeche men, picking up sections of the Seventeenth Battalion that had been sent to reinforce him. Since most of the officers and men of the force in being were Mendecistas, this left the regulars of the Light Battalion, the Mestizo settlers, and the priests very much on their own, to do what they could in self-defense. These movements were closely observed, each unit counted as it marched out, man by man, from behind the trail-side foliage.

The Maya must have felt that their saints had been working over-time, and they were quick to take what was offered. Tixcacalcupul fell first, ending with a massacre that included a priest who lost the privilege of his group by particularly greedy land stealing. This vic-tory gave them the adherence of the Valladolid district, everything but the city itself. Then they turned south, finishing off several neg-lected settlements, and finally, after a two-day siege, took Tihosuco. Trujeque, who had been left in command there, was able to get his people out safely to Peto, which left the Maya supreme in the area between that city and Valladolid, a distance of over fifty miles, with only the empty jungle behind and the restive Cocomes before them.*

In Mérida, Cetina was faced with the complications of politics; while the Méndez forces massed, the Maya victories daily reduced his popularity. In this dilemma, he did the one thing he knew best— he marched. On October 25, not trusting his soldiers to fight the political enemies who were closing in on the capital, he announced that he was going against the Maya and led his army as far as Izamal, where he stopped to see what would develop. That same day, the city sent commissioners and submitted to the Méndez party. Now his revolution was reduced to the fifteen hundred Meridanos under his command, and with no other course open, Cetina continued to Valladolid, sending envoys asking Rosado to join him in fighting Indians. This offer was refused; a battle was fought before Valladolid and Cetina again took to the woods, a defeated refugee.

* These Maya were called "Cocomes" after the Cocom family, which had once ruled all Yucatan from Chichen Itza and had moved to Sotuta after being overthrown; their present home, the ancient province of Sotuta, was the locale of the Quisteil revolt of 1761. The ancient grandeur of the Cocom had been recalled by the republication of Cogolludo's *Historia de Yucatán* in 1843, and the 1761 rebellion was much discussed in the contemporary press. Creoles thus anticipated trouble from the Cocomes some years before it came.

Too much blood had been shed for this to be the end of things. Cetina collected several groups of survivors in Tizimin and vowed vengeance without quarter against Rosado, for the alleged shooting of prisoners. Furthermore, he now talked openly of joining with Jacinto Pat, and a proclamation was printed for him offering the Maya chief five thousand pesos and the tools of war if he would unite with the Barbachano forces. This was too much for his troops, who saw universal destruction in such a course; less blinded than their leader by factional hatred, they began to desert in large numbers. Reduced to impotence, Cetina distributed his excess guns to the local Maya as a token of friendship, and then, in a final gesture of defiance, he took sixty men and once again seized San Benito at Mérida on December 4. This time the city wasn't interested. He surrendered the next day, thus ending his political career.

These rapid marches, countermarches, and fantastic coups had taken place on the brink of a catastrophe, a catastrophe they had made possible. As Cetina darted back and forth across country like an angry insect, he drew to himself the misguided efforts of the only defense the white man had, the state militia, at that date controlled by Méndez. The weeks, the battalions, the money spent defeating and hunting him down were gone, and what could have been done quickly would now require generations—an army each generation, and the bankruptcy of the state for many years to come. The Maya had been given a breathing space and minor victories at the moment of their greatest need. This brought confidence to the Batabob, faith to the native soldier, and recruits without number. Colonels Bolio, Oliver, and Rosado didn't realize this as they redeployed their troops to finish what they considered the minor threat; and at first it seemed as if they might have been right.

Guerrillas drove out of Peto, smashing Maya concentrations at Sacala and Saban and establishing a fortified camp at Ichmul; reinforcements were pushed forward, and a major effort was prepared there to end the rebellion. It was too late. On December 5, a fusillade roared out of the forest and a general assault on Ichmul, which carried into the streets, was repulsed by the smallest margin. Barricades rose overnight, ringing the town and bringing it under siege. The ring was broken after several days of heavy fighting, when the Maya had exhausted their ammunition. The attackers left but promised a return in eight days, just enough time for the pack mules to make the round-trip journey to the English merchants on the Rio Hondo.

The promise was kept. The charge came with war cries, and when it was stopped the Maya settled down behind their old positions, repairing and extending them. Again patrols were sent to drive them away, but, facing a well-supplied enemy, they were decimated one after another. In the space of an hour, forty soldiers were killed and seventy-five wounded; the exhausted officers found no end to the barricades, no technique against them except bloody frontal assault. This was on December 19, and by late afternoon the garrison was driven back into the town, abandoning its outer defenses. The inevitable stone walls were built that night, within thirty paces of Ladino lines. Attempting to force them was expensive in casualties, and no less so in morale: Ladino prisoners were quartered on the spot and their heads thrown back into the lines where they could be recognized by former friends, who themselves began to wonder about the future. Six days of this reduced the ammunition of the defenders to a few rounds apiece, pushed their nerves beyond the point of reliability, and brought the knowledge that if they waited any longer there would be no escape. At five o'clock on Christmas morning, a breakthrough was made on the southern line; the women, children and wounded were followed by the main party at six o'clock and the rear guard shortly after. By good timing, the lack of Maya ammunition, or the desperate bravery of the soldiers, safe passage was won and the refugees straggled into Peto throughout the afternoon, as Ichmul burned behind them.

Colonel Rosado, leading 800 men to the relief of Ichmul, delayed among the now risen Cocomes; after skirmishing from Sotuta to Tiholop, where he learned that he was too late, he turned back to Peto. This town, with a regular population of over 5,000, crowded now with refugees and a garrison of 2,500 soldiers, was well supplied with food and ammunition, and the Colonel took command. He would use it to replace Ichmul as the base of operations. Cetina had been his torment at Valladolid; now it was a kinsman, Felipe Rosado, local leader of the Barbachanista faction. In an effort to enlist this man on the side of civilization and of Méndez, he offered him the ranks of Colonel and jefe político. This was accepted with the same faith Cetina had displayed earlier, and for the same reason; Felipe Rosado was also waiting, wondering when and which way to leap.

Through January 1848, the Maya moved their forces forward to surround the town, fortifying the village of Dzonotchel, twelve miles east, as headquarters. Prepared now, and organized, Colonel Eulogio Rosado hoped to catch them out in the open, to cut them off from the woods and smash them in one conclusive battle. Using the largest number of soldiers yet committed in the war, he ordered the Battalions Sixteenth Campeche and Seventeenth Chenes to attack straight down the main road, while the regulars of the Light Battalion took back trails to get behind Dzonotchel.

The two Rosados watched the opening movements from the Peto church tower, Felipe not responding to Eulogio's enthusiasm over the apparent early success. He had no reason to worry. The Light Battalion was cut up and stopped in the forest, the main forces were barely able to reach their objective, much less take it, and all came back with heavy casualties. That night, Felipe Rosado called a secret meeting of his partisans to decide whom to support. The men of the Peto militia hadn't seen action during the day, but they would quickly enough be forced to fight such men as their fellow-townsman José María Barrera, the local cacique Macedonia Dzul, and their good neighbor and political ally Jacinto Pat. Rosado had correspondence on his party's negotiation with the Maya, from Cetina or Barbachano himself, correspondence weeks old, not reflecting later local developments. There must have been doubts in the mind of Felipe Rosado, some hesitation about joining what might after all turn out to be a race war; choosing temporary neutrality, he left the next day with his family and followers for his ranch of Sacsucil, some thirty-five miles to the south. He was later followed by a large part of the local militia and by civilians of his party, so that the ranch temporarily became a settlement of some importance, and Peto was proportionately weakened.

There were three skirmishes the following week, one to assist a reinforcing unit, but none of them changed the general situation, which was confused and uncertain. Then a hidden cache of guns was discovered in Peto, and messages between the Barbachanistas of Sacusil and the Maya were intercepted. As the natives attacked they shouted, "Viva Don Miguel Barbachano, Gobernador!" It was probably these cries as much as anything else that demoralized the common soldiers at Peto. They had nothing against barracks life, or an occasional two-week war with no one hurt; but to face death month after month, to face mutilation if captured, so that Don-this or Don-that could loot the public treasury—no, that wasn't in the contract. Despised by their officers, ragged, underfed and underpaid, these men would later show courage when the issue was clear, when they realized that this was a new kind of war and understood the stakes involved; but at the moment, feeling themselves pawns in a political squabble, they began to desert up the main road to Tekax and home. With his citizen army dissolving before his eyes, Colonel Rosado was forced to depend on the regulars of the Light Battalion, but soon even they began to desert, leaving their posts undefended. Without serious fighting he had lost almost half his command, and in a moment of weakness, he decided it was time to go.

On the evening of February 6, word was spread and everyone massed in the plaza—civilians, the walking, and the stretcher-borne mixed in with the supply wagons, artillery, and ambulances—a confused mob, disorganized by the dark and the fear of being left behind. Funneling out through the narrow streets and the narrower wagon road, with misunderstood commands and delays, the column was held to the pace of the old and infirm. They had made only one mile by first light, and panic developed then, with the expectation of attack. The artillery, wagons, and ambulances were dumped, while many refugees collapsed on the ground, indifferent and unguarded. For some reason, the Maya held off. The largest part of these people, some 1,500 well-armed men and the civilians, straggled into Tekax through the late afternoon and evening, to the astonishment of the inhabitants, who were unable to understand how such a force could be defeated by ragged Indios. The obvious answer was to find a scapegoat, and there was talk of a court-martial for Rosado; but events broke too rapidly for this, and the Colonel was swept ahead on his long career.

Shortly before this, three days after the abandonment of Ichmul, the Mazehualob of the Cocomes region had risen, striking simultaneously at the many villages and ranches in their area, killing all they captured, showing what could have been done in a peninsula-wide revolt. At first it was chaotic, the Ladinos fighting and dying at their ranches, uniting when they could, hiding in the forest. Kancabdzonot was one center of resistance; burned on the first day, recaptured on the second by one hundred volunteers, who were in turn besieged, it was held for several days before the defenders fell back to Yaxcaba, which then became the general refuge for those who could make it. Colonel Rosado sent some two hundred soldiers up from Peto, escorting wounded, and they stopped at Yaxcaba, where they were soon joined by the Battalions First Mérida and Orden, dispatched from the capital. These units made a number of raids, operating as guerrillas along the trails. The Cocomes Maya knew the trails far better, and in spite of superior weapons the white soldiers were defeated time after time. Gradually the center of concentration pulled back to Sotuta, with Yaxcaba and Tabi as outposts.

Sotuta was the political capital of the Cocomes district. This honor, however, was disputed by Yaxcaba, and the argument, together with others apparently dating back to the petty wars of pre-Columbian times, had split the two towns completely.* At this time there was also a plot by the Sotuta Barbachanistas to surrender Yaxcaba to the enemy. Lieutenant Colonel Alberto Morales, in command of the area, was constrained to divide the two companies of the battalion Orden that came from Sotuta and Yaxcaba, stationed each in its native place to keep them from open fighting. The thought of white traitors sitting across their supply line weighed heavily on the exposed Yaxcaba company; and when they retreated on February 12, they refused to go to the assistance of Sotuta and marched back to Izamal.

During this period the threat against Valladolid had grown serious. Because of the several efforts of Cetina, the city had been given sec-

---

* A similar antagonism existed between Yaxcaba and the Cupul area to the east. When forced into towns by the conquistadors, the natives had worked the land nearest them, even if it lay in what had been a hostile province. Yaxcaba men made their fields across the border in Cupul, dispossessing the original cultivators for nearly three hundred years. Even into the twentieth century, revolutionary struggles split the villages on traditional lines, with Cupul raiding Yaxcaba and vice versa.

tions of several battalions: the Sixteenth Campeche, the Seventeenth Chenes, the Seguridad Pública, the Light Battalion, and the local battalion Constitución. To these were added Cetina's defeated troops, primarily from the First Mérida, which were reorganized and put into the line. Thanks to these forces, Colonel Agustín León, who had replaced Rosado when the latter went south, was able to disperse the bands that had begun attacking on December 4, 1847. The Maya came back toward the middle of the month to annoy him with walls which they never attempted to hold against assault but which always cost a few lives in the taking.

To work behind these people, to box them up and make the casualties worthwhile, León sent troops to reoccupy the village of Chemax, twenty-five miles to the east and up against the empty forest, a place that had been abandoned in the early days of the trouble. This unit achieved its objective, blasting in with artillery, but it cost them 36 of their 150 men. After acting in concert with several sorties from the city, which were unsuccessful or worse, some Campechanos of this command revolted against their exposed position and forced a withdrawal. Tikuch, ten miles east of Valladolid, was the next to go. The defenders of that place, driven back to the village churchyard, broke through in desperation and at heavy cost, reaching a nearby hacienda; they were closer to the city but still surrounded and near the end of their strength. Rescue came from Valladolid. After 150 men with two cannons were stopped in bloody crossfire, the Colonel himself, with 200 more men and more cannons, reached the survivors, burying the dead and bringing the rest to safety.

After the fall of Ichmul, the Maya no longer combined to concentrate their forces at one place or another, but split into regional groups. They had all the recruits they could use, and the distances had become too great. The southern force, which took Peto and went west from there, was under the general control of Jacinto Pat; the groups that besieged Valladolid were led by Cecilio Chi.

Cecilio had campaigned in the war against Mexico, fighting all the way to Campeche, and had learned his lesson well. First he looted and burned the surrounding haciendas and ranches, taking cattle, cotton, honey, coffee, and money; these resources, denied to the cities that needed them, were sent south to be traded for the tools of war. Next, hamlets and villages were put to the torch, small garrisons crushed with overwhelming strength, and counterattacks were lured along ambushed trails if small enough and allowed to wander harmlessly through the forest if too large to handle. Even when he fortified a village, Chi wouldn't hold it against determined guerrillas. He couldn't afford the ammunition, and he preferred his whites strung out along the trails, where one short rush from cover would put his machete-swingers where they could do the most good. Colonel León couldn't garrison all of the villages in anything like sufficient strength, and so he attempted to keep the initiative with a daily combat patrol several hundred strong. But the white men had only their bugles to signal with, and the Mazehualob had their tunkul, the hollow log drum, whose voice could be heard for miles. The soldiers still met the Maya only when expected, and the Colonel watched distant columns of smoke rise from the forest as his villages went up one after another.

By mid-January 1848, Cecilio felt ready for more ambitious steps. On the nineteenth of that month, a white battalion had successfully taken eleven stone barricades, and found itself overextended. The withdrawal from this trap became a retreat and then a rout, continuing right into the city and bringing on a general assault by an estimated twelve to fifteen thousand Maya. The first rush carried into the barrio and plaza of Santa Ana, where Manuel Antonio Ay had been executed six months before. The women and children ran scrambling for cover in the barrio church. The militia frantically re-formed. Cannons were wheeled into line, pointed down the streets, fired at the onrushing horde, a target that couldn't be missed; and the attack was turned back. The Maya kept a firm foothold in the city, but they couldn't face massed artillery volleys over open terrain, and the stone buildings made good defensive positions. That night, the parochial church was filled with burning candles and heartfelt prayers as the priest, Manuel Antonio Sierra O'Reilly, asked the white man's God for aid. Outside, bonfires lit the streets against night attack. The Maya came two days later, seizing more of Santa Ana, including its cenote, the only source of water in the barrio; then they fortified themselves and blocked off most of the roads for good.

Colonel León's next report read:

> For seventy hours now I have sustained fire without intermission against an enemy who attacks me on three quarters of my perimeter [but who has not] been able to advance a step or occupy one of the many barricades held by my valiant soldiers; [the Maya] have been able to burn some houses which lie in the line, favored by the night, the woods, and their use of the bush. . . . In the one-fourth of the line left open to me are the roads to Calotmul, Espita, and Pixoy, the latter being the line of communication with the capital. This circumstance makes me hope that the enemy, even though [superior in number] to my troops, respects my position and would allow me to retreat, which resolution I will take only in the last case, even though I am persuaded that perhaps I have reached the end of the game.

The Colonel was beginning to hedge, to prepare his superiors for the worst. His next report had to be carried through the lines with bayonets: Valladolid was sealed off under close siege.

Four

The Crisis
1848

AFTER THE COLLAPSE of Colonel Cetina's final gambit, Governor Méndez based his government in the town of Maxcanu. Located on the Campeche road some twenty-five miles south of Mérida, at the intersection of the highway to Tekax and Peto, it gave him several advantages: quick access to news of the fighting in the east, a chance to control events in Mérida without risking entanglement in a coup staged by hostile Meridanos, and an open line to the resources of his southern partisans in Campeche.

Meeting in Maxcanu during December 1847, the congress passed a spate of emergency laws. A new tax was voted on capital, salaries, and the professions, and action was ordered to collect from all debtors of the state. The Governor was given extraordinary powers, both legislative and judicial, and on hearing of the loss of Peto, he used them promptly. Men over sixteen were prohibited from leaving their places of residence—a futile effort to stop the flood of refugees. Amnesty was extended to all rebels regardless of their crimes. Finally, Méndez named a committee of the type that almost inevitably appears when Latin revolutions or civil wars become too bloody: it was set up to compromise with the opposition and was headed by his enemy Don Miguel Barbachano, on the off-chance that the war might still be a political rather than a racial one, in which event it would be mutually convenient to make arrangements through party channels.

Barbachano went to Maxcanu to accept; and after a conference of reconciliation, in which the two men agreed that politics were politics but that the game was getting dangerous, Governor Méndez rode up to Mérida, intending to move his government there. He made a speech to the crowded plaza, from the Palacio Municipal, asking everyone to forget old hatreds and join in the common struggle for religion and civilization. His words were received with enthusiastic cheers; the white men would stand together as brothers. That night Méndez heard rumors of an assassination plot and secretly went back to Maxcanu. Brotherhood wasn't made by proclamation.

Barbachano had agreed to undertake a most dangerous and important mission. On February 15, 1848, armed with a letter from the Bishop to the Mazehualob and joined by José Canuto Vela and other priests, he was escorted to Tekax by the dashing and socially prominent Volunteer Cavalry. This town, on the northern edge of the Puuc range, had become headquarters for the southern command, including the Light Battalion of the regular army and a number of units of the National Guard, all under Colonel Eulogio Rosado.

The Maya were now at Tinum, six miles to the southeast. Nominally led by Jacinto Pat, the original force from the Tihosuco area was now far outnumbered by the swarms of recruits that rose, as if by a law of nature, to bask in the warmth of success; they came from the isolated settlements and the free villages, from Ichmul, Sacala, and Saban, and after the victory at Peto their numbers soared. As field hands joined the advancing rebels, the rich sugar-cane plantations of the area began to burn, sometimes with their masters but always with the nohoch cuenta, the written title of Maya servitude. The field hands, who recognized no authority in the beginning, spent their first weeks of liberty releasing old hatreds with the torch and the machete, looking for excitement in bands of three or four hundred men. Jacinto Pat stayed in Tihosuco, leaving most of the troops under his field commanders—his brother Esteban, Juan Justo Yam, and the Mestizo José María Barrera.

While at Tekax, Colonel Rosado decided to take a page from his enemy's book. Until now, holding the towns and attacking only with limited patrols, he had been unable to protect the ranches and haciendas upon which both sides depended for provisions. This timidity had been expensive. With the February–March harvest time beginning, he had already lost large and fertile areas, was embarrassed by great numbers of refugees, and had difficulty feeding his own men. He decided to let the troops feed themselves from the standing corn and destroy what they couldn't harvest. Two camps were ordered to pursue the new policy, one at Teabo, fifteen miles to the north, and one some twenty-five miles south across the Puuc hills at Becanchen; they received instructions to raid and ambush, to contest lost ground in a fluid manner, and to act in concert with the main body. The northern group had some initial success with the aggressive plan, but the southern force never got off its feet—closely besieged from the beginning, it simply drained resources from Tekax in the form of reinforcing convoys.

At this time, the Ladino army received news that should have removed the last doubt about the nature of the revolt. The Barbachano partisans who had withdrawn from Peto to Felipe Rosado's ranch at Sacsucil were assaulted; some thirty-six of them were killed, the survivors fleeing into the uninhabited jungle or making their way to white lines. A guerrilla was sent from Tekax to check this story. It moved undetected down to the neighborhood of Peto, then south through the hills to the ranch, where the bodies were found and buried. Their return was via Becanchen, but on nearing that place they encountered two white survivors of a death fight, and in revenge, attacked the victors among the still warm ashes of the town, killing a few Maya in battle and the prisoners later on. Becanchen was in ruins and Teabo of limited use, her garrison being needed to protect Tekax itself. The arrival of Barbachano's peace commission in Tekax gave Colonel Rosado an excuse to withdraw, and the counter-raids were abandoned.

The military had failed, so now the politicians and priests tried their hand. Letters urging peace had been sent out, and on February 28 the first returns began to come in. They were not encouraging. The Bishop had spoken of the horrors of war as "Divine Justice" for the erosion of religious faith and the growth of secularism. He was talking to the wrong people; there were no Freemasons among the Maya. One of the replies, expressing horror at the destruction of religious objects and the burning of a native church by white troops, asked plaintively: "Don't they know that we are the beloved of our Lord God, who put us here on earth to worship within our Holy Mother Church?"* More important was the answer received from several Maya chiefs gathered at Tabi:

> And now you remember that there is a True God. While you were murdering us didn't you know that there was a True God? You were always recommending the name of God to us and you never believed in His name. . . .
>
> And now you are not prepared nor have you the courage to accept the exchange for your blows. If we are killing now, you first showed us the way. . . .
>
> Twenty-four hours we allow you to give up your arms. If you are prompt, no harm will come to you, nor to your houses, but the houses and the haciendas of all whites who do not give up their arms will be burned, and they will be killed besides, because that's how they have taught us; thus everything the whites have done to us, we shall do the same and more.

With compromise barred in that direction, all hope centered on Jacinto Pat. His answer from Tihosuco, addressed to Father Vela, ran as follows:

> My most venerated sir and priestly father. . . . I swear to God and to your venerableness, as well as to the holy Bishop, that it is the truth I lay before your superior intelligence: that had there been no damage caused by the Spanish here in the town of Tihosuco, these towns would not have revolted; however, since they have, it is to defend themselves against the killing that the subdelegate, D. Antonio Trujeque, started among us. . . . [He] also began the fires, burning the town of Tepich, and he began to catch the poor Indians as you catch animals in the woods. . . . [The Indians] don't know if the superior government had given orders that they should [be killed], and they won't stop until the government has made a pronouncement. Not for one half of the tax will any Indian rest, but only if the tax is abolished . . . otherwise, life or death will decide the issue, because I have no other recourse. Also, I advise your venerability that I will know what is agreeable to you when you answer this communication. Like-

---

* This horror of church burning was shared by some of the Ladino troops. López Martínez, in his novel *El Ahorcado de 1848*, recounts how a sergeant refused to burn a church which had been "defiled" by the rebels and was being used by them as a barracks; when he was arrested and the church put to the torch, he was said to think, "Civilization burns as well."

wise, I tell you that the cost of baptism is three reales, that of marriage ten, for the Spaniard as well as the Indian, and the same for the salve and the response. This is the last that I shall make known to your venerability. The True God accompany your holy soul for many years.

More civilized and cautious than many of the other leaders, Pat may have been awed by the terrible forces he had helped unleash. His terms were easy to meet: Governor Méndez granted them on March 2, 1848, to the ringing of church bells and happy celebrations. It took time for this news to spread. Terms were offered by the Maya at Sotuta on March 6, and at Valladolid on March 10.

The Sotuta siege had been close and bitter, and the Cocomes had lived up to their reputation. Some Maya of the Tihosuco-Tepich nucleus fought with these people, but it was primarily their show, and they had little interest in taking orders from the eastern caciques. Their treaty conditions had a local flavor: return of the guns taken from them before they rebelled; surrender of the jefe político Bacelia, for whom they had special plans because they felt he had betrayed them; and recovery of the Virgin of Tabi, an image with inherent powers only at the service of its owners, which had been taken to the Sotuta church.

A priest had learned these terms by crossing over the barricades dressed in the vestments of a high holiday, standing his ground there while a brother priest fled before the angry threats. The clergy could no longer expect immunity; that last link between the races was breaking. But the terms were never discussed. Deciding to take rather than talk, the Maya came swarming against the lines that same afternoon, demanding the Virgin of Tabi. The attack was repulsed, as were several others on following days, but the whites had had enough. On March 10 they made a successful breakout, taking the guns and the very nervous jefe político with them back to Hocaba. The fate of the Virgin is not known.

The events leading to peace talks at Valladolid were more complex. Three convoys had fought their way into the city since the Pixoy trail had been closed, bringing wagons and mules loaded with food, powder, and shot, and adding 300 men to the garrison. In February, the month of cold winds and sickness, the northern leaders

—Cecilio Chi, Bonifacio Novelo, and Florentino Chan—met with Jacinto Pat in Tihosuco to discuss the terms offered by the peace commission, the terms that seemed to spell victory for the Maya. They had little trust in the promises of white men, but with powder and shot always scarce, the chance was too good to pass up. Cecilio went back to Valladolid, offering an armistice and terms: reduction of taxes, return of the seized guns, and punishment for his one-time leader Trujeque, all to be personally guaranteed by Don Miguel Barbachano. Colonel Miguel Bolio and Padre Manuel Sierra met with them, risking their lives at each uncertain encounter, when a parley could become a massacre; and the armistice was arranged, with both sides to hold in position while details were thrashed out and committed to paper. This was on February 12.

Anything could have broken this nervous truce, and something was bound to. Chancenote provided the excuse. This village, isolated in the forests of the northeast, had been a Ladino rallying point for its area and had survived through Maya neglect until February 10. On that day 2,000 Maya detached themselves from the Valladolid siege and swept down on the seventy-man garrison. The defenders drew their women and children into the walled churchyard, held out until their gunpowder was spent, and then attempted a breakthrough. A few reached safety in the woods, but the majority were cut down at the wall or slaughtered as the fighting swirled back across the churchyard and into the dark stone church. Wooden altarpieces were ripped from the walls and sent crashing down, to join the priest's vestments and images of the saints in a vindictive bonfire—destruction of the Santos who fought on the white side, revenge for similar white treatment of the holy objects of the Maya. Then the village was looted and put to the torch; this gave 25 men who had hidden on the church roof a chance to escape through the smoke and confusion and bring the story of these new atrocities to Valladolid. This had happened before the armistice, which had been in force for a week when they reached the city, but their tale of innocent children killed and women raped and mutilated before the high altar made a treaty with such an enemy unthinkable.

One hundred men under Colonel Rivero informed the Maya that the truce was over by driving into the village of Chichimila, apparently surprising and defeating them; but the Maya knew nothing about tactics, recognized no front or rear, and the Ladino detachment needed 200 reinforcements with cannons to get out. Determined to find the enemy and crush him, Rivero set off with a combat patrol of battalion strength on February 25, and fighting his way through a series of barricades, moved eight miles southwest to the village of Dzitnup. The village was abandoned when he arrived, but the Colonel soon found his battle. The Maya appeared on all sides, surprisingly well armed, and quickly threw his patrols back on the main force, based at the church. Then a counterattack broke under fire, and his command collapsed in panic with every man for himself; only fear could explain this, for although isolated and surrounded, their losses had been little more than 10 per cent.

Morale and discipline were becoming a problem, and a victory was sorely needed. Plans were laid that night for a coordinated attack at the site of the defeat. Bolio, with a battalion of fresh troops, would return to Dzitnup, while a second battalion waited in the city to act as support. If Bolio found Dzitnup undefended, he was to burn several huts as a signal and march on to Chichimila, supposedly Maya headquarters, to be joined there by the converging second column; should Dzitnup be defended, the second column was to come to his assistance, notified by a lookout in the tower of the Valladolid church. In this way they could be certain of finding the elusive enemy, luring him into battle, then concentrating in full force against him wherever he might choose to fight. It was a reasonable plan.

Bolio assembled his men in Sisal plaza, a mixed force from the First Local, Sixteenth Campeche, and Valladolid battalions, organized into three sections, plus guerrillas and those detailed to protect the wounded, which was important in this kind of war. How important became clear as they marched along the early morning trail; the first body, less than a mile from Valladolid, had a head crushed by rocks, the priest of Dzitnup was found hanging from a tree with his eyes ripped from their sockets, and other bodies showed that castration was a favorite form of mutilation. The National Guardsmen slowed, collected in knots to stare and consider, and had to be forced on by their officers. The Maya appeared only once, to fire a few rounds from behind a barricade and then fade into the forest.

Reaching Dzitnup peacefully, Colonel Bolio gave orders to establish outposts and began to prepare his defenses, basing them on the churchyard.

He was too late. The mousetrap snapped, and in a single rush from cover the Maya closed, chasing the soldiers back through the streets to the church, slaughtering the plaza post that tried to fight it out, and setting fire to the huts to make smoke cover—thus giving the prearranged signal that the village was undefended. Patrols sent to find weak spots came scampering back; a mass attack was ordered, but it was shattered after leaving the cover of the atrium wall, and there was panic. Colonel Bolio was last seen defending himself with his saber against a circle of Maya bayonets and machetes, and hand-to-hand fighting congested the lanes around the plaza as the desperate battalion fought its way to the woods. Over half of them made it and got back to the city in small groups. The reinforcing battalion, seeing the smoke around noon, had marched to the empty village of Chichimila and returned without firing a shot.

These two disasters at Dzitnup destroyed the offensive spirit of the Valladolid garrison. At best, they had dodged bullets from unseen snipers or been taken on either flank while they charged the endless barricades. The fighting had become suicidal, and the soldiers wanted no more of it. Colonel León realized that to go over to the defensive would mean eventual defeat, the surrender of the hinterland that supported the enemy and the loss of herds and crops he needed for his own supplies. With no choice but to prepare for ultimate evacuation, he had a large part of the civilians escorted by troops and artillery all the way to Izamal, the escort fighting back in with supplies.

A last ray of hope came on March 10, 1848, when Miguel Huchin sent word to his godfather Rivero reopening the question of peace. Colonel Rivero, Manuel Sierra, and several other priests and officials went out to meet with the native delegation. This was a mistake. They were seized and brought before Cecilio Chi at Dzitnup, where the priests were separated from the military and Rivero and his officers were macheted.

By the time this happened, on March 19, time had run out for Valladolid. On the previous night plans had been made in military council; assembly areas were assigned, the order of march arranged, and instructions given to the civilians. At dawn, cannons opened up on the barricades of the northwestern Espita trail, which were then carried by a five-hundred-man assault group that drove on to Popola village four miles away, setting up a perimeter defense to support the evacuation. Bugle calls announced that the way was clear, and wagons, carriages, coaches, litters, and carts were waved forward, all loaded with military supplies and the possessions of the wealthy, with the old, the young, the sick, and the wounded.

They were followed by a second regiment of troops and then by the remaining population of the city, over ten thousand people of all ages, skin color, and social position. These were the ones who were too brave, too timid, or too incredulous, to leave with the earlier convoys. But now there were no exceptions. The mayor and the councilmen packed away their records, the jefe político emptied his desk, merchants closed their shops, and housewives collected a few pitiful mementos symbolic of a lifetime, choosing and discarding and choosing again, while their men thought only of the weight and the trail ahead. The aged and senile were led protesting into the streets, not understanding the emergency or how they would be able to walk through fifty miles of forest. These people had spent half the night waiting in the streets north of the main plaza, and in the early morning hours they began to shuffle forward, out through the barrios and onto the Espita trail. Up ahead, the inevitable happened. A carriage, lurching from rock to rock, broke its axle, blocking the way at a spot where the trees were too thick to go around; congestion became a jam and the column was halted.

But by seven o'clock, a good part of the city was cleared, with doors standing open along deserted streets and packs of abandoned dogs running nervously about. This waiting silence was brief. Aware of what was afoot, the Mazehualob slipped in through the Valladolid barrio of Sisal; delayed among the buildings by a skirmish line of soldiers who fought to gain time, they nevertheless reached the Mérida road, burning the southern half of the city as they came. The camps in the barrios of San Juan and Santa Ana were given up, the troops falling back on Colonel León's rear guard, which protected the last of the unevacuated civilians while waiting for the order to withdraw. For a few precious minutes the Colonel held, clearing the streets with canister and grape; but the Maya, respecting his cannons, took to the houses and back yards, climbing walls from one yard to the next, infiltrating behind him, suddenly appearing with rifle or machete, and finally reaching the last of the civilians, who were still lined up four blocks long. The Santa Ana force dissolved into parties of soldiers trying to escape through various streets or buildings, most of them unsuccessfully. The troops of San Juan followed their colonel in a desperate attempt to drive through the horde of natives that held the plaza, but they were smashed and ceased to exist as a unit. Only León was able to keep some semblance of control and get his men clear.

The congested and tormented column was attacked along its entire length, with skirmishing where there were soldiers, slaughter where there were none. For the Maya, it was a grand orgy of revenge, their enemy too scattered for effective defense, and the machete quite sufficient for the unarmed. Dzitnup was nothing compared to this. Colonel León worked his way to Popola, where he found the immense jam of carriages and wagons. His measures were prompt: he had the barrels of gunpowder rolled together and destroyed, to save them from the Maya, and he ordered all vehicles abandoned. Most of the soldiers were completely useless by now, interested in nothing but their own skins and refusing to obey, but a few stayed with León; an artillery officer managed to get one cannon past the burning wagons, and this formed the nucleus of a rear guard, giving courage more by its noise than by its effectiveness.

After three days on the trail, and at the point of exhaustion and collapse, the fugitives had covered the thirty-odd miles to Espita. The Colonel hoped to make a defense there, but on the first rumor of the enemy, the troops had left their positions and fled, and so the weary procession continued to Temax. After a rest, orders were given to march south as reinforcements for Izamal, which caused a revolt in the Campeche troops in the Seventeenth Battalion, who demanded a return to their native city, upon which the northern soldiers cried "a Mérida!" These men were through with war. León was helpless, and he led them on into the capital.

Political failure was something Governor Santiago Méndez could recognize and understand, but now, behind the news that bombarded him in Maxcanu, he perceived the development of an unbelievable disaster. With each exhausted courier came new reports of loss, cowardice, desertions, and the plight of hopeless refugees. Counting his resources, he found he had little left, and on March 25, after hearing of Valladolid, he played his final cards. Three Spanish ships from Havana had landed two thousand rifles, some cannons, gunpowder, supplies, and money at Sisal a few days before, and he thought that help might come from that direction. But then the United States Navy still maintained a blockade of Yucatan, and as the nearest great power, Washington had to be considered; and there was also the British Admiral at Jamaica, who controlled the gunrunners of Belize. So Méndez dispatched letters, identical in form, to Spain, Great Britain, and the United States; each asked for "powerful and effective help" and offered complete "domination and sovereignty" over Yucatan to the first power willing to oblige.*

Méndez had sent his son-in-law, the young author and liberal intellectual Justo Sierra, as envoy to Washington in September of the previous year. Sierra traveled on an American warship from Campeche to Veracruz, where he practiced his diplomacy on Commodore Perry. Arriving in Washington on November 16, his initial contacts were with Secretary of State Buchanan, to whom he appealed for the full recognition of Yucatan as a neutral in the Mexican-American War, for the disoccupation of Ciudad Carmen, the only Yucatecan town held by American forces, and for the removal of tariffs at that port.

In December he won his first and only concession: President Polk agreed to lift the tariff on goods moving between Ciudad Carmen and Yucatan. He refused, however, to evacuate Carmen because he suspected gunrunning there, and he could see no neutrality in the revolts of Colonel Cetina, which he considered pro-Mexican. Yucatan was being ignored by the United States rather than recognized as neutral, in part because Méndez had declared for separation

---

* The incredible idea of offering one's country to a foreign power is not unique in Spanish tradition. Salvador de Madariaga has even coined a word for it—*donjulianism*, after the legendary Count Don Julian, who is said to have brought the Moors into Spain to avenge a personal insult.

and not permanent independence from Mexico, and Sierra had no recognized official status.

Hearing rumors of an end to the Mexican-American War, Sierra petitioned to secure his second major objective—a defensive treaty to protect Yucatan from Mexican revenge. His advocacy was soon applied to more urgent needs. The Caste War had semed unimportant when he left home, and news and instructions took a long time to reach Washington, but reports in American newspapers soon led him to realize the seriousness of the threat. On his own authority, he demanded that the arms embargo be lifted, waged a propaganda war in the press, and asked for direct military aid. He made little progress, but then came mail from Yucatan—new instructions and the month-old offer of sovereignty from Méndez. The Méndez letter was forwarded to the American government, and in spite of Sierra's personal disgust, things began to happen. He was given a personal interview at the White House by President Polk, volunteers from the eastern cities offered their services against the Maya, and he became involved in the intricacies of Whig-Democratic politics.

Seven days later Polk addressed Congress to explain the situation in Yucatan; renouncing the idea of American domination, he nevertheless invoked the Monroe Doctrine against any European power that might accept the Méndez offer. He suggested limited use of U.S. naval forces already present in the Caribbean, but was unwilling to reassign troops committed in the Mexican War. As a Democrat, and thus a member of the war party and a believer in Manifest Destiny, Polk was opposed by the Whigs, who considered the invasion of Mexico an immoral act and looked with suspicion on any temporary occupation of Yucatan, knowing well how such operations tend to become permanent. Sierra struggled bravely against these party politics, pleading the desperate need of his country in articles, letters, and reports, persuading individual senators and congressmen, and speaking before committees.

And then more news came from home—still about a month late, and still bad. First there was the capture and presumed death of his brother, at Valladolid; then a change of government; and finally— just before the Yucatan bill was to be voted on in Washington—word of a treaty between the Yucatecan government and a man the American papers called San Jacinto Pat, who was reported to be a native leader of Irish ancestry. That was that. The bill to aid Yucatan was dropped by its Democratic supporters as having no purpose. Sierra, not knowing what to believe, but knowing that such a treaty would never last, had nothing more to say; the apparent political solution of what he had called race war had made him appear a liar.

The change of government in Mérida had come on the same day the Méndez offer of sovereignty was made. Méndez had taken that step as an ultimate appeal, but considering how long it would take

Governor Miguel Barbachano

the foreign powers to act, he saw one more possibility, the old solution when fighting became too destructive: he wrote to his peace commissioner and rival, Miguel Barbachano, surrendering his office; perhaps the savages were Barbachanistas after all. The new Governor continued his efforts for peace in Tekax, but the usual sort of trouble continued; the Sixteenth Campeche revolted against the change of government, and its officers and men marched off home.

Then, in late March, word came from Jacinto Pat that gave room for hope. After some correspondence a meeting was arranged at Tzucacab, a village between Tekax and Peto. Father Vela, Felipe Rosado, and a second priest, knowing what had happened on a similar occasion before Valladolid, swallowed their fears and left the Tekax lines on April 18. The moment of contact was touchy, but they were directed to a nearby hacienda and the protection of Jacinto's brother Esteban Pat, the Mestizo José María Barrera, and Juan Justo Yam. With this escort they followed the camino real, passing thousands of armed natives, to Tzucacab, where they were met by Jacinto. Negotiations went on through dinner and afterwards, the commissioners sitting in hammocks and continually interrupted by a threatening crowd outside the house, which Pat had some difficulty driving away. Terms were drawn up for Barbachano's consideration, and the white men left in the morning, after a sermon on peace by Father Vela. Reaching Tekax, they were amazed to find the place filled with drunken, looting natives: the army had withdrawn the previous day, supposedly to avoid incidents and make a demonstration of good faith. Putting on a bold front, the commission rode right through the mob, Vela even stopping to pray in the church, and that night reached the new Ladino outpost at Oxkutzcab.

They met with the Governor at Ticul the next day, and after some discussion the terms acceptable to Pat were ratified. They were:

 1. Personal contributions from the native class to be abolished.
 2. Baptism and marriage fees to be reduced and made the same for all people.
 3. The Maya to have free use of the ejido and terrenos baldíos, without rent or threat of seizure.
 4. All indebted servants to be freed from debt.
 5. Barbachano to be made Governor for life, as the only leader trusted by the Maya.
 6. Jacinto Pat to be made governor of all the native leaders.
 7. Rifles confiscated from the Maya (approximately 2,500 of them) to be returned.
 8. Taxes on the distillation of aguardiente to be abolished.

This was a declaration of independence quite different from that of 1821, and even more radical: it specified an immediate social revolution that would bring an end to Ladino exploitation, an end to three hundred years of slavery for the Maya. And Barbachano signed.

The fifth article, permanent tenure for Barbachano, was violently attacked by the Méndez opposition as a betrayal of democratic principles. They expended on this one point all the hatred they felt for the vastly more important economic policies of the first four, expressing disgust that all the atrocities, killing, and destruction should be forgotten in the interests of political gain. For the Maya, however, permanent tenure guaranteed that a new government wouldn't renounce the treaty, as had been done with so many past promises, and the return of their seized rifles was intended to back up that guarantee. The clause about aguardiente was included as an afterthought, as Jacinto remembered the excesses of revenue agents.

For the Ladino side, the treaty had quite a different purpose. Sierra, in far-off Washington, shocked his Democratic supporters by immediately proclaiming the document a temporary expedient, a move to gain time—and he was absolutely right. Expanding on point six, the commission offered a sleeper clause, which was accepted in mistaken vanity, naming Jacinto Pat *Gran Cacique de Yucatán*. This title was emblazoned in gold letters on a white silk banner, which was sent, together with an impressive staff of office, to Jacinto's headquarters in Peto. This was not calculated to please Cecilio Chi or the northern chieftains. Furthermore, the collected rifles, packed on wagons and sent south, were to go to Pat alone, to sustain his new dignity. At best an ally, at worst temporarily appeased, Pat was to give the Ladinos relief and a chance to deal with the other native leaders.

This scheme to divide the Maya worked at first. Cecilio Chi, awaiting results of the negotiations in the village of Tinum, near Valladolid, was enjoying himself. He had been using captured priests (including the envoy Justo's brother, Manuel Sierra) and the assembled loot of Valladolid to indulge his people in a magnificent series of fiestas and novenas. He entertained on a grand scale, with herds of oxen, droves of pigs, barrels of aguardiente, and a profusion of candles and fireworks, putting himself right with the various village Santos, whose assistance he would need in the future. Typical behavior for a savage, said the Ladinos, who of course crowded their own churches for exactly the same reason in times of trouble. But on hearing the terms of the treaty, Chi dropped his revels at once. First he wrote a scathing letter to Jacinto Pat, accusing him of cowardice and treachery. As the letter was being delivered, he personally led his men on a forced march across country into the southern zone, burning Teabo in his wake and slaughtering some two hundred people who made a last stand in the church at Mani, only ten miles from the peace commissioners at Ticul. Next, he sent 1,500 men under his lieutenant, Raimundo Chi, to Peto, where they caught Pat by surprise; entering the town without a fight, they demanded and received the staff, the banner, and the treaty, and destroyed them on the spot. This was the end of treaty-making.

General Sebastián López de Llergo, a veteran of the struggles with Mexico, was named commander of all Yucatecan forces after the fall of Peto, and during the armistice lull he had attempted a reorganization of troops. The various militia companies and battalions were formed into five divisions, and placed in an arc around the capital. Ranged from south to north were the First at Ticul under Colonel Morales, who replaced the exhausted Rosado; the Second in reserve at Maxcanu under León, who had recovered from his Valladolid experience; the Third at Hocaba under Colonel José Dolores Pasos; the Fourth at Izamal; and the Fifth under Colonel José Cosgaya at Motul, holding the left flank to the coast. Later, a Sixth Division would be formed, as the threat to Campeche became more apparent, and an expeditionary Seventh Division also created.

On paper, it was a very neat and tidy defense, but only on paper. The men of the old Orden Battalion still hated their compatriots from the former Sixteenth Campeche; officers still suspected each other, and desertion, cowardice, and exhaustion were still very much in evidence. But this was the army, and with the last hope of peace gone, they prepared to do what they could. The confiscated rifles, recently packed up and sent off to Jacinto Pat in the hope they would be used by Maya against Maya, were now recalled and distributed. Outposts were abandoned, and the First and parts of the Second Division concentrated at Ticul. Governor Barbachano and General Llergo left for the capital while the road was still open, to organize what was left and prepare for the worst—a mass evacuation of the country.

Colonel Cetina, as responsible as any single man could be for the present disaster, now came out of disgrace as the military white hope of the Barbachano party; his hot-headed indifference to odds and his inability to quit were qualities in great demand. Riding into Ticul with reinforcements he had raised at Mérida, he took command of the 1,800-man garrison, inspected and improved the defenses, and ordered redoubts for artillery where the three main roads entered the town. It was guessed that he faced 24,000 Maya (an exaggerated figure, but indicative of Ladino morale) led by the recommitted Jacinto Pat.

The Puuc hills were low at Ticul, but they were high enough for sniper work at long range and so posed a threat to the southern streets and barricades of the town. Faced with this, the Colonel began operations on May 17 by sending a force to dislodge the Maya in the hills, only to find himself under general attack. The attack was stopped, but the sniping continued and the Colonel looked for other answers. First he probed for a day, to feel out the lay of the land. Finding what he thought was a weakness to the northwest, he led one guerrilla and ordered a second one to meet him behind enemy lines in that area; he would close the Maya in a trap. The trap closed, but it was empty, and for their troubles the men were once more subjected to sniping by unseen marksmen, with some 30 casualties on each side.

The Maya were elsewhere that day. They had infiltrated around the redoubt that defended the southeastern road, the camino real to Tekax, and after climbing into nearby trees, were picking off artillerymen as they attempted to work their pieces. Told of this on returning from his fruitless morning sortie, Cetina issued a shot of aguardiente to each of his men and sent them, thus inspired, in a double pincer movement to outflank the attackers while he led his own reserve force directly to the redoubt. Again his trap failed, this time because it was too full, and his men fell back on him in confusion. The Colonel, however, put his cannons to good use, threshing the foliage of the offending trees with grape; the guns taught the Maya caution, and their assault never got rolling.

A force had been stationed at Sacalum, eight miles north on the Mérida road, with orders to attack the enemy rear after the siege had begun. They did that same day, clearing the road with light skirmishing into Ticul and returning to their base before dark. These men, under Colonel González, came back a few days later with wagons of food and ammunition, but on attempting to leave they were stopped cold. A guerrilla sent to assist on the left bogged down in the woods; the soldiers showed a fatal disinclination to fight once away from their officers, and those gentry, with a few notable exceptions, had no taste for leading patrols. González had more success in the morning, when he broke free, and, after escorting the wounded on to the capital, returned with reinforcements and supplies. His next effort was against a Maya depot at the Hacienda Luma. Marching toward it in several converging columns, he was defeated piecemeal. The rout continued to his base of Sacalum, which he lost as well, leaving the inhabitants to be massacred and the place burned. A counter-attack gave his men a glimpse of the mutilated bodies among the ashes, the slaughtered horses and cattle, but they could take no more, and he retreated with them to Mérida. There the energetic officer changed old soldiers for new, raised among the thousands of refugees, and, under orders to reoccupy Sacalum and assist Ticul, marched south.

Cetina, inside the siege line at Ticul, had suffered similar defeats. Every move he made, each new tactic he tried, was paid for in casualties, ammunition, and morale. His patrols frittered away with loss of spirit, counterattacks failed against the ever-tightening siege barricades. He had seen the column of smoke announcing the loss of Sacalum, and, when González failed to return, his ammunition grew scarce. Orders were given to fire only when absolutely necessary. Sensing their predicament, the Maya taunted them, performing their traditional X-Tol dances in plain view; dressed in captured uniforms, or as women, with their faces painted black, they shouted insults and threats, inciting wasteful volleys of artillery. At the same time they sapped their way into the suburbs of Ticul—not, in that stony ground, with trenches, but by lying on their backs and pushing large boulders ahead of them with their feet, protected in this way until they had formed a more advanced wall. The Ladinos lacked the spirit to stop them.

Cetina waited five days for relief. Then the man who couldn't surrender saw that if he didn't leave quickly he never would. The sick and wounded were taken from the monastery, which had served as a hospital, the civilians were warned, orders were given to the various units, and on the morning of May 26 the Colonel led an advance battalion against the northern lines. With their lives depending on success, the soldiers mustered up courage and fought through to the hacienda of San Joaquín, which was to be held as a strong point covering the retreat, just as Popola had been when Valladolid was abandoned.

The troops in Ticul withdrew from their sectors in the prescribed order, covering the civilians, but as had happened so many times before, the Maya followed them with a rush, reaching the plaza and creating panic. With each man thinking only of being left behind, the lines wavered, and the orderly volley by platoons—so necessary with single-shot, muzzle-loading rifles—collapsed. The Maya broke through, their machetes killing soldiers and civilians alike. The rear guard, a militia battalion from Ticul itself, simply ran for the woods, every man for himself. The massacre continued up the road to San Joaquín, where a stand was made by the Colonel. Afterwards the natives were diverted by looting and burning that place, and the retreat continued until dark. The next day the survivors reached Uayalceh, where many died of their wounds, and many more of thirst and exhaustion. Those who could went on to Mérida, 17 miles away.

While being pushed back almost to Mérida in the north, the Yucatecan forces also met defeat in the south. The trouble began in the Chenes region, an area lying within and south of the Puuc range, a hilly, lightly inhabited country, with a few isolated settlements joined by mule trails. It had been overrun in April 1848 by three columns of one thousand men each; under the command of the Mestizo José María Barrera, they had easily routed the poorly organized militia groups and had recruited thousands among the local Maya. A lull followed this initial sweep. While Barrera went up to the peace conference outside Tekax, the Chenes Maya returned quietly to their homes, and a few Ladinos went back to their haciendas to recover valuables abandoned in flight. In some villages the whites were welcomed or ignored; in others, they were put to death with refined cruelty.

This uneasy peace ended after Pat's treaty had been broken in the north. A detachment of soldiers who were negotiating with Juan de Dios May were surprised and cut down. At this, fear struck Campeche. Drummers sounded the call to general quarters, citizens fled to the center of town, and the city walls were manned and artillery readied. The French consul in that place, writing early in May, stated that the local militiamen were so demoralized that they could hardly be made to guard the suburban outposts, adding that he thought that the city would surely be taken. In the bay stood the U.S. bomb-brig *Vesuvius* and several smaller vessels left there by Admiral Perry to evacuate U.S. citizens and give what aid they could. Former governor Méndez begged Perry for the rifles taken by American troops at Veracruz, saying that there were only five hundred left in Campeche; it was later requested that United States Marines be landed, if not to fight the Maya, then at least to enforce the orders of the government on its subjects. The south was abandoned except for Campeche, whose citizens cowered behind their massive wall.

After breaking the treaty, Cecilio Chi massed his men against the Ladino forces in the vicinity of Izamal on the northern flank, taking and losing Dzilam in early May, and then besieging Sitilpech, five miles east of Izamal. On May 14 a battalion left Izamal to reinforce this village. Stopped dead in a fire-fight less than a mile out of town, it was extracted by a second battalion and artillery, the combined group going on to Sitilpech; finding the garrison there decimated and in a mutinous state, the entire force returned to base. Of the seven hundred men who had set out, less than half returned to Izamal alive; it was the worst defeat yet suffered in a single battle, and it brought despair to the Ladino ranks. On May 22, after a week of indecisive skirmishing, the single survivor of a mounted scout patrol sent out on the Mérida road got back with the news that Izamal was surrounded.

The commander of the new Fourth Division at Izamal was Colonel Carmen Bello. He had detached part of his command, under Lieutenant Colonel Méndez, to hold the village of Sitilcum, five miles to the west and on the main road to Mérida; to the north was Colonel José Cosgaya of the Fifth Division. There was personal and political rivalry among these three, with little trust and only grudging cooperation. After the disastrous Sitilpech sortie, Carmen Bello looked for more effective means to defend himself. The fields surrounding Izamal were cleared of brush and trees, and he mounted artillery on the largest of the town's four pyramids, Kinich-Kakmo, to the north of the plaza, from which he fired on the Maya barricades as they appeared. His cannon balls did considerable damage to the loose stone walls, but the Maya simply rebuilt them at night, each time a bit closer to Ladino lines. The Maya tried direct action, too, but their one massed assault was directed against a redoubt that held a seventeen-pounder firing grape, and they were repulsed with heavy losses.

Colonel Bello was receiving regular convoys of ammunition and supplies from Mérida, for every unit that attempted the road had been able to fight through; but the moral collapse of his men was complete, and after six days his nerve gave way. On the night of May 28 he led his force of 1,000 men out of the city, taking a back trail without fighting to Tekanto, from where he watched the city burn. The Maya had been astonished to find the place undefended, and had entered cautiously, suspecting a trap; when reassured, they looted and burned with abandon, stopping only to make their devotions to the famous Virgin in the monastery church.

To General Sebastián López de Llergo, staring at a map of Yucatan in his headquarters fortress of San Benito, the little flags marking the collapse of his army seemed to appear in threes. Ticul on the 26th, one flag; Izamal on the 28th, two flags; and later on the 28th, news from a Belize coaster that isolated Bacalar was lost. Three Maya columns, bursting from the distant half-known forest frontier, growing as they advanced, were reaching for Mérida and smothering his defenses, while a fourth probed the suburbs of Campeche. With his flank threatened, Colonel Cosgaya had been ordered back from Motul to screen the escape route to Sisal and the sea. The troops of Carmen Bello picked this unhappy moment to mutiny, over half of them remembering that they were Campechanos with duties to their families, remembering their city's beautiful wall. Colonel José Dolores Pasos and his Third Division at Hocaba had been cut off and not heard from for several days; the worst could be assumed there. Survivors of the First and Second Divisions rested at Uayalceh and Tecoh, hoping for time to recover strength, but they looked back too often at the cathedral towers of Mérida on the horizon. Not much could be expected from them. To the south, all was uncertain. The Campeche road was still open, but at any moment the General might receive one more courier with word that it had been cut by an enemy unit. In the end, even that would matter little; the last fight would be for Mérida. His responsibility was the capital and the 100,000 citizens and refugees whose lives now depended on his defeated troops.

Refugees always seem to be the old and the very young, and in Mérida these were joined by the sick, the wounded, and the dying. Crowded into the churches, the convent of the Majorado, San Pedro College, and official buildings, there was still not enough room for them; the overflow camped in misery under the arcades of the plaza, their cooking fires making the place seem a gypsy camp at night, a beggars' convention under the tropical May sun. Charity appeared;

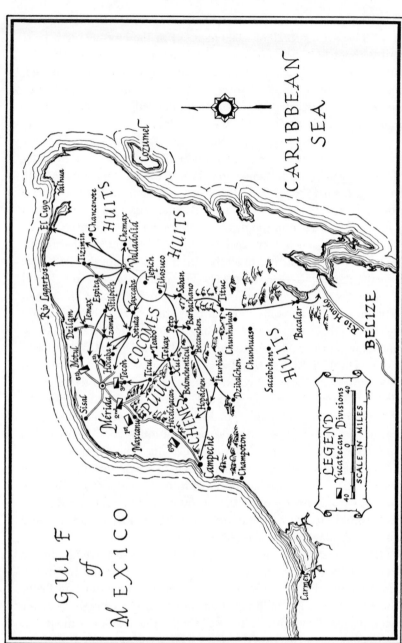

The Maya offensive to May 1848 and positions of the Yucatecan divisions

a commission was formed to feed the multitude and to collect clothes for those who had left their rags on the thorns and branches of back trails and were now kept indoors for the sake of decency. The homes of those who had disobeyed the law by fleeing the state were broken into and used for shelter. And there was the other side of the coin. In Campeche, refugees were forbidden to sell their belongings for fear that they would upset trade, and in Mérida prices were frozen against the profiteer. But that was earlier. As brown-skinned irregulars began to circle the city, inflation magically stopped. Military prospects could be read in prices, and when prices were a tenth or a twentieth of value, the prospects weren't good. Shopkeepers offered their entire inventories at auction without finding anyone to bid.

Rumors swept through the streets that the savages were everywhere. The rumors were believed by those who had seen it happen before, so the refugees wearily gathered their few belongings and joined the Meridanos on the road to Sisal. The wagoneers profited as goods and the infirm were hauled to that little one-street port, to the lighters or canoes that would take them to the off-shore anchorage and the ships of several nations. The government didn't even bother to repeal the law against emigration. People sailed from Sisal, Campeche, or any port they could reach on anything that floated and would take them elsewhere. The island city of Carmen was the nearest and earliest port of refuge, since it was within the state and still within the law; the citizens there forgot about "Gringo Go Home," and petitioned for protection, which three hundred United States Marines were detailed to provide.

In the streets of Mérida and Campeche, there was talk of a general slaughter, an elimination of the white population of Yucatan, which meant over 140,000 people counting the Mestizos, who certainly would be counted. A schooner anchored at Veracruz on May 28 with the rumor that Mérida had fallen. The military spoke of a fighting withdrawal to Sisal, of a defense behind the walls of Campeche; this was the only hope the General could give the Governor. Bishop Guerra left for Havana. Barbachano wrote out a proclamation declaring the evacuation of Mérida, then could find no paper in his deserted secretariat for the printing. He packed his furniture and prepared to leave for the south.

Five

Ladino Recovery
1848–1849

THE FIGHTING MEN, identified by now, were left alone at their posts, the garrison heroes; parade officers were gone, and the last act would be played without them. Fearing the worst but waiting with determination, the veterans prepared to meet the last assault, positioning their artillery and distributing their cartridges, which for once were plentiful. After waiting one day, then two, they began to wonder. At Cacalchen, Colonel Juan José Méndez, now commanding the Fourth Division in place of his discredited superior, Carmen Bello, grew impatient and sent two guerrillas on a scouting mission toward Izamal. These units of 400 men each, under Lieutenant Colonel Gutiérrez and Captain Lázaro Ruz (both of them in their twenties) moved cautiously from experience, but on reaching the burned suburbs of their objective, they discovered an amazing thing: the Maya army was gone. They edged into the place, shooting a few remaining looters, fortified themselves, and sent a courier galloping back to the capital. It was then discovered that Colonel Pasos, with his men of the Third Division, was not lost; he had held the villages of his sector, and had simply been too busy killing Maya to send the usual despairing reports. Colonel Cetina, finding that a little rest did wonders, raided south, surprising Ticul and punishing the enemy before he withdrew via Mani. Mérida went wild with these unexpected victories. Church bells rang, fireworks exploded, and the people learned to smile again. The Governor forgot about proclaiming an evacuation, hoped that others would, and went back to the task of supplying his not-so-hopeless army.

What had happened to the Maya? Many years later, Leandro Poot, son of the Maya leader Crecencio Poot, explained it in this way to E. H. Thompson:

> When my father's people took Acanceh they passed a time in feasting, preparing for the taking of T-ho [Mérida]. The day was warm and sultry. All at once the *sh'mataneheeles* [winged ants, harbingers of the first rain] appeared in great clouds to the north, to the south, to the east, and to the west, all over the world. When my father's people saw this they said to themselves and to their brothers, "Ehen! The time has come for us to make our planting, for if we do not we shall have no Grace of God to fill the bellies of our children."
>
> In this way they talked among themselves and argued, thinking deeply, and then when morning came, my father's people said, each to his Batab, "Shickanic"—I am going—and in spite of the supplications and threats of the chiefs, each man rolled up his blanket and put it in his food pouch, tightened the thongs of his sandals, and started for his home and his cornfield.
>
> Then the Batabob, knowing how useless it was to attack the city with the few men that remained, went into council and resolved to go back home. Thus it can be clearly seen that Fate, and not white soldiers, kept my father's people from taking T-ho and working their will upon it.

Thus Leandro Poot and the native mind. A race had been run between time and space—through March, April, and May, across leagues of trail from the frontier—and now it was lost. These people were masters of the tactics of the Yucatecan bush, but they had no concept of strategic demands, no idea that aid might come from abroad or that the Ladinos might recover their strength. They had beaten the Dzul, taken thousands of rifles and loot beyond counting, and that was good; but now it was time to plant corn. Mérida and Campeche could wait, it was time to plant corn. The habits of a lifetime, the sense of religious duty and family responsibility commanded. With one voice they said "Shickanic" and took the trail east. They were peasant farmers, not soldiers. They had no quartermaster, each man providing for himself, and no discipline except for allegiance to hundreds of petty Batabob, who led only by mutual consent. And so they melted away; back along the main roads past the burnt-out towns, the gutted sugar-cane fields, and the cattle ranches, splitting up along the countless little trails that finally led to a thatched hut, a thankful wife and children, and then to the cornfield.

It was too late for the normal burning; they had to make do with the clearings of previous years, which meant a reduced harvest, but they were content—it had been quite a year. Only a corporal's guard of more disciplined enthusiasts remained behind, attacking Tecoh, Acanceh, and Tixkokob, all about eighteen miles from Mérida, while a few of their brothers in the south burned fields within sight of Campeche.

Success was an exciting thing for the whites, particularly after so many defeats. Discovering the enemy's weakness, Colonel Méndez organized a column of 1,200 men and sent it swinging down the camino real halfway to Valladolid, where it established a base at Tunkas—a *fait accompli*, against General Llergo's orders. From that point, guerrillas probed the back country trails, following the Maya to his cornfields, smashing him in his dispersed vulnerability, burning his villages and settlements, collecting prisoners, horses, ammunition, and supplies. Resistance came as the Maya soldier-farmers became soldiers again, leaving their half-worked fields to besiege the Tunkas camp and a newly established outpost at Cenotillo. They found themselves facing a new enemy; as the Batab Francisco Puc complained to the captured priest, Sierra:

> These aren't the ones who abandoned Valladolid, Señor Vicario; if they [had been there] it would have been impossible for us to triumph; when we besiege them they rapidly counterattack; when we think we will surprise them in our ambushes, we are the ones who are surprised in the rear.*

The Ladino army, with its weakness burned away, had learned the difference between political revolutions, fought mainly with proclamations, and total war. It recovered its racial pride and courage. In spite of this change, or rather because of it, the Maya continued to hold fiestas, calling on ghostly powers for assistance with prayer, fireworks, and alcohol.

---

* The Maya guerrilla tactics, on the other hand, were generally called cowardly by Ladinos—the age-old response of all frustrated regular soldiers. The Maya did not flinch from hand-to-hand combat; there are numerous contemporary references to Ladino dread of the well-handled machete.

Jacinto Pat was also having trouble at Ticul. Probably the most intelligent of the native leaders, with experience and vision enough to see beyond the immediate situation, he had realized that the war would not stop because of the planting and had managed to retain a considerable part of his forces. When the Ladinos recaptured Muna (near Ticul) he pinned them there with a siege, burned their camp at Canchakan, and attacked Tecoh to their rear. Colonel Cetina led a series of long patrols himself, so that the area between the Puuc range and the capital became a no-man's land crisscrossed by raid and counterraid, each side taking the other by surprise, burning supplies and setting ambushes. The skirmishing came to an end on July 29, when Pat, after several defeats, was forced to pull back his reduced forces. It is reported that upon learning that some of the white troops wore boots, he said, "Let's get out of here; the great rich of Mérida have come out to make war." He retreated through Ticul and Tekax toward Peto, contesting each village as he went and almost destroying the overeager white soldiers who pressed on his heels.

Cetina sent his men against Tekax in a double pincer following the two branches of the camino real from Oxkutzcab, each column supporting and assisting the other, with further patrols marching south through the Puuc in a flank maneuver. They captured the city with little fighting, in spite of a double stone barricade the Maya had built for its defense. Prisoners were brought to the main plaza, soundly whipped, and then taken to the second-floor balcony of the municipal building, where they were grabbed by their hands and feet and thrown off, to be caught on bayonets below. One of them, a young boy, was seen weeping and clinging to the legs of an officer; he went over the railing with the rest.

In the middle region, between the Peto and Valladolid roads, there was heavy fighting, with a continual Maya siege of Huhi, eight miles southeast of Hocaba, and destructive raids against native villages and Ladino camps. Unable to take Huhi (which won the title "Little Campeche" for its resistance) and short of ammunition, the Cocomes Maya retreated through their own country, giving up Yaxcaba and Sotuta. These places were occupied by Colonel Pasos and his men, assisted by the Fifth Division from the north—which arrived too late for the battle, still plagued by mutiny and court-martial.

The southern zone around Campeche was isolated from all of this, the Puuc range forming an effective barrier to wagon roads, and thus to fields of operation. Since late May, when the sight of burning plantations had sent the garrison scrambling for the walls (only to find that the smoke was raised by a small band of marauders), militia columns had secured the immediate area but they had made little real progress in the lightly inhabited interior. The existing five divisions were augmented by a sixth, raised from the villages along the Mérida-Campeche road and put under the command of Colonel Agustín León. Sent southeast to join the Sixteenth and Seventeenth Battalions, it engaged in heavy fighting and established a fortified camp well forward at Hopelchen.

The attitude of the western Maya, like the dispersal at planting time, contributed greatly to the Ladino recovery. These people, long adjusted to a status quo of white rule, lacked the sense of outrage felt by their eastern brothers. At the first news of the Caste War, strong measures had been taken to stamp out any ideas they might have had about rebellion. They missed the invigorating sight of burning villages, dead white men, and loot, and when their chiefs were arrested and mass whippings introduced, they retained their belief that the Dzul was all-powerful. Once convinced, they stayed convinced, and on their own initiative offered their services to the white army. Fifteen hundred of them formed in Hecelchacan under their Batab Juan Chi, with equal numbers coming from Dzitbalche, Calkini, and Halacho—all villages along the camino real to Campeche. Others came forward from Motul (northwest of Mérida), from Hocaba, and even from the recaptured town of Tunkas, which had helped in the capture of Valladolid.

In the spring tide of advance, the Maya rebels had gained as they marched, their envoys preceding the columns and incorporating into their mass the local natives, and there had been no real front. Ladino officers had known this as a constant threat; it had given them a continual sense of isolation and exposure and made them eager to hurry back to the cities. For the Maya, it had meant reinforcements, new supplies of food and hidden weapons, and guides familiar with local back trails and enemy dispositions. If all the Maya of the west had risen, the whites would have been forced to evacuate the peninsula.

Chiefs friendly to the whites were given the honorary title of Hidalgo.* As a class, native soldiers fighting for the whites were called *Indígena* natives, to distinguish them from the rebel Maya, or Indios. Armed only with machetes, the Indígenas were primarily a labor corps, transporting food and ammunition on their backs and building defenses. But in a war that had no rear areas, they were also fighting and dying alongside the white soldiers.

A third factor in the Yucatecan recovery was the receipt of vital assistance from abroad. First, in March, came the 2,000 rifles, the artillery, and the supplies from Havana. Charitable organizations in Veracruz and New Orleans sent 300,000 pounds of corn and gifts of money. Then the government seized church treasures, a repository of national wealth collected through the centuries: gold and silver chalices, plates, crosses, candelabras, and the jewels that decorated saints, altars, and reliquaries. All of this was taken, converted into cash, and used to buy military supplies.

Barbachano was quick to endorse his predecessor's offer of sovereignty; he sent new instructions to Sierra in Washington, where the situation was too muddled for any hope; and extended the offer to Havana, where no action was taken, in part because of President Polk's message invoking the Monroe Doctrine. The envoys sent to Cuba then sailed to Veracruz with instructions to deal with the American military if the pending treaty between the United States and Mexico had not yet been signed; otherwise, they were to carry the Governor's letter to the Mexican government. Barbachano had written the Mexican President, suggesting reunion on the basis of Yucatan's earlier demands for federalist principles, but begging for it on any terms, proudly pointing to his own pro-Mexican position and calling the Méndez revolt for neutrality disgraceful. He didn't mention the offers he was making to the other governments; survival is the first law of men or states.

His envoys reached Mexico City eleven days after the ratification of peace with the United States, so the Mexican alternative was taken. They finally found willing ears, their way having been prepared by

---

* The title of Hidalgo, or noble, was a continuation of colonial custom for the older chiefs and an elevation in status for the newer ones. In time, the loyal natives were collectively called Hidalgos.

prominent Yucatecans. One of the first acts of the new President, Herrera, was to award 150,000 pesos to Yucatan; more important, quick action could be taken, for the $3,000,000 the United States had paid for the conquered northern provinces was available and guns could be bought from the departing American army. Five ships from Mexico landed at Campeche in mid-July, delivering 28,000 pesos, 1,000 rifles, 100,000 bullets, and 300,000 kilograms of gunpowder. The rest of the money was to be paid at the rate of 15,000 pesos per month and delivered in the form of military supplies. Yucatecan measures were equally prompt; on August 17, 1848, Barbachano declared reunification, and for that day the response to the challenge "Quién vive?" was to be "México!"

From late May the rains continued off and on through the early summer, making travel difficult in the forest, but it seldom rained for a whole day at a time and the country was not impassable. Planting was delayed that spring of 1848. The Maya could not have completed their most necessary work until mid-July, and they would not have gone back to war for another month if Ladino raiders hadn't forced them to act in self-defense. Jacinto Pat had kept his more disciplined troops in action throughout this period; the loose alliance of northern villages under Cecilio Chi had simply abandoned the field without thought of retaliation.

The native commanders ruled with certainty only the small units of their home villages, and their control over others depended upon personality and success. Discipline was irregular, a mixture of military practices, hacienda custom, and rules invoked by village government. The Batab José Tomás Tzuc received two hundred lashes for losing a position entrusted to him, whereupon he retailed the same punishment to his men at fifty lashes per back. Some of the Maya leaders had held commissions in the state militia, and as time went on a loose system of rank was established, with captains promoting themselves up to general; but true rank was determined by the size of the band that followed each officer. As the rivalry between Pat and Chi made clear, there was no supreme commander.

By mid-August the northern Maya had reassembled, some 5,000 of them under Chi, and marching to the music of captured flute, bugle, and drum, they went off to attack the forward camp of Yaxcaba. That garrison was confident and made a sortie at the first indications of a siege, which was repulsed. A second detachment of 150 men ran into trouble, unable to fight clear; after sustaining considerable losses, it returned to camp under cover of darkness. The easy raids on the Maya were over. In the morning a combat patrol went to a nearby village, intending to destroy it as a potential base for the enemy, but upon entering the place peacefully, neglected to garrison the inevitable strong point, the church. This tactical error was pointed out to them by Maya infiltrators, who seized the church through a side door and dominated the village with rifle fire from the roof and its protective parapet. A second patrol was raked with fire in the streets, and the two units, finding the work too much for them, joined forces and fought their way back to Yaxcaba. Reinforcements were sent to the garrison from the Third and Fourth Divisions, with Colonel Pasos of the Third taking command, but the added weight was not enough. Battle after battle disputed the surrounding barricades, and when they were carried and leveled, the Maya simply rebuilt them at night. Finally, a section of 200 men was sent to break out and bring supplies; when they were stopped, company after company was added until most of the garrison was engaged, at which point the Maya made a general assault, and almost took the place. Unable to recover his defense line in a counterattack, Colonel Pasos retreated to Sotuta.

A siege began at that place the next day, and to avoid a second loss, white troops were rushed up, raising the strength of the garrison to 1,484 men, all well-supplied and well-armed. Either the Maya had shot off most of their powder or their losses had made such work unpopular; at any rate, they melted away into the forest. Heavy companies cleared the area, meeting little opposition, and the old base of Yaxcaba was reoccupied. These forward camps had been purposely kept small so that the troops could live off the country by raiding for corn, feeding themselves and starving the enemy. They were also close enough to give each other mutual support; thus, when Dzitas on the Valladolid road was assaulted, aid came to the sound of the guns from Tunkas and Cenotillo, striking the enemy rear. These tactics had been attempted from the beginning, but with recovered morale, they could now be applied successfully.

Ladino troops in this northern area had made good progress while Chi's men were away besieging Yaxcaba. The Fifth Division advanced to Tizimin and sent patrols as far as Espita and Calotmul, taking prisoners and offering amnesty; Batabob and entire families were coming in to surrender for the first time. The Fourth Division, reinforced by the Light Battalion, drove down the Valladolid road until patrols could see the towers of that abandoned city, and reestablished the several advanced outposts that General Llergo had recalled during the threat to Sotuta.

During this fighting, the Vicar of Valladolid, Manuel Sierra, had been taken from village to village, celebrating fiestas and performing his religious functions, half free, half prisoner. As a Dzul he was hated, but as a priest he was necessary—a fiesta wasn't complete without mass, a cross nothing but wood until blessed. The Maya would be forced to find substitutes, but that would be later. While they had priests, they used them. When the fighting neared his area, Sierra attempted to reach the front, but all moves he made in that direction were closely watched, so he set off to the northwest, working his way through the forest settlements until he made the village of Loche, to find that the reported white raiders had left. A fever stopped him for a time, but then he moved north to the long narrow bay called Rio Lagartos, and in an abandoned canoe paddled west to the destroyed settlement of the same name. Recaptured there by an intercepting canoe of a rebel lookout, he was taken ashore. While his guards slept, he managed to slip away, and with a favoring wind reached safety at the recaptured port of Dzilam, a Lazarus risen from the tomb.

If Jacinto Pat had kept a rear guard to delay the Ladinos at Tekax, he had also been immobilized by agricultural necessities. His return to action paralleled that of the northern forces in September, when he received fresh supplies of powder and shot packed up from Belize. His field commanders, Marcelo Pat and José María Barrera, were determined men; they had paused in Peto to order the execution of a prominent Batab for suggesting surrender, knowing well that for themselves there could be no surrender. On the Ladino front, Colonel Pren had replaced Cetina in command of the First Division, releasing that officer to lead the newly formed expeditionary Seventh; Pren was to hold Tekax with support from the Sixth Division, which had moved up on his right to the village of Xul, fifteen miles to the southwest across the Puuc hills. Heavy skirmishing took up September and half of October, when the Maya concentrated on Xul and, despite heavy reinforcements, drove out the Sixth Division, forcing it to retreat to Oxkutzcab, behind Tekax on the Mérida road. General Llergo came riding down then with reinforcements, to find out what was holding up the advance. Llergo had enough troops to act on a grand scale, and he sent out 600-man guerrillas, which could do real damage as opposed to the indecisive work of small patrols. These units ran into the usual trouble—ambushed, trapped in a sugar-cane field which was then burned to flush them out—but they were big enough to handle themselves. Their success forced the Maya into large-scale attacks against Oxcutzcab and then against Tekax itself, where the assault lasted two days and carried into the suburbs of the town. This was the last effort.

With their gunpowder used up and Marcelo Pat mortally wounded, the Maya burned their camps and retired back down the road to Peto. The best H-menob gathered there, to pray and chant and try their herbs around the bed of the dying Marcelo, but there was a bullet in his spine and nothing could be done about that. The wake was magnificent, a fitting end for the man who might one day have been Gran Cacique de Yucatán—thousands of people sitting out in the dark before the house where he lay in state, lighting candles, telling their beads, weeping, drinking in honor of the dead. Jacinto was drunk, as was customary, but his heartbreak came through as he warned one of his prisoner priests, "Sing well for the boy, *Tata Padre*; I'll kill you if his soul doesn't go to heaven." The troops had come in for the funeral, and afterwards Jacinto reviewed them in the plaza. Then he wearily mounted his horse and started home to Tihosuco.

For General Llergo, the road was open. Maya exhaustion in the north allowed him to use almost his entire army for the coming campaign; furthermore, he could use them in a concerted manner rather than in the separate theaters of the Mérida-Valladolid and the Mérida-Peto roads. Orders went out to the First, Second, Third, Fourth, and Sixth Divisions to attack at staged intervals, sweeping the

Cocomes, and converging on Peto. The Third and the Fourth moved first, since their route from Yaxcaba was the longest, and they fought their way south through Tiholop and Tinum, taking up positions to the east of their objective. From Tekax, the First Division, 1,000 men strong, smashed through Barrera's defenses; making ten miles a day, it reached Peto on October 1 and took it without a fight. The Second and Sixth Divisions, striking from Teabo, were less fortunate; they suffered sniping at the very beginning, were delayed in extended skirmishing along back trails, and were the last in.

This advance moved like a steamroller against the light opposition; of the 3,500 white troops that went into action, only 11 were reported killed and 41 wounded. When a barricade was met along the trail, flankers were sent to either side, men who had learned to take advantage of cover, crawling from tree to tree, supporting one another, in time-consuming but not particularly costly maneuvers. Their muzzle-loading flintlocks were used cautiously in the thick undergrowth, each man reloading before risking another step, machete out, ready for what might be hiding a few feet away. Against white veterans, with their ammunition low, the Maya had to content themselves with sniping and half-hearted ambushes before falling back. But Peto was an empty prize. With the forest so close at hand, there could be no question of trapping the Maya.

Out of their hiding places and into the army lines at Peto poured the refugees: captured priests, disillusioned Mestizos, Barbachanistas who found themselves on the wrong side, Mayas who had always been friendly to the white cause, or suddenly became so, some fifteen hundred in all. The local militia, which had defected during the siege of Peto, was reorganized and formed into five companies led by trusted officers. Municipal authorities were appointed and reconstruction started. Civilization had returned. October and November were spent in securing the district, making certain that rebellion wouldn't spring up behind the lines, establishing a chain of outposts, bringing up supplies. Then came the last push, the one intended to end the war. The Fourth Division led off, taking Progreso and Dzonotchel; leapfrogged by the First Division, the two groups reached Sacala and Ichmul, and on December 13, 1848, they marched into Tihosuco without resistance. The town was undamaged, the streets kept clear of tropical growth, the church and municipal buildings clean and intact. Jacinto had allowed no nonsense in his home town.

It was different in Valladolid, which was occupied at about this time by the Light Battalion and the Fifth Division. There, the churches had been stripped of their saints, retablos, and crosses, and even the bells had been taken from their towers and buried. Private homes were found looted and burned, and the forest allowed to take over. This was a Dzul city, and the Maya, having never lived there, wanted no part of it. Valladolid, once called the "Sultaness of the East," had been raped; her reputation has never been the same.

From Valladolid the northern troops fanned out to Chancenote and Chemax on the forest frontier; then, reuniting, they marched south by separate roads, picking up prisoners and booty on their way, and closed the gap with the First Division at Tihosuco. Military conquest was complete. All points except the isolated Bacalar had been recaptured. Nothing was left to the defeated rebels except the unoccupied rain forest along the eastern coast, an area without towns, without villages, unmapped and unknown to the white man.

Jacinto Pat had retreated to a place called Tabi, Bonifacio Novelo to Majas, Cecilio Chi to Chanchen, all deep in the forest. Each hideout had a cenote and a few temporary huts built by hunters or far-wandering farmers. Now rot set in. The Mestizo secretary of Cecilio Chi had been sleeping with the Batab's wife; the day after the fall of Tihosuco, thinking himself discovered, or perhaps hoping for a reward, he assassinated the native leader. Whatever plans he might have made were never realized. The murder discovered, he defended himself in the hut that served as camp armory, taking advantage of the many loaded rifles, firing from the rafters into the vengeful mob until they cut through the thatched roof and hacked him to pieces. Chi's body was washed, dressed in his best clothes—a handsomely embroidered sash at his waist, his machete at his side—and buried in the churchyard at his birthplace in Tepich. This was the sordid end of the most-dreaded and uncompromising Batab, the spiritual descendant of Jacinto Canek. His wife's mutilated corpse was left to the vultures.

Scattered in small bands around forest wells, lacking powder and shot, the Maya desperately harvested their hidden cornfields, losing those that the soldiers discovered and burned. The rebellion should have been over, but the same innocence of strategy that allowed them to turn back within sight of Mérida now kept them from recognizing their hopeless position. They fought on, making the best of their few opportunities. Convoys were sniped, outposts were rushed, dispatch riders disappeared; and as they recovered their strength and harvested what corn was left, the fugitive Batabob contacted each other, united their forces, and began to act in a more aggressive manner.

Guerrillas were sent to break up these concentrations, and one of them had quite a time of it. A detachment of several hundred men of the Fourth Division, under Colonel Vergara, raided Culumpich, the hacienda of Jacinto Pat, where they discovered a large quantity of aguardiente. An impromptu fiesta sprang from this lucky find, and it continued until all discipline was gone and the entire command roaring drunk, including most of the officers. Perhaps this was intentional; at any event, the Maya promptly attacked, rushing in with machetes to end the celebration. The befuddled soldiers, driven from the hacienda in a rout, retreating in disorganized sections, each drummer and bugler playing his favorite tune, were saved from annihilation by those few who sobered at Maya war cries. An alarm went down the line, and volley after volley was fired blindly into the woods until ammunition ran out, while a small rear guard under a captain engaged and held off the real enemy several miles back. A battalion rescue force sent out from Tihosuco found the scattered platoons wandering aimlessly in the moonlight or sleeping it off in the middle of the trail, tired but happy, their guns lying where they had fallen. The next day, with sore heads and red faces, these men went back to Culumpich to show the flag, and to find some excuse with which to face the infuriated Colonel Rosado.

To cap that story, there is another: the baptism of fire for the American volunteers. These men, primarily from the Thirteenth Infantry Regiment, U.S. Army, had been mustered out at Mobile, Alabama, in the summer of 1848, following the end of the Mexican War. Unwilling to face the drab prospects of civilian life and fascinated by what they had seen south of the Rio Grande, they accepted the offer of the Yucatecan Government—8 dollars a month for enlisted men plus 320 acres of land after peace. This project had been conceived by Justo Sierra to secure military aid and encourage white immigration, but the Americans had more ambitious plans. Remembering how settlers had revolted in Texas and made it stick, how easily a few regiments had beaten the Mexican Army, they dreamed of big things: a Caribbean extension of the United States, or perhaps an independent empire, based on slavery and supposed Latin decadence, with wealth, señoritas, and power for every red-blooded volunteer. They were the first of the American filibusters. Forming under Captain Joseph A. White, who promoted himself to Colonel, they shipped from New Orleans to Sisal in several schooners, 938 of them, and were sent down to Tekax, where the advance party was committed in September 1848.

During the advance up to Tihosuco, the casualty lists began to include such exotic names as "Ricardo Keli." Incorporated in the First and Fourth Divisions, they had never fought as a unit, but at the insistence of Colonel White they were allowed to show what they could do, and they tried their hand at Culumpich. The noise of their heavy boots as they marched, the constant loud talking in the ranks, the pipe smoking and flower picking, all of this was noted with uneasiness by the Yucatecan veteran Juan de Dios Novelo, who was accustomed to more cautious deportment on that ambush-laden trail. And when they met their first barricade, they laughed at Novelo's suggestion of the usual flanking infiltration, fixing bayonets to make a frontal assault, knowing that no Mexican, much less an Indian, could face cold steel. They were wrong. The first volley caught them point-blank, and Novelo had his hands full bringing out the forty casualties, one slung on either side of a mule.

A survivor told of his experiences many years later, with all the exaggeration of the old soldier:

> During the battles of Peto and Ichmul we lost many of our men. At Santa María we lost forty-seven, and at Tabi thirty-six, but at Culumpich nearly three hundred of our bravest men were killed. The Indians there played us a trick; they made concealed pitfalls in the path and placed sharp pointed stakes at the bottom; then they appeared and dared us to come on; we rushed after them with hurrahs and many of our bravest men fell into the pits.

Forty isn't three hundred, and the staked pits weren't used that day according to other sources, but it gives the feeling. E. H. Thompson, who reported this, also heard about the Americans from the other side; here is the testimony of Leandro Poot:

> It was easy to kill the strange white men, for they were big and fought in a line, as if they were marching, while the white men from Mérida and Valladolid fought as we do, lying down and from behind trees and rocks. . . . Their bodies were pink and red in the sunlight and from their throats came a strange war cry, Hu Hu! [Hurrah!] They were brave men and shot keenly. . . . We hid behind the trees and rocks wherever we could, that they might not see us, and so we killed them. They killed many of us, but we were many times their number and so they died. . . . Brave men, very brave. Some died laughing and some with strange words in their own tongue, but none died cowardly. I do not think any escaped. I think they lay where they died, for in those days we had no time to eat or sleep or bury the dead.

Many of the American officers resigned after a week of such fighting, but others stayed on and gave a good account of themselves.*

An answer to these forward camps and the guerrillas came as quickly as powder could be bought and packed up from Belize. The scattered natives gathered, letters requesting aid going to Batabob as far away as the Chenes, near Campeche. At Tihosuco, Jacinto Pat commanded; at Saban, the two Mestizos, Barrera and Encalada. The fights at those places followed similar patterns. After the initial sniping and rushes came the formal order of a close investment: first one encircling barricade to match the white defense, then a second line to give support, and the strengthening of the twin walls by a series of redoubts. These little forts, called *plazuelas*, were the strong points of both siege and defense lines, ammunition depots, and assembly points for counterattack; and they were taken and re-taken countless times as the advantage shifted from one side to the other through that bullet-riddled forest.

At Tihosuco, Colonel Pren established his headquarters in the

---

* Once, when a small group was cut off on patrol, their Yucatecan guide said, in simple Spanish, "Indians in front, Indians behind," and, pointing his finger at a Maya barricade, "to Tihosuco!" The American specialty, a bayonet attack, saved the day.

two-storied Government Palace, a building on the usual Latin plan, with arcaded balconies facing the interior court and bare walls facing out, except for the windows, which had casements decorated with carved shells and cornucopias; although it had survived the first siege, the building suffered now under military necessity, its windows bricked shut, gunports cut through walls, and a rough embrasure built on the roof, not to mention the casual litter, smell, and filth of a combat post. The massive church became an arsenal and powderhouse; even the pre-Columbian pyramid mound on the south side of the plaza was fortified. The outer defenses were similar to those of the Maya, except that they were based on houses and had cannons in the plazuelas. Colonel Rosado at Ichmul and Colonel Juan de la Cruz Salazar at Saban made arrangements similar to those in Tihosuco. Between these three towns were the two Maya headquarters, Jacinto Pat's at Xcabil north of Ichmul, and Barrera's at Uymax, south. From these hamlets they could move together, acting in unison against any of the camps and barricading the trails. If they couldn't always stop the reinforcing columns, they made them pay heavily, finding most of their own ammunition on captured mule trains.

The sieges of Tihosuco and Saban lasted through the spring months of 1849. The Ladinos lost heavily, embroiled in endless barricades. The Maya were slaughtered when they showed themselves, but they almost overwhelmed both towns, battalions of them swarming in among the streets only to be taken in a crossfire from windows and roofs, for every stone house was a fort. Night attacks became common; machetes, rocks, and bare hands were used, and prisoners never survived. This was the major effort of Maya resistance. There were no important battles on the other frontiers at this time, although sporadic fighting continued. Spring came, the second planting season of the war, and that year the cornfields had to be made in virgin forest, as far as possible from the inevitable white raids. Also, the powder was gone, there was little loot to buy more, and the merchants of Belize—Negroes, Englishmen, or Yucatecan refugees—insisted upon cash payment. The fighting died off.

Relieved from their post at Tihosuco, the American volunteers marched up to Valladolid where most of them, including Colonel

White, decided that this was not the kind of war they enjoyed, and, protesting their delayed pay, left for home. Instead of easy loot and frightened Latins, they had suffered 60 to 70 killed and 150 wounded, and had nothing to show for it except a revised opinion of Yucatecans. They must have talked loudly as they left, to cover that not completely honorable departure, because several months later there were rumors that Colonel White was regrouping his men, intending to attack Mérida and claim the lost pay with dividends.

This was not the case. The ambitious Colonel had teamed up with a Cuban, a politician and an out who wanted back in. White and his men were going to put him there, and had gathered on an island in the Mississippi delta when the U.S. Navy spoiled the fun. A certain number of the volunteers stayed on in Yucatan; over 140 of them formed a company under Captain Kelly and sailed with the expeditionary Seventh Division for Bacalar.

Bacalar, 110 miles south of Tihosuco as the crow flies, much farther along the winding trail, had sat out the first part of the rebellion in uneasy isolation. The local Maya had prospered as canoe men or mule drivers in the contraband trade with Belize. There had been little racial friction. This began to change as parties of Maya rebels came down from the north to buy military necessities with the captured loot of a dozen towns, bragging of their manhood and their victories.

These southern Maya began dreaming about those warehouses full of goods. Venancio Pec, one of Pat's war chiefs, tried blackmail first. He explained that he had no argument with these white men, who had always treated him fairly, but please, he would like six hundred and twenty-five pounds of gunpowder, a certain number of rifles, and then he would go away, or else. Captain Pereira of the militia looked to his cannons, positioning them in redoubts, prepared the old fortress of San Felipe, sent his noncombatants to the Rio Hondo to await events on the Mexican side, and said No. Grapeshot caused losses among the hot-headed Maya recruits until Pec showed them how to do it: by rolling boulders forward with the feet as he had done at Tekax, pushing the barricades close enough to make the final assault cheaply. This they did at several points, driving into

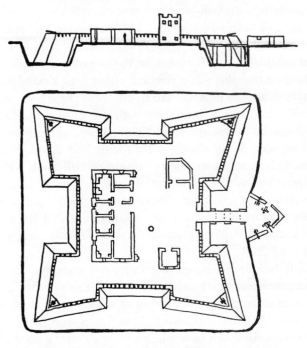

The moated fortress of San Felipe, Bacalar

town. Pereira recognized a professional when he saw one. Remembering that he had no supplies for a siege, he surrendered Bacalar for the lives of his men, who marched out under arms, two files of soldiers with the remaining civilians between.

Colonel Charles Fancourt, the Crown Superintendent of Belize, gave sanctuary to the refugees on his side of the Hondo, and they settled at various places in the northern part of the British establishment, mainly at Punta Consejo. Fancourt then addressed a letter to the new "principal civil magistrate of Bacalar," asking for the protection of English citizens, and in further correspondence he made it clear that the frontier was open for trade. Whether Venancio Pec was a howling savage or a civil magistrate depended on the point of view, and the English were oblivious to the subtleties of local racial distinctions. Creole, Ladino, Mestizo, or Indio were all the same to

them—simply non-English—and this attitude was particularly offensive to the upper-class Yucatecans. This was on the emotional side.
On the practical side, Fancourt refused Mérida's request for guns
and rejected the demand for a ban on the sale of war supplies to the
Maya, holding that this was a political rather than a racial war, and
one in which he was neutral. He had to be. There were no more
than 1,000 white men scattered through the British establishment,
with perhaps 5,000 Mulattoes and Negro slaves, and reinforcements
were a long way off. In March of 1848 some Huit Maya had raided
deep into Belize, attacking the settlement of Hill Bank with bows
and arrows (the only reported use of such weapons). In response,
the Superintendent had been able to send no more than 30 policemen; then reinforcements had come, a grand total of 100 men of the
First West Indian Regiment, equipped with the unnecessary advice
to avoid conflict.

So matters rested. English merchants and smugglers found that
their old customers wanted lead, gunpowder, and rifles, so these
articles were shipped up from Belize in schooners or shallow draft
canoes called "pitpans." Whether these things were paid for with
stolen goods or the spoils of war again depends on the point of view.
The reaction from Mérida was hot, with recitations of the classic list
of acts natural to anyone who would sell guns to an Indian. The least
of the charges was the existence of an English plot to seize the eastern
part of the country—a story believed in Yucatan to this day.* While
a number of Batabob would later come to desire Queen Victoria's
protection, there is no evidence that this imperialistic scheme was
ever seriously considered by the English.

The Maya, driven back from the cities and towns into the eastern
forest, had continued to fight. Governor Barbachano decided that
the English frontier would have to be closed to stop the flow of war
material and isolate the rebels from their only support. This job
was given to Colonel Cetina, with 800 men of the newly formed
Seventh Division, including a company of Americans. They sailed

---

* Yucatecans, convinced that Belize belongs to them, never use its present
name of British Honduras; and Guatemala includes the colony as one of her
provinces, showing it within her boundaries on all national maps—a harmless
enough form of aggression.

from Sisal on the Spanish steamboat *Cetro* on April 20, 1849. After an eight-day voyage coasting around the peninsula (paid for by the sale of Maya slaves to Cuba, of which more will be said later), the troops were disembarked on an island near the mouth of the Rio Hondo to get their shore legs, and were then assigned to one of twenty canoes with a week's rations for each man. Five hundred of them were ferried over to the mainland, to march along the northern bank of the river, guided by Belize refugees, while the canoe flotilla started upstream, supported by the *Titan*, an armed schooner.

The Hondo is a narrow river with heavily wooded banks, but all went quietly until the flotilla poled abreast of a little settlement some three miles from the bay, where hidden riflemen opened up on the lead canoe, pouring more than three hundred shots into it and killing or wounding everyone aboard. Conditions for a massacre were developing, as this canoe and the others drifted helplessly downstream, but the land party hurried to the sound of the guns, flanked the ambush, and order was restored. Protected by the main body, the canoes had no further trouble, passing several undefended strong points, including one at which cannons were mounted, and then reached a small river, the Chaak.

The schooner was left at this point with a guard of 50 men, while the rest pushed on, forced to unload and drag their canoes through the swamps and shallow channel of the Chaak creek, working through the afternoon and night, reaching the lake early in the morning. The land party, after crossing the Chaak, had fought its way around the south end of Lake Bacalar, against increasing resistance. Contact between the two groups was made the second day, the wounded brought off in the canoes. But progress slowed, and when Cetina came up that night, he broke one of his colonels for lack of spirit and ordered a night attack across the water within enemy lines. This was done, and the troops landed quietly, marching undetected to a position behind the town of Bacalar. From that point they charged, and with the Maya facing the other way, massed against the main body, they took twenty-four undefended barricades in one rush and seized the town, the fortress, and welcome quantities of tortillas and beans.

Taking Bacalar was one thing, holding it another. The purpose of the expedition, to deprive the Maya of access to Belize, meant holding not just the town but a long frontier of jungle, swamp, and river. Cetina put everyone to work building a chain of sixteen outposts along the lake, with the greatest strength at the north and south ends, supported by a cannon launch to stop all canoe traffic. A base was maintained at the lake entrance of the Chaak to keep that passage open and dominate the swamp, the schooner *Titan* patrolled the Hondo, and a second schooner cruised the bay shore. In all, this amounted to a blockade of more than fifty miles of waterways, which would force the Maya to pack their supplies over trails of that added distance, trails parallel to Ladino outposts and vulnerable to ambush.

Jacinto Pat quickly recognized the seriousness of this threat. In spite of the planting season and his own precarious situation near Tihosuco, he sent between four and five thousand men down under José María Tzuc. These forces began to harass Bacalar in May and June, mounting increasingly frequent attacks, hitting at the outposts, and finally besieging the town. At three o'clock in the morning of June 29, 1849, they made a general assault. Ladino bugles began appealing for help up and down the lake, as each post was engaged, several of them falling, their garrisons slaughtered. Rescue parties were forced back as the Maya swarmed into the town itself. The troops retreated from one barricade to another, building new ones as they went, all in darkness and complete confusion, but by some miracle they held on until dawn, when the fort artillery drove the Maya out of the city and purchased a breathing spell.

Weeks of continuous fighting passed with no clearcut victory, and the isolation began to work on the minds of the soldiers. A single reinforcement of 100 native Hidalgos had been sent to them; it was supposed to replace the 253 men in the hospital with malaria, the hundreds of wounded and dead. The defenders had been able to buy very little corn from Belize, and they found almost none on raids. Rations were poor and limited. Around five hundred refugees had returned to Bacalar with the troops, but under these conditions they began deserting to Belize.

Cetina was a stubborn man. One day he announced that all who wanted passports to leave the country should speak up. When five or six stepped forward, he ordered them disarmed and shot. Mercy was urged for a father and son, so the Colonel pardoned the boy but shot the father. Another victim was Vito Pacheco, a Mendecista who had been active in politics until Barbachano's return to power, when he had fled to the east coast, where he had supported himself by fishing from a small schooner, and, it was said, by running guns to the Maya. When the Seventh Division appeared he had offered his services, and his boat had been turned into a coast patrol with a 25-man guard. Now, with morale low, a sergeant reported that Pacheco had gone back to his old trade. Colonel Cetina had him brought to the fortress, treated him pleasantly, and then, in the middle of dinner, announced in a friendly tone that this was his last meal on earth—because he was going to be shot. The court-martial and the priest took little time.

By these techniques Cetina convinced his men that he intended to hold Bacalar, even if he had to kill them one by one, and that their only hope lay in obedience. He kept them busy when they weren't fighting. The woods near the town were cleared, a wooden barricade with a ditch was constructed, and the colonial cannons of San Felipe were repaired and remounted. With the addition of a cannon launch to the Hondo patrol, Cetina made a very awkward middleman standing between the English and their customers.

Six

Stalemate
1849–1850

MILITARY VICTORY, by the textbook, is the defeat of an enemy on
the battlefield, the occupation of his country, and the destruction of
his tools of war and means of support. In Yucatan, all this had been
done. Every town, every village on the map, had been reconquered,
held against counterattack, and securely fortified; the Maya had been
killed, captured, or driven from their land, and their supply line to
Bacalar cut. Driven from their homes—from the villages of the Cocomes, from the Chenes, from the areas around Valladolid and Tihosuco—the Maya found refuge deep in the unmapped southern and
eastern forest.

This was not simply the retreat of an army but the forced migration of an entire population, including the old, the women, and the
children; and as such, it was only an intensification of that movement which had been going on for the last two hundred years under
the slower pressure of an expanding population and white oppression.
The poverty of the Maya simplified the movement. Their huts could
be left behind and new ones built from material at hand at the next
camp; their hammocks had no weight, there were no chairs or tables
to worry about, and they never had much clothing; pottery bowls,
jars, griddles, and gourd containers could be replaced and new
hearthstones found. If unknown, the new forest would be similar to
the old, much would seem familiar, and there was no hardship in
clearing a new cornfield for men who had to do this every year. The
only necessities, then, were a machete, a gun with a little ammunition,
and food.

Food was the problem, starvation the enemy that pursued the Maya no matter how deeply they penetrated the forest. Their chief supply was dried and shelled corn, done up in 100-pound sacks (*cargas*), and carried on the back by a tumpline straining across the forehead. The Batabob, those native leaders who had been lucky in the matter of loot, had mules to help, but most of the people—including women and children—were their own beasts of burden. Their corn, the vital seed corn, would make possible new fields and feed them until those fields could be harvested. There were other foods— beans, chili, calabash, sweet potatoes, pigs, and chickens—but they were never plentiful, and what couldn't be carried was hidden in the hope of return. The Ladino counteroffensive had succeeded just as the harvest of 1848 was coming in, and, rolling over the cultivated area, the soldiers fell heir to much of the crop. The planting of 1849 was catch-as-catch-can, with spies watching from treetops for the telltale columns of smoke when the fields were burned in April, marking the direction to set an ambush and trap the farmers. But there was enough for a grim and hungry survival.

Bitterness grew from defeat, hunger, and the loss of the great dream of a Mazehual kingdom. Like trapped animals, the rebels turned to rend themselves: after the murder of Cecilio Chi there was born a new rivalry with Jacinto Pat inherited by the dead chief's two officers, Florentino Chan and Venancio Pec. Pat, more familiar with the world beyond the villages and recognizing that white power would win in the end, sought to avoid further catastrophes through negotiation, contacting a Protestant minister in Belize and writing to Superintendent Fancourt. Rumors of this communication reached Chan and Pec, who remembered the treaty signed at Tekax, the banner and the staff proclaiming Don Jacinto leader of the Maya. That treaty seemed only presumptuous and stupid then, but now, with the emotions of subsequent misfortune, it was considered high treason. On September 3, 1849, Venancio Pec wrote a letter addressed to the captains, sergeants, and Alcaldes, wherever they might be found, denouncing Pat for the seizure of loot from his men, for taxing his people to buy war materiel, and for using forced labor and keeping discipline with the whip. Liberty from such oppression, the letter said, was what the war against the whites was all about. This, of course, was propaganda; each new leader would take up the old methods. The letter also implied that Cecilio Chi still lived and had decided that Don Jacinto, and any who thought like him, should be killed on sight.° In fact, the letter was probably withheld until its argument was academic.

On September 8, Pec appeared at Pat's headquarters camp of Tabi, to find that his quarry had left the day before, traveling down to Belize with 5,000 pesos—to buy guns, or peace, or to seek refuge beyond the frontier, it was said. Pec seized various leaders at Tabi and then hurried south; at the jungle well of Holchen, about fifty miles from Bacalar, he caught Jacinto Pat by surprise and murdered him. It was an act symbolic of the future. The death of El Gran Cacique de Yucatán would be echoed in the assassination of Mazehual leaders yet unborn, in the suppression of repeated attempts to reach some accommodation with the outside world, by those whose world ended where the jungle stopped.

Venancio Pec and his band now became dominant in the north and Florentino Chan in the south of the coastal strip of jungle that remained to the Maya. They weren't in a position to exercise much control. Dzul columns and the natural independence of village life worked against central authority. Each village unit had considered itself a family, self-sufficient and united against outsiders, and this feeling was only partially broken down by the common struggle. If this meant inefficiency on the offense, it also meant that each group could survive emotionally unsupported on the defense, that each group had to be separately crushed. At the outset, each village had fought together, organized in militia companies of no standard size, running from 50 to 300, under officers ranked on the Ladino pattern.† Many of these companies were decimated, and the survivors joined

---

° Pec's reference to Chi in the present tense might have been an error in the Spanish translation, but it was more probably a deliberate effort to win the support of Chi's followers. The date of Chi's death has been disputed, but no writer places it later than May 1849 and the best evidence points to December 14, 1848.

† These village groups were not small. Pedro José Ix, a first captain, reported in December 1849 that he had led the former inhabitants of Oxkutzcab to safety at the rancho of Dzibilum, somewhere in the eastern forest; the people under his command numbered close to 4,000.

other units, mixing and merging according to the fortunes of war. As the Batabob were killed, captured, or lost influence with the loss of their men, new leaders took their places; a leader's prestige depended much on personality, but allegiance always remained with the company, the unit that had replaced the village. Zacarías May fought his separate battles in the Chenes, headquartering at Machanche, below Iturbide; Angelino Itza sat out the war with his people at Chichenha southwest of Bacalar, supporting himself by renting timber land and selling mahogany to the English loggers; and countless minor chiefs, many of them Mestizos, acted in equally independent fashion.

Bonifacio Novelo, that expert at survival, still haunted the Valladolid area from Cruz Chen. Pat's officer, José María Barrera, continued in command at Kampocolche, and Pedro Encalada had found himself a new home at Locha, where he would long remain. These Mestizos, men who had been in on the original rebellion—misled Barbachanistas, or deserters to what must have then seemed the winning side—had authority out of all proportion to their numbers. They were better educated, accustomed to dominating the full-blooded Maya, and often they had regular army experience. There was no logical reason to consider them traitors to the white race, but they were so considered by the Ladinos, and always shot when captured. These men and their bands were forced to remain on the defensive after the unsuccessful sieges of Tihosuco and Saban frittered out. It was not a passive defense. A raid was made right into the streets of Valladolid, the small forward camp of Map was overrun and supplies and weapons captured, and the white raids that continued through the rainy season usually found a warm reception.

The greatest Maya success of the season was at Tituc. This place, about thirty miles south of Saban, was occupied as the point of departure for a march across country to Bacalar, to be led by Colonels Pasos, Pavia, and Juan de Dios Novelo (promoted from Captain since his experience with the American volunteers). These officers, with 535 men, were besieged at Tituc for sixteen days, attracting Maya from the Saban siege and other places, before deciding to give it up as a bad job and retreat to Saban. A few miles out of Tituc, a strongly defended barricade stopped them long enough for the column to pile up in confusion; they were immediately taken all along their flanks, resistance collapsed, and it became a scene from the war's beginnings. Maya profits included 100 pack horses, 78 mules with all they carried, 48 cases of cartridges, many rifles, and much other equipment. Of the 535 men who marched from Saban, 204 returned, many of them wounded. Colonel Juan de Dios Novelo was not among them; he had gone down, sword and pistol in hand, his back to a tree.

This victory and the capture of Map was the work of José María Barrera, whose stock soared among the tribes. He further improved his reputation by picking up a lightly guarded convoy of ninety mules, and by frightening off a second march on Tituc. But he drew Ladino attention with all of this, and the army sent two columns after him, one from Tihosuco to his headquarters of Kampocolche, and the other from Saban to Tabi. When caught, he lost his horse and even his machete in the fight and barely escaped through the brush on foot. These actions were part of a series of aggressive revenge raids that came with good weather, smashing the eastern Maya and forcing them back to the coast.

Ascensión Bay took on an importance after the Bacalar supply line was cut. It was centrally located for the trade of gunrunning, close to the customers and dotted with islands and swampy inlets that gave concealment. These advantages were quickly discovered by the English and turncoat Yucatecans, and small schooners began making regular trips to the bay. It was a risky business. The Mexican Navy had a patrol; and the entire coast was dangerous because of its nasty, unpredictable winds. But the profits balanced the risk.

Ascensión was thus a natural place for the Superintendent of Belize, Charles Fancourt, to meet the Maya leaders. After receiving Jacinto Pat's letter expressing an interest in peace, Fancourt had proceeded to get approval from Mexico to act as intermediary. On November 15 he sailed up to Ascensión, where the shore was crowded with thousands of Maya, come to see the chief of the friendly Dzulob. In a conference with Venancio Pec and Florentino Chan, Fancourt heard the familiar complaints of oppressive taxation, of atrocities committed by soldiers at the front regardless of orders from the Mexican Government, and learned that the chiefs would only accept complete independence of the land they now held. Pec even asked that they be taken under English sovereignty, and when this was denied, he suggested going to England to confer with Queen Victoria. Fancourt promised to transmit the Maya terms to Mexico and sailed home.

The Yucatecans were eager for peace, and they set up a commission of priests, under José Canuto Vela, to make whatever contacts they could and to arrange for surrender of the fragmented Maya bands. The priests were in a difficult situation. Horrified by conditions at the front—especially the slaughter of prisoners, combatant or otherwise, and the systematic raping of women—their complaints made them thoroughly unpopular with the troops, and the only way they could reach the Maya was to go along on raids, which ran against the purpose of their mission. And the natives had lost all respect for them. The more friendly answers to the letters of the priests said, "Go away, and then there will be peace." But the army couldn't hold off. It was one thing to control the country, but another thing to find workers for the land; with former servants now the enemy or serving in the army labor corps, the state was dangerously short of corn, and the soldiers were forced to become self-supporting by stealing the rebel harvest. They accepted prisoners when this was possible, but they continued to raid, regardless of attempted treaties. The Ladino officers, with an army of seventeen thousand, knew that their enemy was beaten and believed that it would take only one more concerted effort to finish the war; they were unwilling to be tricked or delayed by the chance of armistice.

Full use was made of the dry season, September 1849 to April 1850. Guerrillas of 400 men gave way to columns of 1,000 each, which united to fight when there was opposition and then split up after it was crushed to search out the new cornfields, hidden supplies, and scattered fugitives. The columns marched at will, down below Iturbide, past Becanchen, repeatedly to Kampocolche, where they established a forward camp, to the eastern shore at Ascensión, to Cruz Chen. During this period they collected 500 guns, 800 horses and mules, and over 4,400 prisoners. It would seem that the military knew best. Yet these captives were primarily noncombatants, women, children, and old people, who had been surprised in their refugee settlements; from the same reports, only 51 men among all these thousands were taken with weapons in hand and only 152 were killed. Although perhaps not completely accurate, these figures were enough to show the truth: there was more glory than substance to the victories. The raids canceled out whatever might have been done through negotiations. Only isolated results were achieved by the priests— one hundred Maya here, fifty there, as hard-pressed petty chiefs gave up, accepting the amnesty cards distributed by released prisoners.*

And if thousands of rebels were taken, tens of thousands were still in the woods, hardened by their suffering, convinced by broken treaties that for them there was no surrender. Typical was the case of José María Barrera, who received an offer of mediation from the curate Vela, seconded by Colonel Novelo, an old comrade in arms and fellow Barbachanista, urging surrender to their now victorious common party—as if that mattered after all this time. At first Barrera refused, knowing patrols were out looking for him; but when a fifteen-day truce was arranged, he wrote that he would assemble the local chiefs and come to the camp at his former headquarters of Kampocolche on May 4. But Venancio Pec had gone down to Belize to buy supplies, where he forgot defeat, the war, and his responsibility in aguardiente instead, and couldn't be reached; Florentino Chan simply refused Barrera's invitation.

All of this was reported to the regional commander, Colonel Octavio Rosado, who, as much as any one man, had started the war with his execution of Manuel Antonio Ay. The Colonel rode down to Kampocolche to be in on the end. May 4 and May 5 passed with no sign of Barrera and his chiefs, and on May 6 Rosado decided the whole thing was a trick to gain time; overriding the priest's objections, he angrily ordered his guerrillas into the woods. This force surprised one camp after another, bayoneting 72 natives, collecting 228 prisoners and much booty, and losing only one man to rifle fire and two to the machete. Barrera wasn't found. It was a great victory for the Colonel; unborn generations of Yucatecans would fight and die

---

* These defeats were hard on the rebels. Captain Francisco Cob wrote to his commander, Calixto Yam: "Tell me, sir, if there is any force [left] to persecute those who have caused so much disaster, because if there isn't, I will go off into the woods to die. Now I have no other hope." But despair was not universal. Venancio Pec also wrote to Yam at about this time: "Let me deal with those who come this way, and throw yourself on Saban and Tihosuco . . . with the firm resolution to finish with these towns, so that we will see the results as soon as possible."

because of it. Vela had written Barrera at the last minute, warning him of the coming attack, disclaiming complicity, sending a sad farewell; but of course the letter arrived too late.

The threat of extinction had brought forth a tremendous military effort; now there was the question of who was going to pay. A large part of the Mexican grant of 150,000 pesos had by necessity been spent on rifles and ammunition (American rifles and ammunition which were surplus anyway, so the money spent by the United States to give legitimacy to Manifest Destiny came home again). This left little for food. An arrangement was made in August 1848 by the Yucatecan government with Yucatecan merchants to import three million pounds of corn, 500,000 pounds of beans, 600,000 pounds of biscuits and other foodstuffs, the merchants to supply the money and payment to be made out of import duties. These supplies quickly ran out, the duties didn't bring in the anticipated amount, and no new contracts could be made. Heavy taxes were imposed through these years, but with agriculture and commerce ruined and fewer taxpayers on the rolls, that source soon ran dry. Worst of all, in April of 1849 the Mexican allotment came to an end.

The most striking suggestion of the ruin caused by the rebellion lies simply in the figures showing the loss of population between 1846 and 1850. The tabulation by Departments is as follows:

Department	1846 Census	1850 Census	Loss
Mérida	118,839	91,299	27,540
Valladolid	97,468	23,066	74,402
Izamal	72,096	67,423	4,673
Tekax	134,000	35,505	98,493
Campeche	82,232	82,232	0
Total	504,635	299,525	247,118

In short, the population of Yucatan dropped by almost half. The Departments of Valladolid and Tekax, which included all of the frontier except the southern Chenes region, lost approximately seventy-five per cent of their residents, and the Department of Mérida lost more than twenty-five per cent. A survey of the Valladolid district in 1862 showed that 19 towns, 124 haciendas, and 211 ranchos had been sacked and abandoned, most of them by the early 1850's.

We must leave even the questionable accuracy of these figures when we try to account for actual people. An informed guess would put the number of living rebels in 1850 at around 80,000. Some 10,000 Maya and Ladinos sought refuge at Belize, and a few thousand more (which we will not count) fled to Guatemala; and perhaps 10,000 Ladinos shipped overseas to Cuba, Tabasco, or Veracruz. This leaves 147,000 persons still unaccounted for, and these must have been the dead: thirty per cent of the population killed by the gun, the machete, starvation, or disease. No H-men had forecast such a disaster.*

Yucatan's only natural resource had been the land and the people to work it. Now the land was recovered, but not the people, and there wasn't enough food for those that survived. Taking their chances with snipers and the machete as they harvested rebel Maya fields, the soldiers weren't happy to see that same corn wasted on captive savages. They didn't take prisoners except under direct command, or occasionally for the five-peso reward.

With these facts in mind, Governor Barbachano took a step for which his name is still remembered in Mexico. He began selling the Maya to Cuba. There were many apparent justifications: it saved their lives; they were rebels and thus liable to the most severe punishment (execution, or as was decreed by Congress, ten years' banishment); they were sent on a ten-year work contract; and finally, the state needed the money. But still, it was slavery. The first contract was for twenty-five pesos a head; 140 were shipped to Havana on March 5, 1849, and 195 on May 15; and the resulting 8,375 pesos were used to transport the expeditionary Seventh Division to Bacalar. The arrival of the prisoners at Havana was reported by the Mexican consul to the national capital, and when the Mexican press screamed for Barbachano's head, he reluctantly ordered the trade stopped. No tears had been shed for the captives sent to Veracruz, because this was within the national frontier, but for them it was just as bad. Un-

---

* This is a conservative estimate of its dimensions. In a contemporary report, Regil and Peón (from whom the tabulation above is taken) noted that the officials involved in the 1846 census had good reasons, such as tax assessments and military quotas, for undercounting their districts. After a careful survey of inaccuracies in the census, they estimated the total population in 1846 at 575,362— which would raise the total loss to 274,906 and the percentage of the population presumably killed to 35 per cent.

fortunately, Mexico already had enough sweated labor of its own. A newspaper article soon proposed that 10,000 Maya be sent to Cuba, and a $500,000 advance on their salaries be used to support widows, orphans, and disabled veterans and to make loans to businessmen and revive commerce. It was an idea too attractive to forget.

Yet the matter of the Maya slaves reminded Mexico of the desperate situation in Yucatan. She renewed the subsidy, raising it to 16,000 pesos a month; more, she sent soldiers, three hundred of an advance guard and a new commander, the Comanche fighter General Manuel Micheltorena, to replace General López de Llergo. The Mexican general arrived at Campeche on February 5, 1850. He first traveled up to Mérida to be feted at a ball and meet the important people; then, taking over his new command on February 11, he set off on a tour of inspection, escorted by the socially elite Volunteer Cavalry. There was an air of finality about this move, a suggestion that one more campaign could end all the troubles. (How many times the Yucatecans were to think along those lines!)

Micheltorena traveled first to Valladolid and then down to Tiho-suco. Well protected, he visited a number of forward camps, the bases for raids into the forest, congratulating the successful colonels, learning the details of jungle warfare. The veteran Colonel Octavio Rosado was made Corps Commander of the Forces of Restoration in the southeast, General Cádenas in the north. These woods, so different from the blue distances and barren mountains of Chihuahua, must have seemed alien to Micheltorena, and he doutless realized that there was more for him to learn than to teach. He could only advise his officers to continue the good work while he busied himself with supplying his army.

And supply was the chief problem. As the rainy season approached, the more accessible enemy cornfields had been plundered or harvested and the crop hidden. The soldiers marched out on many a hungry raid, only to return with new holes cut in their belts and nothing for the civilians at home. There were occasional acts of insubordination or mutiny, settled by firing squads, but most of the men grimly stuck to their tasks. And so they marched to the south and the east through that third spring of the war, on into the rain, the flooded trails, the mule-stopping mud, with empty stomachs, clothes that never dried, infected scratches that never healed—sick, starving men in search of a sick, starving, shadow enemy. The largest operation of that spring was the march of 700 men under Colonel Patricio O'Horan, from Kancabchen south to Bacalar. They found some corn in that unmolested region and killed 177 natives, whose undermanned bases they also raided and burned.

The isolated Bacalar garrison had suffered even more from sickness and starvation. Colonel Cetina sent his second-in-command by sea to Mérida, begging for the relief of his 800 survivors. Instead, Lieutenant Colonel González returned with a 500-man reinforcement. With this new strength, a guerrilla of regimental size was organized; it was to break through the siege lines and penetrate up the Hondo, traveling by canoes, disembarking when necessary to take river-bank defenses. On their second morning out, they reached the settlement of Cacao, which was little more than a deserted house; there were signs of occupation on the Mexican side of the river, and on the other side a disordered heap of gunpowder barrels guarded by a forewarned Englishman, standing safely in the forest of Her Britannic Majesty.

There had been almost weekly complaints that year to Superintendent Fancourt that "the Spanish" had been arbitrarily stopping peaceful English timbermen on the river and seizing goods intended for their Hondo works. These were the goods, these the works.

The guerrilla canoes hurried on upstream, sighting another merchant or mahogany man, who unfortunately escaped to warn those ahead, at the main objective of Agua Blanca. A short skirmish secured his camp on the northern bank, netting 40 Negro prisoners (60 got away), several wagons, and a vast pile of cut mahogany logs. The master of all this reappeared shortly, venturing out from his shore in a canoe, vigorously waving his flag. When assured of safe conduct, he quietly offered the Mexican commander 8,000 pesos for the wood and 500 pesos for his Negro workmen, who were slaves in all but name. This was refused, but the officer accepted a luncheon invitation on the south bank, where he was treated to a free view of cases of new guns and powder. Again the bribe was refused; the wood was burned and the Negroes taken back down river and to Bacalar. To the Yucatecans, this was fair punishment for the piracy of their forests and gunrunning; to the English, their subjects were only making normal lumber contracts with local authorities, carrying on normal trade with one faction in a civil war. Orders had obviously been given to keep to the north bank and treat the Englishmen gently, since the emotional satisfaction of giving them what they deserved would clearly not be worth a bombardment and possible occupation by English forces. With this last raid, Colonel Cetina was relieved, together with his veterans (except for those who were too sick to travel and probably never would). He embarked for Sisal and Campeche, pausing, in a departing flourish, for a raid ashore at Ascensión Bay.

While guerrillas were combing the woods for prisoners and food, the enemy they couldn't find was busy elsewhere, accepting the losses he couldn't prevent. In the predawn hours of November 4, as Tekax was preparing for a fiesta, the Maya made a lightning raid; they rushed the armory with little fighting, seized the guns and ammunition they had come for, and vanished before anyone knew what had happened, leaving behind a few incidental dead, a few burned houses, and a grim precedent for the future. The small garrison at Xul was wiped out. A surprise attack at Bolenchenticul carried to the plaza, but the church was stoutly defended, and the attackers were cut down as they tried to hack their way through the door. Hopolchen also escaped by a slim margin. While the Ladino armies could march where they pleased, to the eastern coast or down to Bacalar, they did so at a risk to their bases, for they were operating in a terrain that had no front, no rear, and no vital objective, against an enemy who was far from through. It was a dull and maddening war of attrition. Victory seemed impossible, but defeat was unthinkable, and little more than survival was the prize for the side that could hold on the longest.

The Coming of the Cross
1850–1852

WHEN MAN DECIDES to be unpleasant to his neighbors, the gods are always on his side. Spiritual mobilization in time of war is more than jargon from pulpit and platform: it is a human need. Saints, ancestors, heroes, prophets, and gods are mustered by bugle and drum; national myths, philosophies, and religions are invoked in terms that the simplest citizen can understand; metaphysical lines are tightened for the blow. If the adversaries are more or less equally matched, they go into battle each confidently praying to his own god, and a limited defeat is no reflection on that god, but merely on the devotion and energy of his followers. When they pray to the same god, one side may lose, but the god remains secure. But when one culture is obviously inferior and recognizes the fact, then faith is threatened. Man has made gods not in his own image, but according to his own needs; and when the needs change, or go unfulfilled, the gods must change as well. The new fact of foreign superiority and domination must find a place, must become naturalized and explained in local terms on a spiritual level.

Thus the natives of New Guinea, during and after the Second World War, explained the total discrepancy between their own Stone Age culture and the unlimited wealth of the Allied armies as theft by the white men of the gifts intended for themselves, the gifts sent by their ancestors. An existing ancestor worship, belief in an island of the dead across the sea, and the natural feeling that somehow they had been swindled produced what is called the Cargo Cult. A belief developed that some day the ancestors would return in a great fleet of ships and set everything right, and the natives have attempted to speed that day by destroying their own food supply, to force the ancestors to act before famine destroys the nation. There is a tidy logic in this, but it is the logic of magic, a transformation of human desires into natural law, a pathetic cry for help.

In much the same way the American Indian, in the 1870's and again in 1890, after decades of defeat and dispossession by what seemed an unlimited horde of white men, turned to the Ghost Dances. The Indian wasn't afraid of war. His problem was manpower, and this he would solve by invoking, through the magic of ritual dance, the only available source, the Indian dead of all past generations; with that army, using traditional Indian weapons, he would drive his enemy from the country. Then he would dance the slaughtered buffalo herds back to life, and the good times would return.

The primitive man's world view is all-embracing, bringing every fact of life within a comprehensible, self-contained system. There are no alternatives. Either the system is true, or his ego, his culture, and his world are shattered. It would take a Martian, with extraterrestrial logic, to duplicate this shock for modern man, with his multicultural, multireligious background. The Cargo Cult, the Ghost Dance, and a hundred similar nativistic revivals are the last rallies of folk religions against materialistic world civilization.

In 1850 the Maya were losing the same game, losing their priests, their wonder-working images, the vital elements of their spiritual life. Attempts were made at replacement. A clay figure surrounded by candles and decorated with flowers was found by a Ladino patrol at Kancabdzonot in the early days of the Cocomes rising. The soldiers called it an idol, saying that the savages had gone from treating holy images as idols to using idols in fact. But this is part of the game: I am religious; you are superstitious; he believes in magic. It was not magic yet, only a substitution for a stolen Santo, perhaps the Virgin of Tabi which figured so strongly in the treaty terms of that region. Likewise, in that second year of the war, one Macedonio Tut put on captured vestments and acted the priest, using the chants he had learned as a seminarian. These were isolated incidents that came to nothing, but they pointed the way.

For three hundred years the Maya had worked on an adaptation of Christianity, giving up their early gaucheries, such as the crucifixion of children in churches and churchyards shortly after the Conquest or the serving of mass by unordained native priests using maize tortillas for the Host and gruel for wine. They had reached a compromise, but one with many survivals. About one such survival, not much is known. The Maya had speaking idols. A hollow figure had been built into a temple wall at Cozumel with a secret passage for the priest. Another endured with the pagan Itza at Tayasal until it was destroyed, along with the town, 130 years before the Caste War. The Books of Chilam Balam, well-known in 1847 and guarded to this day by the Mazehualob of Quintana Roo, were dictated to the Chilam, or prophet, as he lay on the floor of his house, by a spirit voice coming from the thatch roof. After the Conquest, in 1597, a native of Sotuta named Andrés Chi continued in the same tradition, announcing himself as Moses and claiming to be guided by the voice of the Holy Ghost. Chi's technique was no better than his Bible study; the Holy Ghost was dragged out of his hiding place in the thatch of Chi's hut—a small boy, who because of his youth was spared his master's fatal end at the hands of the authorities. There is no certain record of voices among the Yucatecan Maya after that, but it is most probable that they continued to speak in a whisper too low for white ears. The highland Maya of Southern Mexico and Guatemala have similar traditions. When the Mam tribe planted coffee trees instead of corn, ears of corn were said to speak, warning of hunger and misery. Talking saints and talking chests have frequently turned up among the Tzeltal and Tzotzil Maya; the most famous were those of Pedro Díaz Cuscat, which helped bring on the Caste War of Chiapas.*

---

* In 1868 in the remote mountain village of Chamula, in Chiapas, a Maya peasant, Pedro Díaz Cuscat, made himself a wooden saint, which, he announced, had come down from heaven to help the poor Indio. Calling it too holy for profane eyes, he kept it in a chest big enough for both the figure and himself, and soon the Santo began to talk. When the local curate seized the carving and preached on heresy and superstition, Cuscat made several more and said that they had been born to his assistant, Augustina Gómez Checheb, which made her the "Mother of God." He went further. Long ago the Ladinos had crucified a man and created their god, and the people of Chamula, he said, should do the same. On Easter Sunday 1868, the new Christ, Domingo Gómez Checheb, a boy

The anthropologist Kroeber has described well the moment when a native culture feels itself doomed, either by direct military action or the superior attractions of a more developed society:

> At this juncture a prophet is likely to arise and picture a wish fulfillment: a release from the human impasse by supernatural mechanism. . . . Therewith a revivalistic movement of return to the good old days is launched. The prophet's motivation may range from sincere delusion to desire for power, fame, or even money, or be compounded of these. His converts follow him because of the stress of their social unhappiness.

This is precisely what happened in Yucatan. José María Barrera, driven from Kampocolche, led his harried Maya band to an uninhabited forest cenote forty miles southeast of Saban, called Chan Santa Cruz, or "Little Holy Cross." A place known and occasionally used by Huit tribesmen, it was said that there was an aura of sanctity about it, and that it harbored a miraculous cross with the power of speech. Whether these reports came only after the fame of the shrine was established during the Caste War is uncertain.

The cenote itself was insignificant from a practical point of view. It lay in a dell, tucked between steep, rocky hillocks, a grotto perhaps fifteen feet deep and eight feet wide, the floor of the chamber filled with several feet of water that maintained its level despite heavy use. But the inconvenience, the low, dark entrance, the small size, and hidden quality were exactly the features that appealed to the Maya imagination, characteristics that would make this a "virgin" cenote par excellence. There was, in fact, a larger and more useful cenote a half mile to the east. It would be natural to find a cross at such a "virgin" place, and there was one here.* It was only three or four inches long, lightly carved in a mahogany tree that grew at the

---

of ten and a relative of the "Mother of God," died in torment, nailed through his hands and feet to an elevated cross while the faithful worshiped him with incense and aguardiente. The Caste War of Chiapas was almost inevitable after this act of fanaticism. Cuscat had probably heard rumors of the war in Yucatan, but he need not have known any of the cult details; he was working with a substratum of ideas and beliefs common to all the Maya people, including child sacrifice, hidden votive objects, and holy voices.

  * There is a common Maya association between water and the Cross. The Zinacantan people of Chiapas, for instance, consider their waterholes sacred and use them as locations to celebrate the day of the Holy Cross in May.

edge of the grotto—the work of a wandering hunter or, some say, of José María Barrera. It was the original "Little Holy Cross." This would also be a natural place for the survival of celestial voices, lying as it did among the least assimilated of the Huit Maya, beyond the frontier, deep in the jungle, safe from the eyes and ears of the white man.

If there was a speaking cross, Barrera used it; if not, he adapted one, using traditional means. A wooden cross was produced, displayed on a platform of poles that stood on the slope of a hill just to the east of the grotto. There the hopeless fugitives prayed to God for release from oppression, and, the ventriloquist Manuel Nahuat being among them, God answered: His children should continue to resist the impious enemy; they should have no fear, since He would protect them from Dzulob bullets, and they should now attack the village of Kampocolche. Barrera stage-managed the divine promise and command, but his personal motives and the details of how it was arranged were unimportant in face of the collective need. The solution offered by the voice resolved a problem so emotionally charged that there could be no question of skepticism. Here was proof that God was on the side of His Mazehualob children.

And the need for faith sustained the faith through the massacre of the Maya at Kampocolche. They rushed the place in the dark, armed with God's promise of immunity from gunfire, ignoring the bullets for a chance to use their machetes; almost succeeding, they refused to give up when a counterattack threw them back from the village, and they persisted until the cold light of dawn made clear the broken promise and the dead. This was on January 4, 1851.

Learning of the cult from prisoners, Colonel Novelo led a guerrilla of 220 men by secret trails and surprised the shrine on March 23. Manuel Nahuat fell after killing a Ladino captain but Barrera escaped. The soldiers were amazed to discover a village of more than a thousand people where before there had been nothing, with other settlements clustered in the neighborhood. The Colonel reported that he could have brought in several thousand prisoners if he had had sufficient men to guard them. He did collect the assembled military supplies, the offerings, and the cross. It was hard on the Maya, but their faith would have more to swallow.

Barrera was not finished. The ring of settlements proved the magnetic attraction of the Speaking Cross, drawing the fugitive Maya from their hidden camps regardless of risk, to crowd around the cross and warm themselves in this new hope. With the ventriloquist act broken up, Barrera worked with a secretary, Juan de la Cruz Puc, a Mazehual of Nabalam; the Holy Word was next transmitted through him in the form of a letter. The letter, as reconstructed from the synopsis given by the historian Baqueiro, ran roughly as follows:

> Because of the sacrilegious murder of Nahuat, the Crosses will never speak again, except to the Seraphim and the Apostles. The Crosses were taken to Kampocolche, where the Dzulob asked them to speak, but this was not possible because the hour had not arrived and they would speak only with the Patrón [Barrera]. But now the time has come for them to communicate with their sons, the Mazehualob, and to tell them that the Dzulob will be severely punished for the damages caused by their troops. The Mazehualob must now rise and take vengeance for the spilt blood; their avenging horde must go to the church at Yalcoba, where the Crosses now are, assemble the inhabitants of Chan Santa Cruz and the neighboring villages, and reach an agreement with the Governor, who lives in the ruins of Chichén Itzá. [A reference to the legendary Itzá King promised in the books of Chilam Balam.] The Mazehualob should have no fear, because not One, but Three mysterious personages will take command of the situation. The hour has struck in which the Mazehualob will put the *gavilán* (the rooster windvane) in the high towers of the cathedral of Mérida [an act symbolic of conquest].

The letter was signed with three crosses, purporting to have come from the Crosses themselves, but it also carried the signature of Juan de la Cruz Puc as interpreter.

This brings us to a confusion of numbers. The historian Baqueiro, while in doubt about the rumors and stories of the founding of Chan Santa Cruz, assumed that there were originally three crosses and used the plural to describe what was captured and taken back to Kampocolche, where they were later described as seen by the troops. The letter cited above also uses the plural for the captured crosses, yet says that there are now "not one, but three," and that the three had just arrived at Yalcoba, eighty miles north of Chan Santa Cruz, having traveled directly from heaven. This was probably a mistake of dates; there would be many raids on the shrine, many substitute crosses, three or four groups captured in the first year, and the clearest reading would be that the three crosses appeared after the loss of the original. These three were described as daughters of the Cross, the one carved on the tree being the "Mother of the Crosses." They were dressed in *huipil* and skirt, as befitted their sex, and adorned with brightly colored ribbons. There was no contradiction for the Mazehual in the crosses being at once feminine, God, and the Holy Trinity; it was one of his personal adaptations of Catholicism.

Barrera was working overtime to build his religious esprit de corps. He turned up with an image of the Virgin, which had traveled the now familiar road down from heaven, but it didn't inspire faith; the idea of the cross, based solidly on the familiar cult of lineage and village crosses, was more successful. Possibly the Yalcoba location was a false lead planted to divert Ladino interest, but at any event Barrera quickly had the crosses installed at the accepted shrine of Chan Santa Cruz, where he built a defensive system of stone barricades around the place and maintained patrols against another surprise.

The patrols were needed. Knowing the religious calendar, the Ladinos waited until May 3, 1851, the Day of the Holy Cross, which had a logical significance for the new cult, and then attacked, 153 men under Colonel González. The expected fiesta was under way, but the distant explosion of a signal bomb gave Barrera time to evacuate his people, delaying the soldiers briefly at the walls, sniping, then fading back into the forest. Barrera had an estimated 1,400 men by this time, but he lacked guns and ammunition for a fire-fight and could ill afford another Kampocolche. He left the enemy an empty prize and set up an open siege that night, using his own walls. The white guerrilla was too small for the isolated position and pulled out the next day, having accomplished little. As would happen so often later, it had nothing to report except the continued growth of Chan Santa Cruz.

Traditionally, the Day of the Cross brought the rains, and this third rainy season of the war was the first of them in which the Dzul drew back to his camps. This gave José María Barrera time to consider the other aspects of survival. First came the question of food. It was too late for the burning of new fields, and the Mazehualob, as they had for the past three years, would have to make do with what was available, planting the exhausted clearings and the hidden patches prepared in spite of the fighting. The question was whether to plant the seed corn and starve now, or to eat now and starve later. Most of the wild game had been run off or shot out. There would be the too-familiar diet of wild roots, the bland yellow pulp of the Kunche, the milk of palm nuts—all symbolic of famine, food scorned in prosperity, but all too rare when needed. The lucky bands would scrape by, the others would starve.

Barrera realized that he must find a replacement for the ventriloquist, a new and effective technique, if he was to hold the survivors to his cross. His answer was a thatched church with an inner room called "La Gloria," for the altar on which the Crosses were kept, a sanctuary forbidden to all except a few assistants, guarded day and night. The congregation met in the main, outer room. This arrangement added mystery and glamor to the hidden Crosses and was in keeping with the local tradition of using a substitute Santo for procession when the genuine article was too holy for public view. It was also necessary to keep the secret of the voice. A pit was dug behind the altar, and there crouched a hidden spokesman who used a wooden cask as an echo chamber to amplify, project, and give resonance to his voice. Those who heard it said that the words of God seemed to come from the middle of the air. Remembering the will to believe, Barrera would manage. Starvation or not, the Crosses received a rich harvest of offerings: wax, corn, poultry, pigs, and money.

It was a very human divinity. A captured dragoon, surviving captivity because he was a musician (music teachers being almost as necessary as priests), was invited to a friendly card game with José María Barrera at the door of the church, and won twenty-eight pesos. The next day he was ordered before the Crosses, condemned for sacrilege in the house of God, given twenty-five lashes, and fined twenty-eight pesos, the fine to be spent on candles. When asked what punishment was laid upon Barrera and the other players, the dragoon explained, "Nothing, because they lost." Nevertheless, this soldier believed in the authenticity of the voice, as did many of the Mestizos and Indios in the Yucatecan army.

On through the rainy season of 1851 the Cross spoke, a hollow quavering Maya voice of God, bringing hope to the defeated, re-assembling the scattered, giving spiritual food to those who were dying of hunger. It gained for Barrera a certain control over the eastern bands, from Valladolid to Bacalar. But its voice didn't carry to the north coast or to the Chenes; and far to the south, in Chichenha, its authority was threatened that summer. Barrera received word of peace negotiations with Guatemala and hurried south, picking up his lieutenant José María Tzuc, commander of the Bacalar siege, en route. What he found was not to his liking. The Yucatecans had already attempted to make peace directly through their own priests, and then through the English at Belize. During the rain-enforced truce of 1851, a third avenue for negotiations was opened by a long patrol from Colonel Baqueiro's forces in the southern Chenes, which marched south along seldom-used trails through the uninhabited forest, skirting rebel Maya areas, to meet the mayor of the village of Petén, in Guatemala.

The mayor, Modesto Méndez, was also a Colonel and an explorer, having discovered the vast Maya ruin of Tikal two years previously. He needed all his talents as a politician, soldier, and woodsman to undertake Baqueiro's commission. Together with a priest, he crossed the trackless northeast Petén to the rebel Maya village of Chichenha. When the astonished Maya asked how many troops were with him, he replied that he had only a priest and the protection of the Virgin Dolorosa and that he had come to bring peace. His courage paid off. After two days of negotiations he signed a treaty with the Batab, Angelino Itza.

This was the situation when Barrera arrived. The treaty was not alliance with Guatemala, as had been rumored, but surrender to Yucatan. The terms were generous, but it was still surrender. Priests were to be sent among the rebel bands to organize elections and bring indulgences and a benediction from the Bishop—which did not sit well with a man who had three crosses in his pocket and claimed the direction of God. Barrera walked out on the conference, inviting Colonel Méndez to visit Chan Santa Cruz. Considering the atmos-phere, the Colonel showed good sense in declining. Instead he sent the signed treaty of the Chichenha group directly to Yucatan, helped celebrate a fiesta to peace, and went safely home. He had done more for Yucatan than any Yucatecan had so far been able to manage, even if the results weren't immediately forthcoming. Barrera returned to Chichenha a month later with 500 men, burned the village, and carried Itza and his chiefs off as prisoners. This ended the treaty and started a war that would last as long as both groups survived.

More than the rains had kept the Ladino army at home. On that same Day of the Holy Cross, May 3, 1851, General Rómulo Díaz de la Vega had arrived in Yucatan to replace the disgusted Micheltorena, Mexico's substitute for the monthly subsidy. The subsidy hadn't been paid since March, and no more was coming. Something had to give. Yucatan had 17,000 men under arms, almost every male citizen who could carry a gun, and with their numbers taken away from productive labor and off the tax lists, commerce was ruined and the state bankrupt. General Micheltorena had asked for 300,000 pesos for four months, promising to end the war, but the state could scrape up only 70,000, and apparently the General was looking for a way out. He made a flowery statement to the effect that he would gladly give his life for his country, for that was his duty, but that he could not give up his reputation, which was the property of his family, because one generation has no rights over the future. His honor thus established, he resigned.

With less bombast, the soldiers tried the same thing. There was a plot among the Bacalar garrison to seize that post and give it back to the Indians, and a mutiny at Yaxcaba over starvation rations. In both places, the offenders were taken to the whipping post and then to the firing squad. The troops were fed up, and the officers were hesitant to turn their backs on those who had shouted "Kill the officers!" Relief was necessary, and the new general arranged it. For the frontier, three brigades were organized under General Cádenas and Colonels Rosado and Molas; their reserve was the Light Battalion, the Sixth Line Battalion (Mexican regulars), a cavalry company, and a battery of artillery, all commanded by General Llergo. There are no accurate figures on the size of these units, but they were a small part of the army. The great majority of exhausted, rebellious soldiers were sent home and assigned to what was called the Sedentary Reserve.

Home meant many different things to the soldiers of Yucatan.

For the men from the old militia units of the First Local and the Libertad, it would mean the triumphal palm arches in Mérida and Campeche, welcoming speeches, and a last parade before the big drunk, that rite of passage back into the civilian world; there would be skyrockets, aguardiente, vows of eternal friendship with the hated sergeant, more aguardiente, then someone's sister or a whore and then a long, long sleep, closing the most vivid part of a man's life, leaving him to wake late and hungover, facing a future that was seldom as planned. Others met their future before the drunk and with little celebration. For the Seventeenth Chenes, the Eleventh Tekax, the frontier Orden, and the Constitución of Valladolid, the return was through burnt-over cane fields to sacked and gutted villages; or, for the luckier ones, to a fortified town with barricades, walled-up windows, and orchards leveled for a clear field of fire; it was a return to garrison life. For them the reserve wasn't sedentary. For them home was a pile of ashes, a dead wife or parents, children or family missing, packed up and gone to no one knew where. Many of these eastern men set out to search among the refugee camps, asking for news, and they never came back to the places of their birth.

As the Maya retreat had been a folk migration to the east, so now the Yucatecans began to move west, pulling back from the frontier. No military posts were given up. It was rather a matter of a family here or a disgusted veteran there deciding that the price was too high, that the constant fear at night or while working the isolated cornfield was too heavy a burden. Gradually the eastern provinces were depopulated, and the frontier receded from Chemax to Valladolid, from Kampocolche to Peto and Tekax. Those soldiers left in the reduced army of three brigades defined their sagging morale with more rioting; three hundred of them were arrested at Valladolid and six of their ringleaders hung.

The last major action of the spring had been the raid on Chan Santa Cruz in May, which was followed by isolated skirmishes during the rains. As the roads and trails began to dry out, plans were prepared, orders sent to mobilize local reserve units, and the Sedentary was to be enlisted and equipped. General Vega started on an inspection tour in mid-December 1851, traveling across the northern part of the state to Valladolid and then down to Tihosuco. There were no local reserves. No lists had been drawn up, no supplies gathered; and the active brigades were in a state of moral collapse. The veterans of three years of jungle fighting didn't want any more. The threat of the death penalty simply drove them from the state or kept them hiding in the bush; it couldn't stop them from deserting at the first good chance. Yet there was a job to be done, and the border settlers knew it. If they were ever to know peace, to work their fields in security and live without fear, the last bands of savages must be crushed. Reluctantly and slowly they gathered, some persuaded, some driven; and Vega finally had his army prepared for the march by February 19, 1852, two months late, at Tihosuco. This was to be a clean sweep, similar to the actions of the previous year, over familiar grounds. Lieutenant Colonel Ruz, operating from Valladolid, would scour the northeast coast. Colonels Ruiz, O'Horan, and Baqueiro were sent south to Locha, which had become a nest of trouble under the Mestizo leader Pedro Encalada. Leaving Ruiz to work that area, the other two took their battalions on to Chichenha. These maneuvers were more than raids. They lasted for months and covered hundreds of miles and deserve the Spanish term *entrada*, after raids of similar length and duration in the time of the Moorish wars.

The flanks thus disposed, General Vega led his main body of 600 men under Colonels Rosado, Novelo, and Mezo to the outpost of Kampocolche. There the troops stared at the captive Crosses, still dressed in their sad finery, and exhausted themselves digging for buried treasure: sixteen attacks by the Maya, carried out with religious fanaticism to comply with the direct command of their God, had been explained by the story that José María Barrera's wealth was hidden somewhere in the village. There were blistered hands and aching backs, but no gold. Then, with scouts sent out to give cautious and experienced cover, the ranks closed, discipline returned by necessity, and they took the Santa Cruz trail. It was a peaceful two-day march, and they reached the rebel village on February 24; flanking companies swept out to cut off fugitives as signal bombs ordered evacuation, and the village center was taken after being held briefly by barricades and the Ladino fear of hidden pitfalls.

Chan Santa Cruz had grown since the previous year. New groups of huts had sprung up, maintaining an isolation of several hundred yards from each other, reflecting their separate origins; there were three or four hundred of them in all, with eight or nine centering on the plaza for the leaders. There were also three barracks, very well made, and the church, where the device of the pit and barrel was discovered and laughed at by relieved and superstitious soldiers. The village had been decorated with palm arches for religious processions and fiestas, but it was a place of death. Each cluster of huts had its own fresh graveyard. Felipe de la Cámara Zavala told how he found a young boy dead on a path, another child still moving a little further away near a hut, and inside the hut a limp figure in the hammock, long past seeing through his open, staring eyes. There was nothing to fear in that place, only horror at human suffering, and, for those who could still feel such an emotion, pity for the rebels.

The mahogany tree on which the cross had originally appeared still stood by the edge of the grotto cenote—the "Mother of the Crosses," said to be uncuttable, able to turn the edge of any axe. It had given birth to several sets of crosses, all of which had been captured, and General Vega determined to cut off the source by cutting down the great tree. He assembled his 200 prisoners to witness the act, to see if it could turn his steel, and afterwards he asked if it had fallen like any other tree. "Possibly it is so," they answered, "but the Crosses can't be fooled." There is no arguing with an Indio, it was said, but no matter: clearly, this band of fanatics was starved out, the prisoners weren't worth keeping, and Chan Santa Cruz was finished. So they turned the prisoners loose and headed south on April 1, looking for someone to fight.

Dividing into several columns, the Yucatecans picked up 300 captives, who were more trouble to find than to take, reassembled at Bacalar a month later, and then joined Colonel Baqueiro's command at Chichenha. The Colonel had previously learned of the suppressed treaty and had been collecting prisoners in the normal manner. He had also established garrisons on the Rio Hondo and at Cacao and Agua Blanca, thus sealing the frontier and stopping all trade. In the north, Lieutenant Colonel Ruz had had the same experience, working out of Valladolid. His campaign had been more an exploration than a war, a game of hide-and-seek with a starved, defenseless enemy; the rebels had made a few token raids on reduced garrisons while the columns were away, but nothing more. Their objectives accomplished and the rains again coming on, General Vega declared the season closed, collecting his outposts and concentrating his scattered units. The army marched back to its regular camps, and the Sedentary Reserve went gratefully home. After two months without news, Mérida expressed its relief with salvos of artillery, victory salutes from the cannons of San Benito.

Eight

The End of the Caste War
1852–1855

THERE WERE ALARMS and skirmishes in the eastern forest during the rainy season of 1852, including a July retaliation raid that carried into Chan Santa Cruz, but Yucatan was bored with the Caste War. There had been too many victory celebrations, too much expense. As early as February of 1849, an article in the Campeche newspaper *El Fénix* had suggested that the rebels be left to rot in their wilderness, which could never be policed, and that the Ladinos concentrate their efforts in the west. This idea grew as the military budget continued to cripple the state. Colonel Rosado, after what he had seen on the spring entradas of 1852, reported that the war was over and that all efforts should be spent on restoration and reconstruction. The largest part of the Maya who had initially borne arms were now reclaimed, including many thousands of the eastern Huit tribesmen and their families; they had been settled in new villages of sixty or seventy huts, each with a Ladino in charge, each with a church.

The fortified towns began to relax. Bricked-up windows were opened to let in the light, barricaded arcades were cleared, in some cases prematurely, and garrisons were replaced by local inactive reserves; new thatch appeared on roofless buildings, and new huts sprang up from the ashes of the past. There was a symbol for this restoration. The principal bell of the parochial church of San Gervasio in Valladolid, 472 pounds of ancient iron, was missing when the city was recaptured. Now a Maya came forward to show where it had been buried. It was uncovered, carted back to the church, hoisted up to the tower and rehung, its resonant voice annnouncing the return of peace.

Destruction and population loss had been heaviest in the Departments of Valladolid and Tekax, and this meant the loss of subsistence crops, as well as cattle and sugar. Sugar and sugar products had been the prime export of Campeche, one of the main sources of capital on which its imports were based, and her long-term decline was intensified. Mérida, with a large hinterland, less dependence on sugar and on trade, and with the large fortunes of old landed Creole families to stimulate recovery, was not so badly hurt. Refugees replaced the early losses, and there was work enough for all hands. While corn was the first necessity, the need for a cash crop quickly became apparent, and the one crop that would grow in that rocky northern soil was henequen. Its cultivation was well launched before the war, when the crop earned over thirteen per cent of the state's export pesos, and necessity pushed forward its development at high speed. Once the threat to Mérida had eased in 1848, inflential hacendados had demanded and won exemption for their field hands, and even for their mules—this in spite of total mobilization. So the rows of henequen plants grew and were extended throughout the war. Jobs were waiting for the discharged soldiers and Hidalgos, under the old debt law, and many ruined Mestizos found themselves working side by side with their full-blooded brothers. Members of the Sedentary Reserve were attracted to the large haciendas, where the master could protect them from recall to active duty, while the individual farmer had no defense. The importance of henequen was underlined by the state government, which in 1852 offered a reward of 2,000 pesos for the invention of an efficient rasping machine to replace the crude hand methods of separating the fiber; they had in mind a machine which, like the cotton gin, would make large-scale commercial exploitation possible.

War can be a stimulating medicine if not taken in too large a dose, and after the first crisis, there were many men who found Mérida more exciting than chasing rebels through the eastern bush. The city resumed and expanded upon its earlier brisk cultural life. The bare, unsightly Plaza de Armas was planted with palm trees and Indian laurels, walks were laid out, gardens planned along the best European lines, and a wall with a cast-iron fence and gates was added to keep mules and natives out. The Palacio Municipal was reconstructed, with the handsome façade and clock tower brought to their final form, and new buildings were going up in the suburbs. An Academy of Science and Literature was founded in April of 1849, and its literary journal, *El Mosaico*, was run by the returned envoy to Washington, Justo Sierra; an art class was taught by Gabriel Gahona; two public libraries were opened with donated books, new plays were produced, and concerts held once again.

Unfortunately, there were also politics. Barbachano was confirmed in the office given him by Méndez through an uncontested election in August 1849. Opposition then developed among the outs, its intensity moving in inverse ratio to the Indio threat. In 1850 the dissidents made an illegal attempt to get their men elected to the Chamber of Deputies. They also won over the Commissioner General, a federal agent who collected taxes and paid the army, which is to say he distributed the loot; with this much power, he was a natural enemy of the Governor. The opposition then enlisted General Díaz de la Vega and, by chain of command, that part of the army not under Barbachanista officers. With such backing, they did better in 1851: five deputies to Barbachano, three to Méndez, two personal friends of General Vega, and two neutrals who managed to slip in. But this was small-time politics. Sniffing the wind from Mexico, Méndez chose to sit out the gubernatorial contest of 1852. The old war horse Antonio López de Santa Anna, exiled since 1848, was on his way back, riding again into Mexican politics on the Jalisco insurrection. Once in command, he arranged state governors at his pleasure. Yucatan waited its turn. Uncontested, Barbachano won his fourth term, but no one expected him to serve it out.

The first dissent came under a surprising name. Colonel Cetina, that congenital revolutionary and long-time Barbachanista, started a revolt in Mérida's Plaza de Armas. Just what he intended to do, besides express some personal annoyance with Barbachano, is not clear, for his movement was swallowed up in the general excitement. The city council declared for Santa Anna, offering the governorship

to General Vega; the legislature came out for Santa Anna and Barbachano; and the Mérida garrison, with military simplicity, for General Santa Anna, period. No one paid any attention to Cetina. There
was confusion in the streets, a choice of bandwagons, and a torrent
of talk—a mid-century Latin gear-grinding as the state tried to inter-
pret the changes of power in the Mexican capital. Barbachano and
Vega went into conferences with the various cliques and read dis-
patches from Mexico; although the General hesitated and an interim
Barbachano man held office for a time, Don Miguel was through.

General Vega took office on August 7, 1853. By that time a
cowed legislature had second-guessed with a vengeance; the direct
vote and judicial amparo were voted out, and restrictions on the
press, on the rights of assembly and petition, and on business were
voted in, along with a stern law against conspiracy. The army
amused itself with new names: Grenadier Guard, Horse Grenadiers.
After a long tradition of civilian liberalism, Yucatan had surrendered
to the caudillos. Again there were cheers, skyrockets, bell-ringing,
and band-playing in the plaza; but there were grim faces and tears
behind closed shutters.

Thus far, politics had little effect on the smoldering embers of
the Caste War. Bankruptcy, lack of food and ammunition, and low
morale had kept reports dull through the spring of 1853. The front-
line officers were more concerned with events in Mérida, aligning
themselves according to political philosophy. But there was some
good news. It was reported that the arch-enemy and traitor José
María Barrera, the inventor of the Speaking Cross, had been killed
on the last day of 1852. A raid to Ascensión Bay had trapped a
smuggling schooner and several rebel chiefs. Finally, there were
rumors of a new peace with the Maya at Chichenha, and Colonel
Novelo mustered relief troops and supplies for Bacalar and marched
south to investigate this.

José María Tzuc, successor to Angelino Itza as Batab of Chichenha after the latter's defeat by the soldiers of the Cross, asked
Superintendent Fancourt of Belize to help him make peace. Messages traveled from Belize to Mérida and back, and Gregorio Cantón
was sent to negotiate for Yucatan; after several days of talk, a treaty

was signed on September 16, 1853, at the Government House in Belize. Cantón conceded a great deal. No taxes were to be paid by the Maya, even after a moratorium of ten years; Indios were to be allowed to retain their guns; and a general pardon was extended to include even the hated rebel Mestizos and the few turncoat white men. Civil rights were guaranteed. The Maya rebels could stay where they were or move back to their old villages, to be judged as their own people saw fit. This declaration of status quo, by which Mérida gained no authority, was given because it was no longer considered worth the danger or expense to hunt the Maya down. The first of Cantón's terms, a face-saving but meaningless submission of the Maya to Mexican authority, was worth all the rest to the weary Yucatecans. It took the proud gentlemen of Mérida a little time to realize this, but the treaty of 1853 endured. The Chichenha and other nearby groups became known as Pacíficos del Sur (Peaceful Indians of the South), and their Batabob were pro forma Mexican officials. A final point of the treaty gained what had been attempted five years before at Peto, to set rebel against rebel: Chichenha was to maintain 400 armed men to use against the beaten but still dangerous bands of rebels at Chan Santa Cruz.

Well content with these results, Colonel Novelo, who had worked behind the scenes from Bacalar, collected the Yucatecan troops who were to be relieved and started north. The march proceeded without incident, and after forty days in the field, he must have looked forward to the relative luxuries of a layover at the frontier post of Uaymax. But when he arrived, he found the post vacant; it had been sacked. While the soldiers poked around the ruins, wondering how this could have happened, scouts found an old man who had been hiding in the woods. He was from Sacalaca, and his story was pure horror: civil war, plague, and Indios. His town of Sacalaca had fallen; Saban, Dzonotchel, Chikindzonot, Ichmul, Tihosuco, Tixcacaltuyu, Santa María, even Yaxcaba, all had fallen. The frontier had collapsed. The Indians were everywhere.

This again was the price of politics. The day before the treaty of Chichenha was signed, Colonel Molas, hounded from his command by a mob of agitators as a Barbachanista, had come out against Gen-

eral Vega and for a return of liberal federalism in Yucatan. This was
a young revolution. Molas himself was only thirty, but old enough
to have fought with Iman fourteen years before, for the same cause,
and like Iman, he made his declaration at Tizimin. He was joined by
Colonel Manuel Cepeda Peraza, a twenty-four-year-old with eight
years of service behind him; he had been a teenage captain, with two
years in grade as full colonel, and all those years had been spent
in fighting. A militarist regime in Mérida drew natural opposition
from thousands of veterans with a natural distaste for officers; these
veterans, joined by Barbachanistas and others always ready for a go
at the government, answered the call of the young colonels. They
quickly dominated the northeast, including Valladolid, and set off
for Mérida, all on the classic pattern. General Vega imprisoned
Barbachano, together with eight of his partisans, in San Benito, and
then, as the danger mounted, he shipped them off to the fortress of
San Juan de Ulúa.

Vega's appeals to all loyal officers were quickly answered. Colonel
Rosado stripped his southern frontier defense zone and Lieutenant
Colonel Oliver came posting up from Campeche, both Mendecistas
fighting the old fight. They arrived to find their opponents with a
lodgement in Mérida, working toward the center of the city, block
by block. They hit them from behind, and Molas and Cepeda withdrew toward Izamal in what became a rout. The Fourth Horseman
now made his appearance, in the form of cholera. Word of this
traveled faster than the retreat; the defeated troops found the doors
of Izamal closed to them, the town already fighting the plague.
Cepeda fled to the north coast, caught a boat to the United States,
and lived to fight another day. Molas delayed too long for a man
with 500 pesos on his head; he was caught, and, according to the
revised rules of the rebellion game, was stood up against a wall,
along with several of his officers, and shot. It was a victory for the
militarists, but a hollow one. Colonel Rosado—whose execution of
Manuel Antonio Ay had helped start the Caste War, and whose im-
patience with José María Barrera had perpetuated it—fell to the
cholera at Izamal, where his old friend the curate Vela buried him.
His second in command also succumbed, and then his soldiers, by

platoons and companies, both there and in Mérida, hundreds of them in a single day.

And then the Indios came. Tacdzibichen was celebrating a fiesta when its time ran out; only one survivor from there reached Tixcacaltuyu. But Tixcacaltuyu was next, then Santa María, and then Yaxcaba, well into the Cocomes. The weakened frontier was giving way, as it had in 1847. But this time there was a difference. The plague-ridden troops at Izamal, convinced that they might just as well die fighting, hurried south under Colonel Maldonado to join Mérida reinforcements at Sotuta. Colonel Léon came up in strength to support the stubborn garrison of Tiholop, and went on to fight a stiff battle at Xcabil. This stopped the invasion, which was only a massive and opportunistic raid through the center of the line with nothing to back it up, a raid by Maya who looked like skeletons and lived on faith and fanaticism. León entered Tihosuco without further action. A guerrilla was sent toward Chan Santa Cruz, but they turned back at the news that cholera had already preceded them. The plague was inescapable. Prisoners and their escorts alike fell to the black vomit; Colonel León, the defender of Valladolid, collapsed on the trail and was buried in a shallow, hastily dug grave. Everywhere the vultures grew fat. This was the story Novelo heard from the old refugee at Uaymax.

Along with this general misery there was another special one. The selling of Maya into slavery had been revived, this time without the earlier justification of crowded prison camps. Santa Anna assigned the monopoly on this trade, the latest of his gifts to backward Yucatan, to one of his cronies, Colonel Manuel María Jiménez. Trading began as early as June, immediately after Barbachano's fall, when Superintendent Fancourt reported to his superiors that a Cuban ship, the *Alerta*, had been intercepted carrying 30 men and three girls for sale at Havana. The slavemaster was brought before an English judge in Belize, tried under international law, and given four years at hard labor. Collection was improved by a lack of discrimination; one rebel Maya was as good as another, and so political prisoners taken in the defeat of the Molas-Cepeda revolt—the Maya much easier to catch than the wild ones of the forest—were shipped out. The government was supposed to receive twenty-five pesos per head after paying a fee to the slaver; but between smuggling, falsified records, and free enterprise on the part of all concerned—civilians, the military, and the government—it never quite turned out that way.

The Ladino army went into the field later each year. In 1854, delayed by weakness and lack of spirit, it didn't march until April 1, when the harvest, the enemy's most vulnerable time, was over. This year Lieutenant Colonel Ruz led his command from Tihosuco against the shrine at Chan Santa Cruz. He was said to be using a "flying column," the latest of General Vega's ideas, intended to do with few men and little cost what the General had been unable to accomplish with an army. In fact Ruz led an old-fashioned guerrilla down those fifty familiar miles to Chan Santa Cruz, flanked, barricaded, sniped at every foot of the way by Maya who had profited from the loot of the Cocomes disaster the previous fall. After one last battle, which was bitterly fought, he reached his objective on April 10. This was no improvement. Closely besieged, he persisted for four days in one long fire-fight, and then, with his ammunition to worry about, fought his way back to the base.

This was not last year; the savages were not ready for the coup de grâce. Permanent camps would be in order; Ruz at first contemplated three of them, but when he was able to raise only 350 men for the duty, he decided he couldn't risk it. Concentrating on the shrine then, he went back on May 26, again in the face of a well-armed and aggressive defense. Reaching their objective, the thirsty soldiers found a freshly dug well in the center of the village, and beside it, several hollowed-out logs filled with water. They drank, became dizzy, vomited, and died; Maya voices called out from the jungle siege lines, asking if the water of Chan Santa Cruz was fresh and healthy.

The Maya, experimenting with biological warfare, had polluted a special well with the clothing of cholera victims. If the physiological effects were not so immediate, they were none the less deadly; the psychological effects can be imagined. In an attempt to quarantine the infected, Ruz split his forces, leaving enough men in the pest camp to protect the sick and moving the rest of his men to the other cenote a mile away. If there was a solution, this was not it. The Indios hit first one camp and then the other, until there were only 90 soldiers left who were able to bear arms. A week after his arrival, the desperate officer had litters prepared for his sick and wounded; lacking enough healthy men to carry those litters, but unwilling to abandon them to the inevitable machete, he started back. One Maya attack was all that was required. The helpless were dropped while the able attempted to defend themselves; and the entire command went under, its commander included, and only a few escaped to tell of it. Enthusiastically, the Maya went on to have a crack at Tihosuco. General Vega hurried up reinforcements, the active reserve to Peto and a Mexican battalion to Valladolid, and there was lively action through June, July, and August. In September, a local victory at Tituc encouraged the Maya to attempt Peto, but they had more success in the congenial business of raiding the lightly garrisoned Cocomes region, where they took Tixcacaltuyu and Yaxcaba, both for the fourth time, and left for home with many prisoners.

Vega sent his flying columns to the rescue: Colonel Novelo to block off the Bacalar route, Colonel Pablo Antonio González to the shrine, both leaving Tihosuco in mid-November. There was little to be done for the prisoners. Some two hundred freshly slaughtered corpses were found at Chan Santa Cruz, plus an equal number of skeletons—the remains of Lieutenant Colonel Ruz and his command. After the sickening task of burial, González gave up the idea of using the place for a base; he moved fifteen miles south to the cenote of Xpanha and then east to Yokdzonot, collecting prisoners and raiding for corn along the way. This was a long-term operation to dominate the enemy's heartland throughout the harvest period, a strategy geared to the agricultural cycle. November passed into December, and Christmas 1854 was celebrated in the jungle; the month of January wore on with occasional casualties, a mounting sick list, and sagging morale. To prevent fights, González turned disciplinarian and forbade gambling; he then found himself briefly a prisoner of mutinous officers and executed two captains before he regained control.

Colonel Novelo had been busy to the south. After his early tour near Lake Bacalar, he had established himself at the crosstrails of Pachmul, surprising Maya supply columns of mules and porters coming from the English depots on the Hondo, columns which had thought themselves safe after skirting the Bacalar garrison. He also followed the established routine, collecting prisoners and raiding for corn. With the larger force and the more strategic position, he attracted his full share of Indios, who assembled against him from the most distant points. Learning of this through prisoners, Novelo sent messengers through the jungle to González's camp, about twenty-five miles to the northeast, where they asked for help and a concentration of forces. But there was bad blood between the commanders, and González answered that he had trouble enough of his own. Novelo then recalled his raiders and opened the battle against the massing enemy, attacking their camp on February 22, 1855. The attack went forward too quickly; it was cut off, hacked up, and got back to base with heavy losses. The Maya immediately tightened the siege, and there was heavy fighting for the next two days. On February 25 the Colonel made his final effort, throwing 250 men into a single assault against the barricades. It failed. Obviously, the season was over, and two days later he started his units north.

As always, no matter how close their siege, the Maya let the soldiers break out when they wanted to, preferring to shadow the retreat along the trail, waiting until the column relaxed as it neared security. Then they struck. Novelo's rear guard was surprised and overrun, and some 200 sick and wounded were abandoned; the survivors reached Peto on March 4. Colonel González, inactive during all of this, with little pressure on his line from the otherwise engaged Indios, retired ten days later, without casualties except for many of his prisoners who, it was said, died of hunger and thirst.

It was an expensive year for the army of Yucatan. In 1855 about 1,000 men, perhaps fifty per cent of those in the field, were killed in action, and hundreds more died of cholera or were wounded. Yet for all this, the ultimate solution to the war, once apparently so close, had slipped through their hands again. And so it was simply decided that the rebellion called the Caste War had come to an end. This is the point where its major historians, Serapio Baqueiro and Eligo

Part Three

The Speaking Cross

Nine

The Cross Speaks
1855–1861

THE MAZEHUALOB OF Chan Santa Cruz had drained the cup of suffering, and that suffering had transformed them into a new people, the *Cruzob* (the Maya plural suffix added to the Spanish word for Cross). José María Barrera's Cross was a symbol so responsive to their need that it survived its creator's obscure death (at Yokdzonot on December 31, 1852) without difficulty. The message, not the prophet, had social life, and it was well nourished with martyrs' blood: Florentino Chan was dead; Cosme Damián Pech, killed suppressing the Chichenha treaty; Juan Justo Yam, dead; Venancio Pec, dead (not Venancio Puc, who had a long career to come); and countless thousands of their followers, killed by bullet, machete, starvation, cholera, and despair. And yet the Cruzob survived. For eight years they had fought against a superior enemy, using pits, poisoned wells, poisoned snares, and clay bullets, accepting deadly volleys for a chance to get within machete range, planting corn only to see it stolen, running, then running again when there was no way to fight, hiding in the swamps, starving in the forest when surrender seemed the obvious answer.

The test was too great for many: for those who sought refuge at Chichenha, for the bands at Ixcanha, Locha, and Mesapich, for those who fled into Guatemala or Belize, for the isolated bands that lurked in the forest east of Valladolid. None of these people surrendered in fact, and they kept themselves apart from the Ladinos; but they accepted a status quo in which they were neglected and ignored, allowed to linger on at the fringe of society, eventually to be re-absorbed or die off.

Only the Cruzob, with their unique possession, the Speaking Cross, had made a positive response. The Cross supplied the higher authority necessary to every culture, an authority desperately lacking among the other tribes, causing them insecurity and leading them to hanker after priests, even white priests—a fact revealed in every treaty they made. The spiritual life of the other tribes was controlled, in large part, by foreigners: by the Bishop, an almost legendary figure, residing in far-off T-ho, and itinerant missionary priests. They knew the pain of isolation and spiritual poverty. The soldier of the Cross, on the other hand, was complete. His world centered on Chan Santa Cruz. Between his village and the shrine there was a full and harmonious relationship, giving security, authority, and religious guidance. He had no need to look beyond his territory, except for guns and ammunition; to get those, he could deal with the English on equal terms. This social integrity had enabled the soldiers of the Cross to survive the terrible years of trial; it kept them alive as a militant force, able to take advantage of the break when it came in the form of the Molas-Cepeda revolt, and it gave them the strength to endure cholera and fight off the columns of 1854 and 1855. The Cruzob had won the right to survive.

Now came the planting season, the first in eight years that would be undisturbed. The fields were burned, the rain fell, the seed was planted and grew into ripe husks of corn, with the Mazehual in peaceful attendance; and when the harvest came, he was the one to collect it rather than the Dzul raiders, and it went to feed his wife and children. A measure of normalcy returned to his life, and for this he gave thanks to the Speaking Cross.

The prestige and authority of José María Barrera was inherited by his successor in the office of Patrón of the Cross, an extension of the "patróns" of the Santos at village fiestas. He was usually called the *Tatich*, or Father, but also *Nohoch Tata* (Great Father) or *Ah-kin* (priest). With Cruzob success, the office began to develop along lines that reached back to pre-Columbian times, lines transmitted through village life and heavily charged with traditions of the Spanish Catholic Church. Primarily, the Tatich was a priest, a necessary replacement for the lost Ladino priests, able to perform the sacraments of mass, baptism, and marriage. In time he became the equivalent of a bishop, delegating powers to others and raising the lay Maestros Cantores to the rank of priests. As the inheritor of his position in a renewed apostolic succession based on the Cross, as the interpreter of God's will and the supreme authority in religious matters, he could be compared to the Pope. Barrera's successor is uncertain. Ladino accounts, scanty at best, sometimes confused patróns with generals, and are often contradictory. Juan de la Cruz Puc is one candidate, for he was active at this time, writing letters and signing them in the name of the Cross, as we have seen; but the grandson of José María Barrera, Pedro Pascual, stated that his father, Agustín Barrera, had inherited the rank.

To help the Tatich in the artifice of the Speaking Cross, to provide for the succession and give counsel, two other offices institutionalized the role of the ventriloquist, Manuel Nahuat: the *Tata Polin*, or Interpreter of the Cross, and the Organ of the Divine Word, who was perhaps the man who crouched in the pit, projecting his voice into the sound chamber of the sunken barrel. The natural reverence that the Mazehualob felt for a man wise in the sacred art of reading and writing was reinforced when Juan de la Cruz began circulating letters signed with three crosses and his own name or one of his various aliases—"Lord Jesus Christ," "Creator of Christians," "Son of God." The writing began before the barrel was invented, but it continued as a supplement to the voice for long-range work; and whether Juan de la Cruz parlayed his literacy into the office of Tatich or not, there would always be a third officer under the Tatich —a Secretary to the Cross, a respected and important figure.

After the Tatich and the triumvirate in the hierarchy came the military leaders, the commanders or generals. This was only the theory, for in fact they sometimes usurped power, assassinating or dominating the Tatich. But normally the Tatich was supreme, able to order them to the whipping post along with the lowest of his subjects. He was beyond criticism, personally holy and inviolate. He acted as judge, gave orders to his generals in domestic administration, and, with their advice, had supreme command in time of war. The *Tata Chikiuc*, or General of the Plaza, was the ranking general and lived in a house on the plaza comparable to the residence of the Tatich. Beneath him were all the officers in the army. Unfamiliar with colonels and generals, the Mazehualob adopted the higher title when the Ladinos began using it, skipping the rank of colonel; from general the ranks ran down through major, captain, lieutenant, sergeant, corporal, and soldier. Their idea of army organization went no further than the company level: battalions and regiments didn't exist as such, but were simply groupings of companies; a major was a company commander of higher rank or longer service. There was no general staff or table of organization. There was, however, a department of military intelligence, headed by the *Tata Nohoch Zul,* or Great Father Spy; this man, who kept regular agents among the Ladinos and a weather eye on ambitious generals, reported directly to the Tatich. With the exception of the Spy and the General of the Plaza, all officers led companies. They were elected on New Year's Day, after the old militia pattern, and vacancies were filled from the lower ranks with the Tatich's approval.

As the army company replaced the native village as the object of Mazehual loyalty, the company commandant took up the role of the village Batab, judging minor offenses, maintaining discipline and public morals. More serious cases were passed up to a council of commandants presided over by the General of the Plaza, which was the judicial and legislative body of the Cruzob, and ultimately to the Tatich himself. This company loyalty was also enlisted in the service of the Cross through the organization of the *Guardia,* or Guard of the Saint. This was a combination of the old village Guardia (imposed by the Ladinos to perform communal work service under state control) and the various religious lay brotherhoods. Starting from the necessity to guard the mechanisms of the Cross from curious eyes, the Guardia grew with the military need to protect the shrine village and was formalized with a required garrison of several companies of about 150 men each, which rotated through the year; it was, in fact, the Cruzob standing army. Barracks were built for these troops at Chan Santa Cruz, and what became an annual month of service for each soldier was spent in guard duty, socializing, and, since religious obligations were organized through the companies, in a great deal of praying. Besides the regular tour, most of the companies came in for the two great fiestas, The Holy Cross and The Virgin of Conception. Guardia service was required of every healthy man over sixteen, and in this way each one of them spent a considerable time at Chan Santa Cruz, binding himself to the group through his service and his devotions to the Cross. These patterns and organizations had been developing since the appearance of the Cross. They flourished with military success and took root with peace.

The year 1856 was one of consolidation for the Cruzob, with only a few border actions for excitement, and the dry season of 1856–57 was equally quiet. A new crop was planted and grew. Herds of captured cattle, as well as mules and horses, were fattened and driven down to the Hondo for trade; the profit from this, together with the loot of the Cocomes raid and contracts with English lumbermen for stands of mahogany in the southern forest, produced the best armory the Cruzob had known since the early victories. New guns, kegs of powder, and bullets made them restless; the planted crop, confident; peace, aggressive. Then came a cessation of the Ladino raids and reduction of the frontier garrisons. This had always meant the same thing; and the Great Father Spy sent his children westward to investigate, to slip past the outposts, to mingle with captives of the blood on the plantations and in the towns, to question and to observe. They returned in August of 1857, with interesting news.

Yucatecan politics had been working up a head of steam. General Vega had been ordered back to Mexico by his master Santa Anna in November of 1854. He was reluctant to go, what with his share of the slaving, the taxes, and the bribes; but the orders were explicit, and he left the governor's chair to his subordinate, General José Cádenas, who was quickly replaced by another Mexican general, Pedro de Ampudia. Mexico City dictated according to centralist principles until Santa Anna fell, for the last time, in 1855; then liberalism and federalism triumphed, and Yucatan looked about for a native non-military leader. Barbachano was considered. He had suffered imprisonment under Santa Anna; but, unfortunately for him, the pity aroused by his term in chains at San Juan de Ulúa was canceled out by circulation of a daguerreotype showing him in the fancy uniform of Councilor, a post he had accepted in the final days of Santa Anna's regime. The picture was seen by too many people, and it ended the political career of Don Miguel. He died in Mérida on December 17, 1859, at fifty-two years of age.

If not Don Miguel, then Don Santiago inevitably; Méndez was nominated, elected, and took office in November of 1855. Cleaning his lenses and adjusting his pince-nez, Méndez set to work like a good bookkeeper to bring order out of the years of revolt, civil war, commercial collapse, and official looting. The state's annual expenses were 408,000 pesos, of which eighty per cent was needed to maintain the army on a defensive basis; revenue from import duties was only 250,000 pesos, and the government was 100,000 pesos in debt. Considering these unpromising figures, Méndez deserves great credit for solving the problem. He adjusted taxes without rebellion, balanced the import-export ratio, and when he left office after two years, the state had only current debts and there was money in the treasury. To his honor, he stopped the slave shipments to Cuba organized by his three military predecessors, ordering a 1,000-peso bond against the issuance of a passport for personal "servants" taken abroad. And to his glory, he gained the ultimate distinction for a Latin politician, or any other: when he died, fifteen years later, he was a poor man.

Barbachano and Méndez now gave way to men of the next generation. Colonel Pantaleón Barrera, publisher, part-time soldier, defender of the Chenes, a Campechano but not strictly committed to southern interests, was elected Governor on July 26, 1857. He was to have his troubles. First, a warning from the frontier, Colonel Novelo reporting: Chikindzonot sacked and burned, 71 people killed, more driven off into captivity, and the troops too weak for an effective response. There was a revolt against a fraudulent vote count, an unpopular military draft, and general restlessness focusing at Tekax. Then came a revolt, of the proclamation style. Colonel Cepeda Peraza, home from exile after the liberal victory, together with Colonel Novelo, made a show of force for the government. No blood was shed, but the bitterness remained.

The main problem was Campeche. The pride of that "patria chica" had suffered under the growing prosperity of Mérida, which stood in sharp contrast to southern bankruptcy. Méndez, Barbachano, and the new Governor Barrera had all been Campeche men; but all had been seduced by northern money, or so it seemed to the unhappy merchants of that port. They didn't like a Mérida-appointed judge and a Mérida-appointed chief of customs (a lucrative post, held by Méndez's brother), and they wanted exemption from the draft for their sailors, as there was exemption for henequen field hands in the north; and mainly, emotionally, they didn't like Mérida. A separatist organization had started negotiations on a national level before Méndez's last term, and his refusal to accept the idea of a divided Yucatan was to make him a hated exile in his old age.

Liberio Irigoyen, the southern candidate defeated by Barrera at the polls, demanded a recount by seizing the armory and wall forts of Campeche, intending to negotiate from a position of strength. While messages were going back and forth a second movement erupted in the city, separate from but confused with the first, making more explicit demands; each was a symptom, not a definition of the separatist disease. When the leader of the second group, Pablo García, was told that no other part of the state had risen to his support, he cleared the air by announcing that the district of Campeche could no longer live under the same government with the rest of Yucatan and that a legal separation was necessary for the incompatible parts. This point of view, never expressed but a vital force in Yucatecan politics since Independence, was at last out in the open. As the movement became serious, Barrera reluctantly assembled his forces. Stripping the frontier as usual, he sent Cepeda Peraza in command to join Colonel Baqueiro at Hecelchacan, from there to march south and contact the Campeche militia at Tenebo, twenty-five miles from the port. There wasn't much enthusiasm for this: the enemy commander was Cepeda Peraza's brother; the walls of Campeche had never been taken; and no one wanted to be killed when negotiations would inevitably decide the issue after a careful comparison of forces and perhaps a face-saving skirmish.

This, or the essential parts of it, was the story brought back and reported to the Great Father Spy. The General of the Plaza and the higher officers met with the Tatich in council, where candles were burned and prayers said to the Speaking Cross. The Cross spoke, and when it had finished, orders were sent to the villages for the companies to assemble.

So it was that on September 14, with most of the Ladino soldiers of both factions blustering at each other in the extreme southwest of the state, a column of troops came marching into Tekax. They approached from the southwest on the Xul road, marching in step, rifles at right shoulder arms, and well-dressed by local military standards, with ribbons on their hats and red and white striped jackets. They were, their officers announced, Campeche troops, come to liberate Tekax from the dictators of Mérida. The few citizens on the road, still hot over their own recently suppressed one-day revolt, joined in the cries "Viva Campeche and Irigoyen! Death to Mérida and Barrera!" There was nothing unnatural about the dark complexion of these troops. In spite of past lessons, Hidalgos still formed a large part of the militia. The Tekax garrison, a company of eighty men, were mainly southern sympathizers, and their captain, Onofre Bacelis, had disarmed them on learning of the approaching force. No Campechano himself, and under orders from Mérida, he fortified himself with a platoon of trusted men in a building above the plaza, intending to fight the rebels without danger of a mutiny. His men opened fire as the first of the enemy appeared, but as they continued to file into the plaza, rifles slung upside down *a la funerala,* and formed under the galleries, several thousand strong, the shots came to an uncomfortable halt. The enemy officers then exposed themselves, taking off their hats to salute the captain; their numbers convinced Bacelis that his military obligations were at an end, and he left with his men by the back door, broke through the soldiers in the street, leaving part of his coat in their hands, and escaped. The preliminaries thus skillfully arranged, Crescencio Poot, the Tata Chikiuc of Chan Santa Cruz, ordered the massacre to begin.

The townspeople had closed their shutters and barred their doors, fearing a skirmish in the streets and stray bullets. Now doors were battered down, walls climbed, windows entered. Machetes served better than rifles for close work against the defenseless, and the householders with swords and pistols could only delay the inevitable: there was the wailing of babies abruptly terminated, the screams and curses of men or women, muffled in back rooms where they attempted to hide, or loud under the sun in the patio or the street. Some, understanding the cries in time, had reached open country; some hid in caves, in the stink of sewers or outhouses; and some lay still among the dead, mutely suffering inquisitive kicks, blows of gun butts or machetes, while flies buzzed about and settled on the drying blood. More than a thousand were killed.

Sergeant Pedro Ruiz and some fifteen to twenty men, apparently part of the disarmed garrison, recovered their weapons and defended themselves as best they could, moving from house to house in the confusion and eventually reaching a strong building of two stories on the plaza.* Distracted by easier prey, the Cruzob had bypassed these soldiers, but around three o'clock in the afternoon, with the massacre complete, the raiders attempted to talk them out of their hole, offering them their lives if they surrendered. This fooled no one, not after the events of the past hour. Unwilling to make what would be an expensive assault, the Cruzob waited until dark, then piled looted furniture under the gallery, and set it on fire. As the supports burned and the upper balcony collapsed in flame, the soldiers retreated to the stone shell of the building, firing into the mob through the light of the flames, scattering the enthusiasts. There were insults and threats and bullets, but no assault. The soldiers waited grimly through the night, faces black with smoke, too stunned by what had happened to think of anything but the necessity to die fighting. From their half-burned ruin they watched the campfires of Poot's army spread across the plaza, listened to the singing, the guitar playing, and to what was done with the women. They saw the seventy-year-old curate Marin passing from fire to fire, denouncing the murderers and the chiefs, without a hand being raised against him. Sergeant Ruiz and his men rested on their guns until dawn, when rescue came.

There were other white men alive in Tekax that night. Some Cruzob spies, caught some time before the attack and left in a cell to starve to death, had been saved by a merchant of the town, Anselmo Duarte. He gave them food and put them to work digging a well for his garden. When the Maya army arrived, the spies reported this treatment; Duarte's house and store were protected by posted sentries, and he and his family escaped untouched.

Crescencio Poot had little time for such details. He had organized

---

* It was probably from the upper gallery of this same building, the Palacio Municipal, that Indio prisoners had been thrown, to be caught on bayonets below, when the town had been recaptured nine years before.

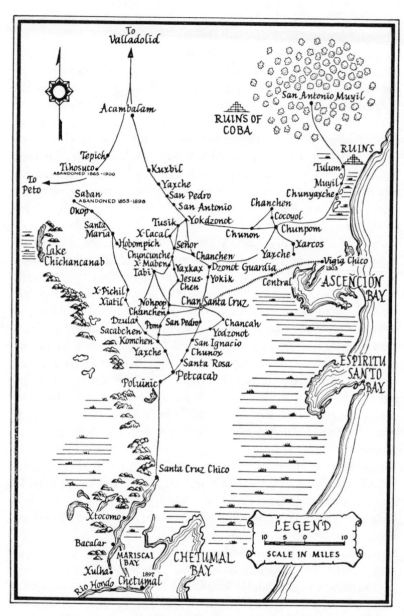

The Cruzob area, 1855–86

his ruse to perfection; he had moved his army through the lightly inhabited Chenes below Peto without detection, coordinated his approach and cover story to fit political rumors based on very accurate intelligence, and bluffed the white men out of any real defense. Killing Dzulob was what he had come for, and like them he made little distinction as to age or sex; children grew up to be soldiers or mothers of soldiers. He also knew that the white reaction would come quickly, and he acted with speed. The warehouses of local distilleries were emptied; hundreds of barrels of aguardiente were loaded on horses and mules, which were then hurried on the trail south into the Puuc hills. Shops were stripped of their hardware, machetes, axes, pots, skillets, and bolts of cotton goods; weapons and gunpowder were taken from the armory and private homes. Money, jewels, and watches were left to individual looting; the Cross would harvest them later as offerings. His army spent the night in Tekax. Some of the men went too far with the aguardiente and argued over women, but they were veterans, and their discipline under the circumstances was excellent: the sack was completed by early morning.

Captain Bacelis had spent an uneasy night in the neighborhood a few miles away, collecting some eighty men; he was beginning to suspect that this was not a matter of politics. At dawn he addressed his small command: "Muchachos, if they are rebels who are in Tekax, we are not obliged to fight against unequal numbers; but if they are Indios, I offer you the chance of doing what you see me do." A bloody refugee ended all doubts as they approached the town; and dividing into three little bands, they went in from different directions simultaneously. Bugles sounding, the few men impersonating a regiment, they fired one volley apiece and made a bayonet charge. Fortunately for the captain and his brave men, they met only stragglers, drunks, and disorganized looters, and drove them off. What they found was sickening: the mutilated dead, the dying calling for water, the naked women left where they had been raped. It took five days to bury the dead. Pursuit was impossible for the captain and the handful of men under Sergeant Ruiz, and no other force was near enough to help. Crescencio Poot got clean away. By mid-December, a concentration of Cruzob was down at the Hondo, trading horses, mules, and aguardiente for guns and gunpowder with refugee Ladino merchants.

There were wild rumors in Belize as the year drew to an end: fear of an attack from Chan Santa Cruz, of an attack from Chichenha intended to destroy the refugee town of Corozal. Corozal had absorbed 2,000 more fugitives of mixed origin in 1857, and many of them had come from Chichenha. Sometime during the year there had been a second assault on that place by the Cruzob, and although it was beaten off, it convinced the Pacíficos that the region wasn't healthy. Some fled across the frontier, others moved down near it to a place called Icaiche, more remote from the soldiers of the Cross. Five hundred Pacíficos were reported mobilized under a Ladino officer at the year's end, but nothing further came of this.

The focus then, if confused, was on the south; and it was inevitable that after the sack of Tekax, which brought the Cruzob a new realization of their strength, the Cross would speak again. Cruzob forces appeared on the Hondo on February 15, some 1,500 of them, with more horses and mules to trade for a last increase of munitions; and then at a late hour on the night of February 20, they surprised Bacalar, taking the town in twenty minutes under the leadership of Venancio Puc. The garrison there—300 soldiers and 250 women and children— was utterly demoralized by lack of supplies and relief, which had been held up by the civil war; they were surprised in spite of the rumors that had been circulating for two months and in spite of the known presence of Cruzob forces. Their commander and some of his men fled to the Chaak outpost and crossed the river, turning in their loaded guns in exchange for the protection of the British Crown. The rest made the mistake of surrendering, remembering how they had been allowed to withdraw unharmed to Belize ten years before. A large number of them were massacred that same night.

The Magistrate of Corozal, a man named Blake, who had business contacts with the Cruzob, hurried up to help the survivors. He offered 2,500 pesos in ransom to Venancio Puc, but found that he had to deal with a higher authority: the Speaking Cross, or a substitute, had come down to rule the captured town. That night the Englishman watched the Maya assemble before a house in which the Cross was kept, listened to the praying and a military band until around eleven o'clock, when the prisoners were brought out—men, women, and children—and forced to kneel in the street. Over the children's crying, he heard "a squeaking, whistling noise." The Cross wanted 4,000 pesos.

Blake went back to Corozal for the money, returning on March 1 with Captain Anderson of the Second West Indian Regiment and a message from the Superintendent of Belize. But neither the message nor the money had the desired effect on the Cross; that night it gave new orders. As Henry Fowler later reported it:

> Some of the women and children were separated from the rest, amongst whom was a young Spanish girl well known in high circles. A procession was then formed and marched off to the east gate. First came a strong body of troops, then alternately, in Indian file, a male prisoner and his executioner, who drove him on with his machete holding him by a rope; next came the women, thirty-five in number, driven and held in a similar manner; then another body of soldiers closed the rear. The Englishmen were not allowed to follow. The procession halted under a clump of trees about one hundred and fifty yards off and soon the butchery commenced, shrieks were heard, but in ten minutes all was over.

Several nubile young girls were saved for the Batabob out of this blood bath, and eight children were spared. One child, a girl of seven, hid in a small cave right in the middle of Bacalar for five days, living on roots, fleeing to the river on a stormy night.*

Some Englishmen had been on the wrong side of the river when the Cruzob first came south, and Blake now demanded that they be released. Puc offered to exchange them for the former commander of Bacalar, Perodomo. Apparently rumors of the revolt of another kind of Indians against their white masters had reached halfway around the world; the Cruzob general taunted the English about their defeat at the hands of the Sepoy mutineers. All of this made the northern part of Belize very uneasy, the Hondo being a narrow river, and protection was demanded. It arrived in April, 167 men of the Second West Indian and 130 local constabulary. An effort to enlist refugee Ladinos came to nothing. But if the Cross was arrogant, it wasn't

---

* Her name was Herminia Robelo, and she lived to be interviewed in 1935, the last survivor of Bacalar.

1 Balam Na
2 Chikinik
3 Tata Chikiuc
4 Kampocolche Cah
5 Town Cenote

Chan Santa Cruz in the 1860's

foolish. Once the English were antagonized, it would have to get military goods the hard way, and so trading started again after a time and relations slowly returned to normal.

Bacalar was stripped of everything of value, the material forwarded to Chan Santa Cruz, and the place was used only as a fortified base to protect the Hondo trade route. A regular road was cut for this purpose, from the river to Bacalar and then north to the shrine. With the south secure, some enthusiasts attempted the north, making their way secretly into the parade ground of the Valladolid garrison, where they were caught seizing cannons. There was a bloody little battle, but apparently this was only a raid; the Cruzob withdrew, holding their own, until pursuit was given up after some ten miles of trail.

The twin victories of Tekax and Bacalar had been ordered by the Speaking Cross, and would have been inconceivable without its protecting hand; and as the Maya made offerings of thanks to the gods for good harvests, they now set about making an offering on a far grander scale. The first home of the Cross had been an open-air pole altar on the slope of a hill fifty paces east of the grotto; the second had been a two-room thatched hut, probably on the same site. But the steep little hollow had become too small for Cruzob assemblies and the surrounding hillocks proved inconvenient as building sites for an increasing population; and so it was decided to move the shrine to more level ground a quarter of a mile to the southeast, halfway to the other larger cenote. But a mystic quality would continue to pervade the little valley where God had first come to the Maya. A stone oratorio or shrine was erected near the first home of the Cross; it was some twenty-five feet high, walled on three sides and open to the west, looking down on the grotto. Fiestas were held there and delinquents assembled before the shrine to receive whippings at the order of the chiefs. The valley was then called *Chan Kiuic*, Little Plaza, and also *Kampocolche Cah*, Kampocolche Village, in memory of the original home of some of the Cruzob, which lay in that direction.

The new church was laid out along ambitious lines, over 100 feet long and 60 feet wide. Foundations weren't necessary on that scanty soil; some leveling was sufficient. Stone lay everywhere at hand and mortar was easily reduced with heat from limestone boulders in open-air kilns, a technique unchanged in thousands of years. And the walls began to rise, massive, richly mortared, growing in sections, with pauses to let the mortar cure, flanked by five reinforcing buttresses on either side. The buttresses supported an equal number of low arches, on which were placed horizontal rows of wooden poles; the poles served as forms for a thin layer of mortar, and when that hardened, for more layers, until there was a ponderous, self-supporting concrete vault forty feet high. A protected walkway ran the length of each long side of the roof, a feature typical of Yucatecan churches, intended for defense. Four stumpy, never-completed towers gave stability at the corners, the southwestern one mounting the looted bells of Bacalar. A single arched portal, and above it a door with a balcony, pierced the bare façade, and together with side doors, let a dim light into the interior. The Balam Na (House of God) was a somber, crude, impressive achievement for ex-serfs and half-breeds of the lower class.°

Flanking the church on either side were one-story wings, each enclosing a line of rooms with arcades in front and behind, which would be used as schools and barracks; to the rear was a high-walled compound with several service buildings. The church and schools edged the plaza to the east, a plaza whose rectangular shape was broken by a block of buildings on the south, forming a smaller plaza, enhanced by a fountain to which legend would give the role of whipping post. The plaza was nearly flat, rocky, cleared of trees and bushes, and complete with the traditional sapodilla tree, the center of every Maya town—in this case, the place of execution. To the west was built the residence of the Tatich, called *Chikinik*, or West Wind, a building some 100 feet long, arcaded fore and aft, with guard and reception rooms and private living quarters. There was also a similar palace for the General of the Plaza, a council house, at

---

° Alfonso Villa Rojas has written that the chapel in the valley of Chan Kiuic was also called Balam Na and was the second of the Cruzob churches, replacing the original thatched structure. This seems unlikely: the building has no provisions for the sound effects required of the Speaking Cross, no element of secrecy, and the ground falls off too steeply in front for the addition of a thatched nave. Balam Na was the general Maya word for church. The principal one at Chan Santa Cruz was sometimes called Nohoch (Great) Balam Na.

least seven barracks for the rotating companies, and a prison, all surrounding the plaza. Sixteen regular blocks, counting the church compound, were laid out on the Ladino plan, wide streets crossing at
right angles, superimposed on the more casual Maya settlement pattern. Around the plaza, and adjacent to it, the civic buildings were of
stone with flat roofs; the rest were thatched huts, aligned on the
streets, or grouped within the blocks, each block enclosed by dry
laid stone walls and filled with fruit and shade trees. Five natural
rocky hillocks, some thirty feet high, lay scattered through the town,
and they were fortified in the manner of the plazuela redoubts of the
Tihosuco siege; several lines of rubble walls encircled the suburbs,
with outposts to guard against surprise. For spiritual defense there
were four thatched chapels, one to each direction, and sentries with
orders to kill any domestic animal that entered the sacred confines
of the town.

Appropriately, the heavy mass of the Balam Na dominated the
skyline, an unexpected sight over the treetops after days of travel
through wilderness. The town itself was a secondary, if vital, offering
of thanks to the Cross of Victories, an outward replica of a Ladino
town ordered by a half-acculturated Tatich and run by the Guardia
companies, with whips and chains for those who were insufficiently
grateful. And there were the white slaves. The wasteful slaughter
of Bacalar would not be repeated by a more confident Cruzob. By
Ladino count, 500 prisoners were taken in 1859 but only 200 of them
killed. Women were kept in a thatched barracks in the church compound and used as domestic servants by the Tatich and commandants, the more attractive ones also serving in the higher-ranking
hammocks. Men were parceled out to work the fields, to cut wood,
burn lime, and haul stone for the new buildings, and to serve as
teachers of music, Spanish, reading, and writing. It was a very complete reversal of roles: the master had become a slave and the slave
a master, with whip and gun in hand. Most prisoners were of the
lower classes, Mestizos and poor white frontier settlers of the type that
couldn't escape military service; and many were Maya—Hidalgos,
subdued villagers, or members of a rival rebel band. These Maya
were treated somewhat better than the other slaves, and children of
all races were brought up as free citizens of the group. But there

were occasional members of the upper class, men and women, who suffered far more than the others and died easily from the unaccustomed labor, the poor food, and their despair.

Still enmeshed in politics, Yucatan could do nothing for the captives. After the disasters at Tekax and Bacalar, the frontier ravages continued unrevenged as interest settled on a partial solution of the Campeche problem: the formation of a new state, the frontier running between Maxcanu and Kalkini, southwest to the middle of the peninsula and then south to Guatemala, with Carmen and Laguna de Términos included. Governor Barrera had resigned in favor of his military commander, General Peraza, who signed the treaty of partition. Details of the divorce were carefully spelled out. Campeche was to pay one-third of its annual income to help cover expenses of the Maya war, which, with her Chenes back country long since neutralized, would become the exclusive problem of reduced Yucatan. Duties were to be the same at Carmen, Campeche, and Sisal, with tax-free movement of goods within the peninsula, and there was to be mutual extradition of deserters. In other words, the status quo was preserved, with some concessions to local control, local pride, and local politics at Campeche. And of course none of the terms were met.

As there were enough people to disapprove of this solution, two rebellions quickly blossomed; one in Campeche was stifled, and one in Yucatan, led by Colonel Pedro Acereto, succeeded after a little fighting and much politics in deposing General Martín Peraza and installing Liberio Irigoyen as Governor. Irigoyen turned out to be a vest-pocket dictator, attempting to consolidate his power by making wholesale orders of exile; he shipped out General Peraza, Colonel Cepeda Peraza, who was getting familiar with the trip, former governor Barrera, and many others. Among the exiles were those who went the hard way, to Havana, with a work contract signed for them and no arbitration allowed in the cane fields. Slaving had been revived by Barrera and continued by Peraza, and again it drew on the ranks of the opposition party, Maya or Ladino. The law said only that "rebels" could be taken, and for those on the losing side without influential connections, the law was applied in full vigor, the profits going to the successful candidate and his cronies.

Figures on a clandestine trade are hard to come by. One man, Gerardo Tizon,was later accused of shipping several hundred people; he admitted to 374 in court, where the question was not moral, but financial. Under Barrera's administration, Tizon had arranged a Cuban loan of 30,000 pesos and 500 rifles, with a one per cent commission for his trouble, the principal to be redeemed with Maya prisoners at 25 pesos per head, children free. The traffic didn't really get moving until General Peraza took office, when the price went up to 40 pesos for men and 25 for women, with shipments made from the small ports of Rio Lagartos, Dzilam, and San Felipe on the north coast. Irigoyen, with political raw material at hand and production costs down, ran the market up to 160 pesos for men, 120 for women, and 80 for boys and girls. There were many private ventures as land- and serf-poor hacendados began liquidating their surplus. The trade became more public, with the government fort at Sisal used as a holdover station: ships picked up human cargo at Campeche, convoys became a common sight along the roads, young men of the best families were caught with their servants, headed for the nearest port. Gabriel Gahona drew a caricature entitled "Una Indiera," showing a woman of means leaning against cages of Indians, cages labeled for shipment to Havana.

Irigoyen was too heavy-handed. Rebellions multiplied until Colonel Acereto, who had put Irigoyen in, got tired of putting them down and made one himself, together with old Cetina taking a curtain call from Campeche. Pablo Castellanos was the lucky one this time, a good man apparently, who stopped the slaving; but he was quickly out. Next Colonel Acereto installed his father, Agustín Acereto, and after Irigoyen, it was a popular choice. The principles invoked during all these maneuvers are hardly worth talking about. This was politics of the most blatantly personal sort, revealing a complete and tragic breakdown of civic life; it was the reign of petty caudillos who wanted the loot, assisted by a people used to war and an overabundance of bored colonels who didn't want to fight Indians but couldn't give up the easier delights of military life. So much for anarchy. Aceretos, father and son, had gained a breather, and they set out to do what their predecessors had very publicly intended, but never quite got around to: avenging Tekax and Bacalar.

Supplies were assembled and troops were enlisted, armed, drilled, and massed at Valladolid, some 2,200 soldiers and 650 Hidalgos of the labor corps; and they all got down on their knees in the main plaza to hear one final collective mass on the morning of January 2, 1860. In command was Colonel Pedro Acereto, the victor of many a civil engagement; Colonel Virgilio was his second, and he had two colonels and a commandant for each of his three sections. It was a brave sight that morning, this largest single force that had ever gone out against the Cruzob, and it was a confident army that paraded from the plaza to the music of bugle and drum under the eyes of its commander, and the governor, his father. They marched south to Tihosuco in two days, which was good time, most of them being veterans of a generation's fight, and then on into the enemy jungle, scouts fanning out, guns ready, crowding the trails. It took them eight days to reach that center of superstition and fanaticism, Chan Santa Cruz, but they had only an occasional brush with the supposedly invincible savage. Where was he? They gawked at the new temple, the arcades around the plaza, homes of the Tatich and the General of the Plaza, the whipping post and execution tree, and decided that this legendary place was not so much after all; and they wondered what had become of the Cruzob.

Perhaps it was a failure of the spies, the surprising quickness and size of the invading force, or, more likely, an intentional plan; but at any event, the Cruzob frontier companies had fallen back, delayed a bit with sniping, added up the columns of soldiers, and reported. Then Crescencio Poot gathered up his people. From the Bacalar garrison in the south, the active companies near Peto, the Guardia of the capital, from all the villages and little settlements they came, each man grabbing a gun, powder and bullets, a machete, a gourd of water, a sack of cornmeal, all forming by units and companies, heading for the shrine. This was no indifferent scattering of isolated tribes that had been invaded, but a unified body social, whose heart had been threatened; when a messenger came panting up to a cluster of huts he carried an announcement rather than a command. Poot made no piecemeal commitment. When the Cruzob came, it was all at once. A mounted company of Ladino scouts had the misfortune to make the first contact, several days after the occupation of Chan

Santa Cruz; they were ambushed and barely got back to the army, fighting on foot with heavy losses. Immediately there was a general assault from all quarters, with no lack of guns or ammunition; and the monstrous sound of those volleys immediately convinced the more experienced officers that it was time to get out. With equal or superior firepower and unquestionably superior spirit and conviction under fire, the Cruzob made attack upon attack over the bodies of the fallen, and organized Ladino resistance collapsed.

Within a few days, rumor of the disaster reached the frontier with small parties of badly mauled stragglers. The uneasy governor had Tihosuco reinforced to hold the escape route and sent an expeditionary force by sea to Ascensión Bay with orders to search out and assist his son. Doubt was ended and the worst fears justified when the Colonel himself showed up at the Tihosuco barricades with the 600 survivors of his army. He had lost 1,500 men, 2,500 rifles, all of his artillery with its ammunition, 300 mules, a great quantity of supplies, and his military band. The band was captured intact, together with its instruments, and its members began teaching music to young Cruzob students. The details of Ladino defeats are hard to come by; the fighting which followed that first rush on the camp, the month before Acereto returned, the adventures of the expeditionary party, all seem lost to history. Like so many before him, the Colonel had learned that his campaigning in the petty revolts of the west had no meaning or application against the Cruzob, and neither he nor his followers wanted to talk about the experience. And for good measure, with surplus arms and feeling their strength, the Cruzob took Chichenha, killing the Pacífico men and marching the women and children off to Bacalar.

There was also the question of prisoners. Governor Acereto had continued the Cuban loan to field his army, selling futures on expected victory. When the fortunes of war went against him, he followed precedent and paid off his contract with peaceful Maya of the northern villages and an occasional Mestizo. This was the last large shipment of slaves. Prosperity in the henequen fields and a labor shortage killed the trade. Early petitions to rid the peninsula of ten thousand savages were now replaced with complaints from the Mérida wealthy that their workers (outrageously enough, even

indebted workers) were being seduced or stolen, and that soon the
haciendas would be without men, families without servants, priests
without congregations, fathers without sons. Then the great Benito
Juárez, humanist, liberal, constitution writer, and himself an Indian,
was elected President of Mexico. In March of 1861, he sent a commission to stop the trade, search out the guilty, and bring them to
justice. No punishments are recorded; too many people in high
places were involved, including five governors; no one could remember any details; no definite figures could be found. A report of the
United States Census Bureau, made in 1899, stated that only 755
Maya were in Cuba at any one time, in contrast to the rumors of
many thousands shipped. At the time of the report, 38 years after
the trade ceased, only one slave was located, hiding in a swamp.

The defeat of Colonel Acereto's army discouraged any idea of
Ladino reconquest for a long time. It was followed the next year by
a series of border eruptions. Ekpedz was attacked and Sacalaca
totally destroyed. At Dzonotchel the inhabitants hid in the stone
rectory with doors and windows barred, to wait out the raid; but the
Cruzob cut away the rafters that supported the massive lime cement
roof, crushing the lot of them. Repeating his deception at Tekax,
Crescencio Poot slipped an army past the frontier patrols, marched
it secretly up through the Cocomes to the Mérida road, and then
paraded into Tunkas from the west. Thanks to the continuing military anarchy, one more column attracted little attention; detachments blocked all streets, and the entire resident population, some
600 people, was marched off into captivity. There is a legend that the
raiders split up at Chichén Itzá, dividing the loot and prisoners and
hanging the undesirables from the gateway arch of what has become
known as Thompson's Hacienda. Thus 600 persons, each with a life,
with plans, with hopes of his own, were lost. One of them was the
young wife of a militia colonel, and he spent years at Valladolid and
the forward camps attempting, and after many years succeeding, in
arranging her ransom. Most of the others lived out their lives, briefly
or with long endurance, as slaves.

These raids cleared the border country and created a buffer zone
of deserted forest. The towns of Ichmul, Ekpedz, Saban, Sacalaca,
and many others were abandoned; their streets were overgrown,

first with tough savanna grass, then bushes, then trees, until they were covered by dense forest, their plazas and arcades hidden among the foliage. The saints of once proud churches stood exposed in their niches, looking out on the verdant rubble of a collapsed roof, weathered by sun and rain, forgotten except by some passing hunter who might stop to pray. St. Peters and St. Sebastians became like the Guardians of the Wild Places, sharing what piety came their way with other gods, as these lost buildings shared the forest with other, much older ruins. And the surviving towns suffered the blight of fear, which killed all hope of growth. Peto suffered under sporadic attack, frequent sniping, and kidnapping; Tihosuco and Tixcacalcupul were inhabited only by soldiers; Valladolid stagnated; and uneasy dread hung over Yaxcaba, Sotuta, bloody Tekax, and unhappy Tunkas. The Cruzob had secured their position, destroyed all forces that had come against them, killed or captured over 4,000 people in the last three years, taken countless rifles and other loot, crushed their native rivals, and opened the trade route to Belize. The Cross had spoken well.

There had been a series of minor incidents on the Hondo—sniping back and forth, cattle stealing, and kidnapping—caused by the fact that northern Belize was filled with Ladino refugees, and provocation was inevitable. To English complaints, the Cross dictated a letter of explanation instructing Puc and three of his officers to add their signatures. One militant refused, proving that faith didn't extend to those in on the secret; so the Cross gave a new command, ordering the recalcitrant to suffer fifty lashes. By the time this matter of discipline had been straightened out, the offender's name added and the letter delivered, new incidents had occurred; so the English Superintendent wrote a much stronger note, and on March 14, 1861, commissioned Lieutenant Plumridge of the Third West Indians, and Lieutenant Twigge, Royal Engineers, to deliver it. They were told to have nothing to do with the Speaking Cross or any other such nonsense—instructions easy to dictate in the security of Government House. The two lieutenants, their dignity very much in mind, smartly uniformed with swords at their sides, crossed the Hondo, leaving the British authority behind; when they entered the domain of the Mazehual God, the fun began. The commandant of Bacalar was drunk and impertinent, and caused them an unnecessary delay. They profited by this wait to hire an extra interpreter, a Ladino named José María Trejo, who was involved in the usual refugee business of selling guns to the Indians. They neglected to tell him the details of their errand. Trejo discovered these, to his horror, after their first day's journey, at the village of Santa Cruz Chico on the northern end of Lake Bacalar. Knowing the casual way of Venancio Puc with a machete, he flatly announced that they would all be killed if they delivered the letter. After some argument they went on, each deciding that he knew best. There were further delays as they traveled north along the freshly cut road, past the villages of Petcacab and Chunox, as outpost guards stopped them and waited for orders from above; but after about a week's travel they reached Chan Santa Cruz and were taken before Puc.

Through Trejo, they explained that they were the representatives of Her Majesty's Government and had come to negotiate differences with the leader of the Santa Cruz Maya, giving him the Superintendent's letter. Puc told them that they would have to talk to God, as he had no power himself. The officers reluctantly agreed, stating however that they wouldn't wait more than two days. Puc shrugged his shoulders. God spoke only when He was ready. Plumridge and Twigge were disarmed, down to their swords, which they claimed were part of their uniform, and escorted to a barracks hut. They had arrived at eight in the morning and had the entire day to remember all the stories they had heard of bloodthirsty savages, of human sacrifice before idols. At midnight they were led out of their quarters, taken through a large crowd that filled the plaza, and into the Temple of the Speaking Cross. The building was crowded with chanting, praying Maya and was completely dark. Directed to a spot before the altar, they were forced to their knees. Behind the altar was a curtain. As Plumridge reported:

> At that moment the soft music and singing that till then had pervaded the building ceased and was followed by a deafening and prolonged sound similar to thunder when heard at a distance. This, too, ceased, and in the midst of the silence that followed was heard a rather weak voice, which seemed to originate in the midst of the air and which spoke in the Maya language.

The stage directions had improved. Trejo nervously translated in a low whisper:

> Tell me, what you have come about? Have you come about that letter that was sent me? That letter was a very insulting letter. If you have come to make me pay for the cattle, tell me so. You have come to pick a quarrel with me; the letter says that the Queen will send troops against me. If the English want to fight, let them come, in thousands if they like. If this is the case, say so, and I will dispose of you at once.

The lieutenants told Trejo to reply that they had come in peace with a peaceful message and required a peaceful answer for their chief. When this was translated the Voice of God angrily said that it would give no answer, peaceful or otherwise, and repeated, "Tell me at once, have you come about that letter?" Then José María Trejo, unwilling to commit suicide, took over on his own. In his most humble Maya he told God, No, they had come to make peace and arrange trade. God demanded one thousand barrels of gunpowder at the usual price, which Trejo said could be managed. When the Englishmen found out what was going on, they objected, telling Trejo to say only that they would carry this message back to Belize, nothing more. The letter forgotten, the interpreter went on to promise that the gunpowder would be delivered in six weeks, and the interview came to an end. It had not gone as planned from the English side. Between the two interpreters—one serving the Cross, the other, Plumridge and Twigge—there were misunderstandings that would take a long time to straighten out.

The emissaries' troubles were not over. Puc threw a fiesta for them the next day, and Twigge reported that he was forced by the drunken Puc to swallow a spoonful of cayenne pepper. Trejo told it differently; according to him, the lieutenant offered a highly spiced paté to the unsuspecting native, and the cayenne pepper came afterwards. Once the party got going, it was difficult to stop. Puc sensed the Englishmen's attitude and resented it, threatening to kill them if they didn't enjoy his hospitality. Plumridge had anise seed pressed on him until he vomited; and, all thoughts of dignity gone, the lieutenants found themselves drunkenly hugging and kissing their drunken hosts, dancing and singing to the general delight.

There were three days of this before the badly shaken Englishmen were allowed to leave, with warnings that the "promised" gunpowder had better arrive or else. Plumridge and Twigge would never forget their interview with God.

The Superintendent took a dim view of the encounter when he read their report. The country was thrown into a panic; barricades were prepared in the streets of Corozal, rumors spread, and all trading stopped. This lasted only long enough for the Ladino merchants to find that the Cruzob had no intentions of invasion, that they were seriously concerned about the trade stoppage, and that they, too, had been deceived by the false translation of José María Trejo. So the Superintendent wrote a second letter to Puc, demanding a complete apology for the humiliation of his emissaries and granting him free passage through Her Majesty's territory for that purpose. The archives of British Honduras hold no evidence as to who was expected to deliver this letter or whether it ever was delivered, and no record of an apology from Venancio Puc.

Ten

An Empire and the Cross
1863–1866

JOSÉ MARÍA GUTIÉRREZ DE ESTRADA, Campeche born, citizen of
the world, aristocrat, and diplomat, launched the next offensive
against the Cross, if indirectly, as he achieved his life's work in bow-
ing before an Austrian Archduke, thus becoming the first to make
obeisance to the new Emperor of Mexico. This was on October 3,
1863, in the reception hall of the Miramar Palace, on the Adriatic
coast near Trieste. From that moment of glory, Gutiérrez could look
back on two decades of struggle and exile for an ideal. He had seen
his country torn by a succession of greedy caudillos, robbed, plundered, weakened, and reduced to anarchy. He felt that since so many
generals acted like kings, Mexico might do better with a real one; he
believed that there was more freedom under a peaceful monarchy
than in a republic of political bandits. He found out about freedom
of the press when he published these ideas in Mexico City in 1840;
he was lucky enough then to trade the prison cell of a liberal administration for European exile. And the caudillos went their merry
way, with all the results he had predicted: President, Excellency,
Serene Highness, their titles successively more impressive as they
followed one another in passing through Cortés's old palace; and
the price was two major Indian revolts, by the Yaquis and the Maya,
two foreign invasions, and the loss of one-half of the national territory to the United States, with the apparent prospect of falling under
the expanding colossus of the north. Under the weight of all this,
others remembered Gutiérrez and wondered if perhaps he was right;

they finally agreed that he was, and sent him a commission to look for a candidate.

They could have found no better envoy. Gutiérrez hadn't suffered in exile. Twice married, both times to countesses, both times to money, he was at ease with the upper aristocracy, with the manner and the means to make himself heard. Spain was the first and most natural hunting ground, but after he found no one available there, a search in the *Almanach de Gotha* turned up a man of the highest rank who had nothing to occupy his time and possessed the requisite energy and romanticism to consider founding a new dynasty: Ferdinand Maximilian, Archduke of Austria. Feelers were put out, an interview arranged, and Gutiérrez told His Imperial Highness about the snow-capped volcanos, the guitar music in the night, the dark-eyed women—all of which was quite true—and, with less honesty, how joyfully Mexico would receive him as monarch. Maximilian accepted. There was, however, more to it than that. The United States would never allow Europe to intervene, but the U.S. had its own problem, a civil war. Certain liberal fanatics and other such riff-raff might not know what was best for Mexico; in fact, an army was necessary, and a fleet for transport. England, France, and Spain would undertake to supply this requirement; they had debts to collect and intended to take a little more for the expense of collecting. So it was arranged. Gutiérrez traveled down to Rome with Maximilian, where he had the unique experience of entertaining a Pope and an Emperor at lunch—which wasn't bad for a Campeche boy. Banquets, fireworks, parties, all this was fine, but Gutiérrez, remembering the harsh realities of Mexican politics, began to worry about the easy-going, unrealistic man he was sending there. After listening to a statement of Ferdinand's political intentions, he said, with more than conventional meaning, "God protect the Emperor." A coolness soon developed between them; Gutiérrez refused to accept any position in the new regime and remained in Europe.

When the French fleet dropped anchor off Campeche, it found the Yucatecans at each others' throats as usual, with Mérida troops besieging the walls of that port. Political division of the peninsula had solved nothing; habits were too deeply ingrained, and rebels traveled north and south in the old familiar way. There had been eight governors in four years, and with the treasury stripped, the army without equipment or morale, roads still blocked by barricades of the Caste War or taken over by the forest, the Yucatecans were ready for Gutiérrez's cure. Mexico had already submitted. Governor Navarrete of the state of Yucatan declared for the Interventionists when his henequen trade was stopped by the blockade of Sisal. Governor García of Campeche had no choice. On January 22, 1864, Yucatan became a department of the Empire. Navarrete became Military and Political Prefect of the entire peninsula until the arrival of Maximilian in Mexico City in June, when José Salazar Ilarregui was sent as Imperial Commissioner.

Three years before, President Juárez had sent a commission to study the troubles of Yucatan, and it had recommended reunification of the two states and the dispatch of a non-Yucatecan, impartial, and honest governor with national troops to back him up and restore order. Now, under a very different administration, these points were met. Ilarregui, a mathematician and engineer with no local prejudice or enemies, set to work. He abolished the much-abused National Guard, organizing in its place reserve battalions under Imperial control; he suppressed all exemptions from military service, and recalled political exiles, including three governors and Colonel Cepeda Peraza; and he re-established the long-needed colonial office of Protector of the Indians. This was the Imperial honeymoon, with logic prevailing under the still untarnished prestige of the Emperor, and it seemed that a new and glorious future had actually dawned.

At the head of the list of unsolved Yucatecan problems were the Maya. In the last days of 1864, the Mérida newspapers announced the arrival of some exotic birds of passage: Aide-de-Camp Boleslawski, Captain Kaptistynski, and Lieutenant Waldherr, of the Emperor's General Staff. These worthies came to discuss ways and means with Ilarregui. Leading citizens and the local military met in the governor's palace to familiarize the foreigners with the situation. The military positions at the time were as follows:

A "line of the south," with headquarters at Tekax, held the southeastern camino real, with garrisons at Peto, Dzonotchel, Ichmul, and Tihosuco. The "line of the east," with headquarters at Valladolid, defended that place, Espita, Tizimin, and probably Tixcacalcupul. Valladolid's lifeline, the northern camino real, was protected by the "line of the center," with headquarters at Izamal and detachments all the way back to Motul and Cacalchen and forward to Tunkas and the ruins of Chichen Itza. The eastern force was a 500-man permanent battalion, formerly commanded by Colonel Manuel Cepeda Peraza; its troops were better equipped and had more discipline than the militia forces, but they were not considered as good in jungle fighting. The militia were recruited throughout the state, serving a month at a time for wages of one and a half *reales* per day.

While forward posts like Tihosuco and Ichmul were strictly military camps, the other towns mentioned had settlers, or *Colonias*, who were an important part of the defense force. They kept themselves on an informal but very ready basis, with half of the men under arms at all times, lookouts posted at the highest observation points, and regular patrols combing their districts looking for any sign of raiders. Sentries were also scattered through the forest at strategic points, and when they spotted enemy movement, they would light a fuse on a homemade signal bomb and slip away before it went off. These bombs, which were used for the same purpose by both sides, were made of uncured bull hide strongly corded with henequen fiber, and they could be heard at a distance of three miles.

The Colonias were courageous and self-reliant. They had to be; as regularly as the seasons, the professional soldiers, for whatever they were worth, took themelves off to the more congenial work of military politics, leaving the settlers very much on their own. As the frontier was deep, a continuous line of defense could not be held; nothing could prevent the Cruzob from slipping past the forward camps to strike deeply at the less guarded towns and villages, such as Tunkas and Tixcacaltuyu. Almost all Yucatecan towns were isolated islands of people in the bush or jungle, and this meant that once the Cruzob struck it was almost impossible to catch them before they slipped back into their native forest.

There had been a raid that fall, with 600 Maya working into the Peto district, where they killed 39 and wounded 11 on November 28 and 29. The little village of Dzonotchel, stubbornly repopulated after each of the many massacres it had suffered, was the main objective; but a platoon of 25 militia men and the settlers were warned in time, kept their heads, and with an organized defense maintained themselves. Seldom willing to pay the price of frontal assault, the Cruzob pillaged and burned on a small scale (the corn was ready for harvest) and then withdrew. But this kind of thing made it almost impossible to work the fields, which meant the settlement would have to be abandoned, and no one knew where such attrition would end. A simple increase of village garrisons wouldn't change the picture, and everyone agreed that an offensive was necessary. A commission was appointed in Mérida to study the problem and recommend a strategy.

Talk existed of a peace party among the rebels, now called Indios Bravos, and an effort was supposedly made to contact it. Propaganda and supplies were also furnished to the Pacíficos, who were no longer established at Chichenha. Some of their number had settled at a place called Icaiche further to the south, more remote from the raids of the Cruzob; and after the third bloody attack on Chichenha in March of 1863, the survivors gave up the site for good, joining their relatives at Icaiche. They were encouraged to assert themselves in the disputed northern districts of Belize, cutting off the flow of English supplies to the Cruzob. (An Imperial proclamation had included Belize within the Mexican Empire.) Ladino agents were sent to operate along the Hondo to further this end. Thus the right flank. The center and main effort was planned along the old entrada road, southeast from Tihosuco, using Valladolid as base of supply. Maximilan promised to furnish troops and money, 60,000 pesos a month, and build new barracks and forward camps. For all of this, business and the military could only smile and give thanks to their gracious Emperor. These promises began to be realized as General José María Gálvez landed at Sisal with a battalion in February, and the new area commander, Divisional General Severo de Castillo, took over at the end of April.* Supplies and equipment had

---

* Several years later, as the political wheel of fortune spun the wrong way, Severo de Castillo found himself with a great deal of leisure time in the prison fortress of San Juan de Ulúa, and he made use of it by writing a book—half history, half melodrama—entitled *Cecilio Chi.* Published in 1869, it was the first historical review of the war, appearing some nine years before Baqueiro's history, and if the facts are not all that they might be, it is interesting for the atmosphere and social attitudes it describes. Severo's hero, a young Ladino named Raimundo, marries María Chi, thinking her the daughter of the rebel chief Cecilio. María turns out to be the ward, not the daughter, of Chi; in fact, she is the granddaughter of Jacinto Canek, and thus the "queen" of Yucatan. After many difficulties, the couple escapes to Belize, and Severo de Castillo solves their future, and incidentally expresses his own feeling toward Mexico in this fantasy, by having them sail for Europe, never to return.

been readied by then, the reserves called up, and General Gálvez moved his combat command headquarters to Valladolid. A support battalion was sent down to Tihosuco with orders to start cutting a road southeast into the forest. This was begun about May 1, 1865.

Colonel Daniel Traconis

On the Maya side, the old blood-drinker, Venancio Puc, was missing. Two years before, on December 23, 1863, he had been voted out of office by a plurality of machetes led by the new general, a Mestizo, Dionisio Zapata Santos. His was the peace party mentioned above. It was reported that he intended to repopulate abandoned Bacalar and arrange a treaty with Yucatan, and that he treated the white prisoners in a humane manner. No one could hold power very long at Chan Santa Cruz with such a policy. Zapata's opponents discredited him among the troops, waited until the shrine Guardia was drunk following a wake, and then killed him, together with the prisoners who were suspected of plotting rebellion. The new leaders were General Crecencio Poot, Bernabé Cen, and the indestructible Bonifacio Novelo. Novelo became Tatich, Poot General of the Plaza. They were quite ready to fight; and when the Ladino sappers began their work on the frontier near Tihosuco, the call went out, companies were mobilized, and a powerful Maya force was put in the field.

Colonel Francisco Cantón was in charge of the road-building, and on May 4 he inspected the work, which had progressed a short distance beyond Kampocolche. Aware of the pressure that was building up, he pulled his workers back to the well at Yokdzonot, and hurriedly entrenched himself. Disciplined volleys from behind makeshift barricades stopped the first attack, but his patrols found that the Cruzob had come to stay; they were building siege lines, starting in the east, and, after reinforcements under Colonel Ana-cleto Sandoval came in, they continued to the north and west, cutting the detachment off from the frontier. Skirmishes continued through May, bitter and inconclusive. General Gálvez himself came down to find out what the trouble was, together with 400 men, and found plenty. Cantón heard his fighting progress through the woods and sent out a force to help him, and when it was stopped, another force with most of his best men; this did the trick but at a heavy price, including part of the general's artillery. By June 10, another Apache fighter decided this was not Sonora; Gálvez, finding the Maya too well-armed and inexhaustibly supplied with gunpowder and courage, ordered the Emperor's army home. They almost made it. Six miles from Tihosuco the rear guard under Colonel Sandoval was attacked and routed. Attempting to help, the main body under Gálvez was drawn into the disaster and smashed in turn, losing rifles, baggage, and artillery, and abandoning their sick and wounded to the usual fate. The General was broken and sent home for this, to be replaced by the jungle veteran Colonel Daniel Traconis. The agents on the Hondo managed to divert one shipload of gunpowder from the Maya, seizing 600 pounds and escaping English law on a Sisal-bound schoo-ner; but this was an insignificant item of the flourishing trade. The Pacíficos of Icaiche, instead of raiding the Cruzob lifeline, had fled for the safety of the jungles of Petén.

Then came a pause from war and killing. On November 22, 1865, María Carlota Amalia, Empress of Mexico, arrived at Sisal on board the steamship *Tabasco* and on the following morning made a joyous entry into Mérida, with a thunderous 101-gun salute from the can-nons of San Benito, the ringing of church bells, and the cheers of the populace to greet her. There was a Te Deum service in the cathedral, and a serenade that night, made brilliant with fireworks and illumi-nations. This was the beginning of an eleven-day whirl in which the energetic little Belgian toured the city visiting hospitals, convents, schools, the fortress of San Benito, markets, shops, and factories, watching more fireworks and receiving more serenades. Three balls were given, one by Commissioner Ilarregui for the Empress, one by the Empress for Mérida society, and one for the Mestizos in the galleries of the Plaza de Armas. Every rank of the social order was reached. Various citizens of wealth were made Chamberlains of the Emperor, Ladies of the Palace, Honorary Councilors of State, or Officers and Knights of Guadalupe. Outstanding members of the working and military class were given medals of gold, silver, and bronze. Prisoners in the jail were given good advice. Even the Maya were remembered. Ilarregui issued a bilingual proclamation in the name of the Emperor, inviting the Maya of Chan Santa Cruz and other groups to come to Mérida and make peace, with their personal security guaranteed. (A few natives were eventually persuaded to travel all the way to Mexico City for treaty-signing, but they represented no one but themselves, and although they were from the Pacíficos group, they were killed by fellow tribesmen on their return.)

Carlota left an exhausted, delighted, and very loyal Mérida behind her when she traveled south, 101 more salutes ringing in her ears, escorted by young men of the best families. She became one of the first, and certainly the most prominent, of tourists to visit the ruins of Uxmal, spending two days admiring that lovely site. Campeche attempted to outdo her northern rival, and certainly outgunned her with the fortress cannons. More balls, serenades, visits, and presentations of honors to the leading citizens were crowded into six days. The Empress departed through streets decorated with flowers, hangings, and pennants, and as she passed beneath a special triumphal arch at the head of the wharf, a cascade of flowers, verses, and white doves was released, and at that moment the church bells began to ring. She would remember Yucatan in the hard days ahead, and Yucatan would remember her. Maximilian could not have had a better representative.

With the fiesta over, it was time to go back to work. Imperial Commissioner Ilarregui was called for cabinet duty in Mexico City, and replaced by Domingo Bureau. A new district commander, General Francisco G. Casanova, arrived in early April; and the combat commander, Colonel Traconis, was ordered down to Tihosuco, which was to be the forward headquarters, with his regulars of the Ninth Battalion. There was little activity there during the early summer, only some skirmishing and a light siege; but the Maya began to appear in force toward the end of July, after the planting was in. On August 3, 1866, an army patrol of 200 men ran into a trap, suffering 85 casualties. Colonel Cantón led a second force along the same trail that led to the nearby well of Majas, and suffered a heavier defeat on August 14. From then on, Tihosuco was cut off from outside help, under a close and bitter siege, the defense perimeter reduced to the plaza itself, the church, the government building, and commanding pyramid mound. Supplies ran low, and the troops would eat horse, mule, and dog before they were through. Yucatecans felt a concern they hadn't known for many years. Volunteers came forward, 150 from Calotmul and 300 from the vicinity of Cansahcab. From Mérida itself came 200 young men of the "gente decente," a class that had long left the fighting to professional soldiers and to the poor who couldn't afford to buy their way out of service. The recent visit of their Empress had fired their sense of duty, and to this had been added the oratory of Commissioner Bureau and the "inspired and animated verses" of a local poetess, Gertrudis Tenorio Zavala, whose reading followed the Commissioner's words at the review held on the Alameda of Mérida on the day of their departure for the east.

General Navarrete, with his Second Brigade at Majas, knew of the danger at Tihosuco, and he had heard the gunfire of the two defeats in August, but it took the enthusiasm of the volunteers to stir him into action. An enlisted man, one Corporal Pina, took the suicidal job of slipping through Cruzob lines to carry word of the coming relief to Tihosuco; he mingled with the enemy until he could make a rush for the defending barricades, shouting that he was a friend, and, risking bullets from both sides, he made it. On September 2, some 400 men carrying food and ammunition left Majas under two volunteer captains. They fought most of the way, and the Cruzob maneuvered to bring them under fire from the garrison when they reached Tihosuco the following day, which caused some losses before the confusion was straightened out. Their help was needed. The major attack came on September 15, at odds calculated by the Ladinos as six to one, but at any event made by thousands of Maya who had suffered repeated invasions based on Tihosuco and were determined to take the place. This was not their day, nor open massed assault their best tactic. With sufficient ammunition and restored morale, the reinforced garrison beat them off, and in that victory left their own lines to take the enemy's barricades and pursue and disperse him, burning and looting his camps. General Prieto and the First Brigade at Ichmul had done nothing during this time to help the beleaguered force; and when the General saw the columns of smoke rising in the northeast, he assumed that the town had fallen. Eight days after their defeat, the Maya definitely abandoned the siege, and Colonel Traconis and his men were relieved.

Two victory parades were held, one for the Colonel on November 4, and a second for the troops on November 12, with the buildings along the line of march from the suburbs to the plaza decorated with flowers, pennants, and arches, the men marching with fixed bayonets at shoulder arms, each bayonet holding a floral wreath. The poetess Zavala had many competitors, and the oratory was long-winded and baroque; but the food was good at the open-air banquet given on the Alameda, and the women were pretty, and with so much patriotism and gallantry in the warm night air, nothing was too good for the "Heroes of Tihosuco." It is no reflection on their unquestioned courage, but one fact was ignored: Tihosuco was given up as too exposed for defense, its overgrown ruin becoming part of the belt of disputed territory that separated the Cruzob from Yucatan, and the frontier was moved back to Peto.

The Empire itself was now in trouble. The French army, Maximilian's main support, was withdrawn by Napoleon III in the face of pressure from the United States, where the Civil War had ended and Washington was in a position to put teeth into the Monroe Doctrine. The United States had the largest and most modern army in the world, and Union forces were sent in a threatening manner toward the Rio Grande. The combinations that had made the Empire possible were unraveling. The fugitive President, Benito Juárez, found more and more support, and his small bands became armies marching out of the hills. The Republican movement came to Yucatan from Tabasco, whose Governor supplied ex-Governor García with men and materiel of war, whereupon García headed for Campeche. The eastern lines were stripped to meet this threat, Colonel Traconis embarking on December 19 from Sisal with his Ninth Battalion. It was not the complete battalion; a company deserted at Hunucma, the day before reaching Sisal, proclaiming for the Republic. It headed south to make contact with García, brushing aside a force sent in pursuit, and then declared Colonel Cepeda Peraza commander of the revolution in Yucatan. The Colonel, an often-exiled soldier of the Republic who had been fighting Indians and reactionaries for the last twenty years, was living a withdrawn and inactive life in Mérida. He slipped quietly out of the city and joined the small band of rebels at Calkini on January 17, 1867. After the Colonel's action, Mérida authorities made a number of arrests among known Republican sympathizers, whom they sent to join other dissidents at the penal colony which had been established on Cozumel Island, off the east coast.*

Ilarregui, once more Imperial Commissioner of Yucatan, was like a man trying to put out a dozen fires with a leaky bucket. The force under Colonel Traconis, which he had sent by sea to Campeche, went on to squelch a rising at Isla Carmen, then rushed back to help hold the newly besieged walls of Campeche, and was then recalled because of Cepeda Peraza's growing success in the north. Cepeda Peraza won his equipment and supplies from the Imperial Army, first in company-size engagements and then in larger operations, but he had to avoid battle when Traconis came looking for him with 1,800 men. When Traconis mounted a lukewarm siege of a part of the rebel forces encamped at a hacienda near Ticul, Cepeda struck. Taking a battalion, he slipped through the siege and raided Mérida by night, freeing political prisoners, seizing a large quantity of guns and ammunition, and getting away before the reaction could catch him. Three days later, on March 18, he surprised the rear of the forces

* This place, together with nearby Isla Mujeres, had been settled by fugitives in the early days of the Caste War, on the premise that the Cruzob were not ocean sailors. Isla Mujeres is less than three miles from the mainland.

besieging his men, with great success, and Traconis gradually pulled back to the area of Mérida. Success snowballed Cepeda's forces, and he collected the adherence of Tecoh, Izamal, the port of Sisal; and with 2,500 men in his command, he laid siege to the state capital. Yucatecan civil wars had a way of becoming solved without much loss of life, but for once this was not so. Now Mérida paid the real cost of Carlota's visit, paid for the Orders of Guadalupe, the medals of gold, silver, and bronze, and the smiles of Her Imperial Majesty. For once feeling ran hot through all the ranks, not just in the inflamed imaginations of revolutionary officers. It was the Empire against the Republic, and men were ready to die for principles. Colonel Traconis, hero of the fifty-day siege of Tihosuco, with the eyes of the world upon him, was ready to outdo himself, and he did: the siege of Mérida lasted fifty-five days, with the fighting house-to-house and block-to-block and losses of over 500 men on each side. The colonel undoubtedly knew of the plan to transfer the capital of the Empire to Yucatan if things became too difficult in Mexico, to make Yucatan the hub of a new Empire that would absorb the unstable states of Central America; and he was determined to hold his post. Colonel Cantón had been given the responsibility of holding the frontier against the Cruzob, but with his cause in serious trouble he raised five or six hundred men and led them against Cepeda Peraza, first at Izamal, and then, fighting through the siege lines, into Mérida—which only added to the number of mouths in that ill-fed city.

A character from history made a brief appearance at this time. A steamship carrying López de Santa Anna, being deported once again from Mexico, this time by the winning Juárez, stopped at Sisal; and the old general, hearing that a "Peraza" was besieging Mérida, took it to be General Martín Peraza, his old partisan in centralism, and sent a message ashore with a plan of cooperation. This was a mistake. The commander of the port sent two customs boats out to the steamship, which was an American ship, the *Virginia*; Santa Anna was seized and carried ashore to the Sisal prison. When Cepeda Peraza learned that the archenemy of liberty and of Yucatan was in his control, he ordered him shot, and was only dissuaded at the last minute because Santa Anna had been taken from the protection of the United States flag and an execution could cause international complications. Santa Anna was shipped back to face Juárez.

General Manuel Cepeda Peraza

While the soldiers sniped at one another from the rooftops of Mérida, made short and bloody rushes across the exposed streets, and smashed up the architecture with cannon fire, Maximilian was captured at Querétaro. This was on May 15. Although the Empire was reduced to a few city blocks in a provincial capital, the defenders of Mérida refused to believe that their cause was lost, and went on fighting; there were local problems of pride and hate to be settled. But the end came at last. The civilian population was starving, ammunition was expended, and the Emperor's fall could no longer be denied. Colonel Traconis was replaced in his comman by General Navarrete, which spared Traconis the humiliating task: under instructions from Imperial Commissioner Ilarregui, Navarrete asked for terms. Cepeda responded with a guarantee of life, liberty, and protection of personal property, subject to the dictates of the central government, with free passage out of the state for leaders of the Imperial party. It was enough, and the treaty was signed on June 15, 1867. They were lucky to surrender to Cepeda Peraza. General García, who in the meantime had completed the conquest of Campeche, shot his prisoners, General Espejo among others; and he sent first a commission demanding death for Ilarregui and then a squadron to intercept him off Sisal. For Cepeda Peraza, now Governor, this was a question of honor; he told the

Campechanos that he would defend his prisoners by force if necessary. Ilarregui sailed for New York, and General Navarrete and Colonels Cantón and Villafana for Havana. And as they sailed, Ferdinand Maximilian's dream ended with the volley of a firing squad on the slope of the Cerro de las Campañas. Carlota was soon to enter her own fifty-year dream of gray afternoons, shielded, we can hope, by her madness, in the quiet halls of the Chateau de Bouchout in Belgium. The creator of this story, José María Gutiérrez de Estrada, escaped the last sad pages; he died of old age at the end of March of that year, in France.

Eleven

The Empire of the Cross
1867–1900

IT WAS LONG before sunrise when the Maestro of the guard company swung himself out of his hammock and crossed the plaza from the barracks to the church, which was deserted at that hour except for the lone sentry, keeping perpetual watch over La Santísima. Candles guttered on the altar, illuminating a number of small crosses, some of them dressed in huipils, others decorated with mirrors, colored papers, ribbons, and sea shells. La Santísima itself was hidden in a wooden chest. Over the altar was a canopy of red silk. The boy acolytes, or "angels," yawned. A few soldiers of the guard, including those who paid for the service, drifted in with their large straw hats held across their chests, heads bowed, and they knelt on the bare floor in the public part of the church. Then the Maestro Cantor began the mass, the "Chan" or little mass, chanting Latin to the best of his ability, undisturbed by the fact that many of the words were just sounds to him, because this was the language of God, who does understand. The host was a thick tortilla of corn and honey. Mass was said in the regular Catholic form, with the Our Father, Hail Mary, Salve, Credo, General Confession, and Act of Contrition, all carefully, correctly remembered by former acolytes or sextons to Dzul priests of the previous generation, and taught by them to their children. Very little of the ritual was lost.

After service, the Maestro Cantor and the soldiers went back to their barracks, where breakfast was being prepared. For the soldiers it was the beginning of a long and lazy day. They would attend a second mass around eight o'clock in the morning, when the band would play in God's honor various sacred pieces, polkas, or whatever else it knew, and in the evening there was the Rosary. They might be called upon to run errands, but for the greater part of the day they would lounge in their hammocks, twisting henequen into rope, weaving bags or some similar task simply to pass the time. Mainly they would talk, gossip, and remember the adventures of their last raid. Gradually the town came to life. There was the pat, pat, pat of women's hands as they flattened dough into tortillas, the rasping of stone pestles as corn was ground to flour. Most of the barracks servants were Dzul slaves; one might have been the mistress of a wealthy hacienda once, another the wife of a colonel, another the town beauty who listened to the guitars outside her window in the evening, wondering which of her suitors she would choose. There was no choice now. They blackened their faces over cook fires, strained their muscles with heavy water buckets, and shared the hammock of the officer to whom they were assigned. Then the cocks crowed, forest birds answered, the sky paled, and the dawn came to Chan Santa Cruz.

By this time the Tatich, if he had not officiated at early mass, would have completed his devotions in his private chapel before a cross heavily ornamented with gold and jewels. And the Tatich was none other than that indestructible Mestizo, Bonifacio Novelo. Twenty years before he had been a hunted refugee, "the assassin of Valladolid." Now, at the other end of the social and moral order, he led an independent nation, controlled an army and great wealth, and was the high priest, the pope of his people.

> He is a man of about sixty years of age, immensely stout and of a lighter shade than the generality of the Indians. His expression of countenance is decidedly pleasing. He was dressed in a many-colored cloth of Indian manufacture. White loose cotton drawers trimmed from the knees downward with rich lace, sandals of embroidered leather and a scarf, also of Indian manufacture, around his waist, while around his neck was hung a massive gold chain with cross attached.

This description comes from John Carmichael, who traveled up to the shrine city from Belize in the fall of 1867. As the Yucatecans were cheering Colonel Traconis and his men, Carmichael found the Cruzob, with more justification, in the midst of a victory celebration. He and the six-man bodyguard assigned to him by the Bacalar commandant were stopped by a picket on the outskirts of Chan Santa Cruz, held there for half an hour, then escorted into the city by José Crescencio Poot, a company of two hundred soldiers, and a thirty-man band. Triumphal arches were thrown across the streets as for fiesta, well-equipped sentries presented arms at each cross street, and a thousand soldiers were massed in the plaza. The Englishman was much impressed with everything he saw, and particularly with Bonifacio Novelo. The Patrón asked him if he hadn't been afraid to make the trip, going on to say:

> The Yucatecans give us a very bad name for treachery and cruelty, but whatever our conduct may be towards them, I can assure you that our feelings are nothing but those of friendship towards the English, and the time may yet come when we will give you proof of our sincerity.

Novelo laid claim to all of Yucatan (with the diplomatic exception of Belize), control over an army of 11,000 including allied tribes, and a treasury of 200,000 pesos plus jewelry and gold ornaments of great value. There was exaggeration in this, but the Patrón obviously ran a going concern, and he took advantage of this visit from the outside world to inquire about another monarch, Queen Victoria, and "her relations with her subjects, English law and punishment." He said that the use of ventriloquism to make the Cross speak was the work of evil men and a thing of the past, and that his people worshiped God through the Cross. Novelo no longer took an active leadership in the field, but spent much time in his palace or the church, living aloof from his people, a pattern that future Patróns would follow. Captain Carmichael gave credit where credit was due. He was no Plumridge or Twigge, and Novelo was not Venancio Puc.

This mission had several purposes. With the victory of the Cruzob over the Emperor of Mexico, the Governor of Belize wanted to reassure himself as to Maya-English friendship. Secondly, Belize had suffered from Mexican agitation of the Icaiche Pacíficos. Luciano Zuc, the Batab of Icaiche, died in December of 1864 and was succeeded by Marcos Canul, after the move from Chichenha to Icaiche.

Canul continued the policy of taxing English loggers and making raids across the Hondo. In May of 1866 he surprised the settlement at Qualm Hill, British Honduras, killing two who resisted and carrying off 79 prisoners; his own force was only 125 strong. A Prussian, Gustav von Ohlaffen, took on the risky job of ransoming these people, beating the price down from $12,000 to $3,000 and getting them safely back to Corozalito by July 1.

Refugee Maya had settled in the western jungle of Belize, after the various defeats of the Pacíficos at the hands of the Cruzob, and founded a number of new villages, the principal one called San Pedro. As early as May of 1863, the chief there, Ascensión Ek, had petitioned the Governor for arms and ammunition to defend his area against Chichenha, but it took three years and Canul's raid of 1866 for approval to be granted and the guns sent. A border patrol under Captain Delamere, on learning that Canul was headed for San Pedro, went there first, to learn what had been feared: Ek was playing them false, and the guns would be used not against but in alliance with the Pacíficos. Ek warned Delamere to leave, which he did because of the odds against him. Canul then went down to San Pedro, and 42 men of the Fourth West Indian Regiment were sent to cut him off. On December 21, 1866, they made contact along the trail one mile out of San Pedro; after thirty minutes of fighting, the English suffered five dead and sixteen wounded, and they fled with their commander, Major MacKay, all the way into the town of Belize.

In January of the following year the San Pedro and Icaiche Maya moved deeper into the colony, taking the village of Indian Church, which had been evacuated and left under the guard of seven policemen. Poisoned rum had been left as a present for the raiders, but they weren't naïve in such matters; they had one of the prisoners drink first, and lost their thirst on seeing his expression. They left letters demanding rent, not only for disputed border districts but for Orange Walk, Corozal, and Belize itself, the old Yucatecan claim, at a total of 19,000 pesos a year, with the alternative of complete destruction. The Crown Colony went into a panic. The Governor's barge was kept ready to sail day or night, and refugees swarmed into Belize town. An old Negro heard a noise in the bush, fired his gun at a grazing ox, and shouted "Indians!"—which sent everyone rushing for the wharf with valuables and children in hand, and there were red faces later. But forces had been set in motion; appeals for help went out to Jamaica and Cuba for ships in case evacuation became necessary, and a militia was organized, armed, and sent north to assist the detachment of the West Indian Regiment. A punitive column of 313 men attacked San Pedro on February 9; besides the men they had a rocket tube, or launcher, which sent incendiary missiles into the thatched roofs of the village, and these pyrotechnics promptly returned the Maya to a state of respect for Her Majesty's law. Rocket warfare was then taken to San José, Santa Teresa, Chorro, and other little hamlets, all with equally satisfying results. Few people were hurt, the huts could be easily rebuilt, and the area was so thoroughly pacified that the militia was discharged in April.

This took care of the San Pedro Maya, but not Marcus Canul, protected by his ninety miles of jungle and swamp. So Carmichael went up to Chan Santa Cruz to seek Cruzob support, and Bonifacio Novelo gave him every assurance. In a letter dated October 30, 1867, Novelo warned the Governor to guard Corozal, promised to block the Icaiche trails or at least give the alarm, asked permission for hot pursuit of the enemy onto Belize territory, and said that he would turn over Canul if he caught him.

The Icaiche Batab denied any intention of invading Corozal, but when the troops were withdrawn from the frontier, the raiding picked up again, particularly when a border survey, following a northern branch of the Hondo, worked within nine miles of his village, absorbing 150 square miles of what he considered Icaiche territory. There were continual English protests to Campeche about the activities of Canul, a pro forma Campeche official; these brought only half-hearted assurances that Canul would be curbed—when in fact Campeche lacked any power over him—and futile comments on the illegality of Belize and on the 100,000 people killed because the English had sold guns to the Maya. So matters continued until April 18, 1870, when Canul with 116 men occupied Corozal with the cry "Mexico forever!" There were approximately 5,000 people living in Corozal, primarily refugees, both Ladino and Maya, and none of them felt like fighting, so there was none—no killing and no prisoners. The Icaiche men said they were looking for Cruzob and, when they found none, withdrew, whereupon the townspeople who wouldn't defend themselves drew up fantastic claims for their losses against the government which had failed to protect them. Marcus Canul was in the same area a year later, but this time the Cruzob were ready. Within two or three days 500 of them had massed on their side of the Hondo ready for action, and 5,000 more were promised if needed. Fifty of them crossed over to Corozal to make arrangements with the commander of that place, but the sight of any Indians made the English nervous, and they were abruptly ordered off. A few barrels of gunpowder and thanks for much-needed assistance would have been more in order, and a coolness resulted from this undiplomatic behavior.

Marcos Canul made one last raid, crossing the Hondo near Corozalito and on September 1, 1872, attacking the village of Orange Walk. The garrison of that place, 37 men and an officer, was besieged in a one-room barracks, with the Pacíficos sniping at them from behind stacks of cut logs and attempting to burn them out. Help came from some American settlers (several hundred ex-Confederates, preferring the white man's burden to carpetbaggers, had moved to the colony after the Civil War intending to create a new Dixie); they rallied, took the Maya in the rear and drove them off with heavy casualties, including Canul, who lived just long enough to be carried back across the Hondo. His successor, General Rafael Chan, wrote the Governor of this, explaining that he, Chan, had always been against the raids, and begged forgiveness from "our Queen, who had much reason to be annoyed."

But we are ahead of our story and must go back to the second point of Captain Carmichael's mission to Chan Santa Cruz in 1867. In June of 1866 the S.S. *Light of the Ages* had landed at Belize with 480 coolies from Amoy, indentured for work in the lumber camps. The more enterprising of these Chinese didn't take long to get their shore legs and use them. After one look at the work that was expected of them, the working conditions, the bad food, and the absence of rice, 100 of them fled north. Their lot was not good among the Cruzob; they were treated as slaves, distributed among the officers for use as field hands. Yet their initial fears were warranted. Half of those who stayed in Belize died of fever within three years, while most of the runaways survived to old age; and since extradition was refused by Novelo, they lived out their lives in the jungle of Yucatan, joining their blood-line with the Maya, reinforcing that mark known as the Mongolian spot. This was the fate of all but four of them, who went right on running, this time to Mérida, where they opened a laundry.

Extradition had another side. A considerable number of Cruzob had found the Cross too demanding—with heavy labor, military service, and tyranny of the generals—and solved their problem by crossing the Hondo south. Pach Chakan and several other villages near Corozal were populated by these people; about 10,000 Maya of all denominations were in the colony. From 1860 on, La Santísima had sent agents and raiding parties to recover these delinquents, and protests did little good. Then there were the freewheeling loggers who made private contracts with the Cross for timber rights and, once on English territory, refused to pay—which meant more kidnaping, more protests, and more apologies. The Hondo was a narrow, placid jungle river and very easy to cross. These were some of the problems of foreign policy with which the Cross was faced, why it was recognized as a de facto nation by the English, and how it was a sometimes ally of the British Empire.

We have heard something of the second neighbor, Icaiche, a fugitive settlement of the survivors of Chichenha, with its petty wars, an army of 150 men, and a population of perhaps 1,700. The village stood on the crest of a 400-foot hill, protected by a wall of live bamboo trees, with an entrance to the east and to the west, but it was protected most efficiently by its isolation, by swamps where there was no water fit to drink, and by dense jungle. The one trail to Belize was described as a tunnel in certain parts. Wood instead of stone walls was used to divide house lots, and streets were wide, with huts in even alignment. For public buildings there was a church—a hut like all the rest—and a barracks or guardhouse, where loaded guns were kept ready for instant use. The military system of these settlers was similar to that of the Cruzob: companies were based on the old Yucatecan militia—the school in which all the rebels had studied, with officers elected by the ranks—and the commanding officer was a general who served as tribal chief and judge, ordering either the whip

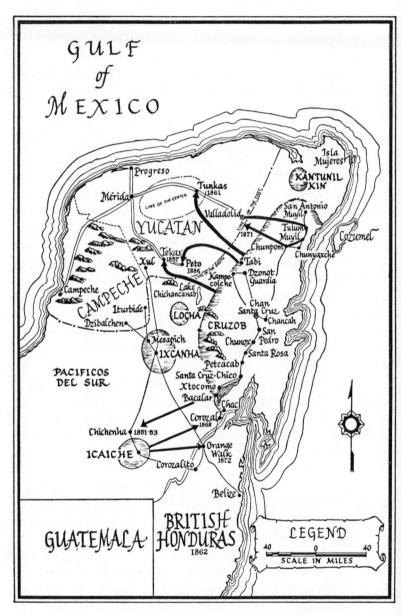

GULF
of
MEXICO

Isla
Mujeres

KANTUNIL
KIN

Progreso

Mérida

Tunkas
1861

LINE OF THE CENTER

Valladolid
/1871

San Antonio
Muyil

YUCATAN

LINE OF THE EAST

Chunpom

Tulum
Muyil

Cozumel

Chunyaxche

Tekax
1857

Peto
1886

Tabi

Xul

Kampo-
colche

LINE OF THE SOUTH

Dzonot
Guardia

Campeche

CAMPECHE

Lake
Chichancanab

Chan
Santa Cruz

Chancah

Iturbide

LOCHA

CRUZOB

San
Pedro

Dzibalchen

Chunox

Mesapich

Santa Rosa

IXCANHA

Petcacab

PACIFICOS
DEL SUR

Santa Cruz-Chico

Xtocomo

Bacalar

Chac

Corozal
1868

Chichenha 1851-53

Orange
Walk
1872

ICAICHE

Corozalito

Belize

GUATEMALA

BRITISH
HONDURAS
1862

LEGEND

40   0   40
SCALE IN MILES

Independent Maya groups, Yucatecan defense lines, and major
military actions, 1853–86

or the firing squad, arranging trade with Campeche or Belize, and was recognized as an independent leader by the Mexican Government. Their religious life continued in the combination of folk Catholicism and pagan beliefs that had been known before the rebellion, with services conducted by Maestros Cantores and very occasionally by a visiting priest. They despised their Cruzob enemies as non-Christian.

Ixcanha, the largest group after Chan Santa Cruz, centered on a village of the same name, and spread over an area approximately thirteen miles wide and forty-five miles long, surrounded by empty forest. It had joined in the treaty of Chichenha and was one of the Pacíficos del Sur, with its chief receiving honorary appointment from Mexico as jefe político and an official stamp for his correspondence. There were over 11,000 Maya scattered through the district, including the town of Mesapich, sometimes considered a separate entity or even the capital, and Chunchintok, later peacefully ceded to the state of Campeche. General Arana, a Mestizo, was the Batab. He was replaced by his brother General Eugenio Arana with the aid of Ladino troops in 1869, surviving in that rank until at least 1894—a record as such things go. Lacking a bloody history, Ixcanha might be described as the most successful of the rebel groups. Its members got what they wanted, which was to be left alone; Mexico was satisfied with the client-state relationship, and distance kept them secure from the Cruzob. A trail was cut down to Santa Cruz de Hondo, leading on to Orange Walk in Belize, but it was seldom used because of the danger from Bacalar and because there was little to trade. Campeche was closer. There was nothing but thatched huts at Ixcanha; the Spanish adobe and stone buildings in the area were abandoned and left to ruin. Religion was the folk mixture run by Maestros Cantores and H-menob. These were the Huits who stayed that way, self-sufficient except for guns and gunpowder, raising their corn, beans, hogs, chickens, and cattle, and trading with the frontier settlements of Campeche for what they lacked, the necessity of that trade keeping animosity to a minimum.

Not much is known about the Locha group, which lay in the neutral zone between Ixcanha and Chan Santa Cruz. Another Mestizo, the Caste War fighter Pedro Encalada, was leader there of some 6,000 souls. Campeche recognition was attributed to him, making him a Pacífico; but he was allied to the Cruzob and his troops counted in their army. He operated with the Cross against Icaiche and was able to trade with Belize along a trail dominated by his more powerful neighbor. There is a suggestion of conflict over the rental of logging rights, but nothing more. A second subtribe, unplaced but somewhere in this area, Macanche, was listed as an ally of Chan Santa Cruz by Bonifacio Novelo. There was also a small isolated group in the northeastern corner of the peninsula, centered on Kantunil-Kin; it was considered Pacífico in 1860, when prisoners were unfairly taken there for the slave trade, and in 1871 Colonel Traconis feared that it would come under the domination of the Cross.

Frontier raids by the Cruzob against white outposts had become almost a reflex action—a standard foreign policy to ensure elbowroom in that direction—and two were made in 1870, in August and December. Ladino response came in a brief interlude of civil peace, when 1,000 national guardsmen and 300 Hidalgos marched out of Valladolid on January 21, 1871, under Colonel Traconis. They left familiar country behind after two days. There had been no fighting in these northern woods for many years, the forest grew quickly—the trails purposely allowed to disappear—and the army became a party of exploration, native auxiliaries cutting a way with machetes. Trails were found on the other side of the wilderness, and a hamlet was surprised far to the north of what had been considered Cruzob territory. Traconis followed this string of new settlements down to Tulum, picking up a few stragglers, but failed to surprise what had become Santa Cah Tulum (Holy Village of Tulum), where, in a rare exception to Maya practice, there was a priestess. Then they turned south, with the villages still evacuating before them. Sniping was the only resistance offered until they reached Chunpom, which was taken after a fire-fight that lasted several hours. That was as far as they went. For reasons unknown, whether restricted by orders or fearing large-scale attack, Traconis turned back without penetrating the Cruzob heartland. Several times on the return march he set ambushes to his rear, counting on the enemy tradition of assaulting columns just before they left the forest, but his bait wasn't taken, and he reached Valladolid without further incident. Reporting to the Governor, the

Colonel emphasized the morale of his men as opposed to the normal cowardice of recent years, claiming that the savages had been taught they couldn't raid with impunity, that their forest was no protection. He frankly admitted the lack of material results—prisoners and booty —and warned that the Cruzob northern expansion must be stopped before they brought the Pacíficos of Kantunil-Kin into their number. He felt a start had been made. It was in fact a 1,300-man reconnaissance patrol, and there was no follow-up. The northernmost known Cruzob settlement was San Antonio Muyil, seventy-odd miles from the Shrine, with patrol and hunting activity, and probably cornfield hamlets stretching thirty miles beyond.

Seen in perspective, there was much similarity between the Cruzob and the other Maya groups that lived outside the Ladino pale. They all had chiefs who called themselves generals and were usually Mestizos or even Creoles; they all maintained a military system based on militia practice, lived in scattered villages, and continued their special religious practices and turned their backs on the white world. The difference, of course, was the Cross. It sustained a social order based on the refusal of peace in any form, and had enough authority to check the tendency toward dispersion of the scattered agricultural villages; from it sprang the only town worthy of that term, the only creative response of the rebel Maya to the attack on their world view. The other groups were incomplete. They used white priests when they could get them, and were aware of their spiritual poverty. Chan Santa Cruz had filled this need, and was spiritually self-sufficient. It had taken the shock of war, defeat, and enforced isolation to give birth to the new religion; partial victories brought growth and strength, and time gave sanction. The creation and realization of the Cross Cult is a unique example of Spanish-Indian cultural synthesis. Other tribes of North and South America adapted Christian beliefs and Western ways to their own patterns, but they did so always more or less under the master's eye; their moves in this direction were tolerated just so far, and they were restricted in their political development. Only the Cruzob acted independently enough, and on a sufficiently large scale, to give us a full picture of real synthesis on more than the village level.

It is tempting to stress the exotic, to look for ancient pagan sources for strange or unusual customs, and it must be made clear that the majority of Cruzob forms, ranks, and organizations had a Spanish background. The name "Cruzob" is, of course, a Maya-Spanish corruption. "Tatich" and "Tata" are from the Spanish "daddy." The military companies, military ranks, religious brotherhoods, Maestros Cantores, village secretaries, and the majority of their prayers came from the other side of the ocean, along with the Xoc-Kin divination, conquest dances, and ideas of disease. These forms and ideas replaced their pre-Columbian equivalents once and for all; there was and could be no true revival. The Cruzob looked back to the world of his father and grandfather, not to that of a distant ancestor who wore feathers, painted hieroglyphs, and studied the stars. The Spanish culture had proved superior to the Maya culture by the fact of conquest, and the defeated people had accepted what was taught them. It was only in the area of agriculture, where the foreigners couldn't improve on local techniques, and in matters of village and family structure that the older practices continued, along with the associated gods and rites.

Within these limits, the evolution of the pre-Columbian, colonial, and Cruzob social hierarchies shows how original ranks were displaced or altered, and how the Cruzob, drawing on four hundred years of colonial synthesis, built their own world in freedom. (See the chart on p. 212.)

The Maya had held slaves in pre-Columbian times, primarily for sacrificial use, but also for economic reasons. A person could become a slave through birth, as a legal punishment, when orphaned, or as a prisoner of war. Under Spanish domination the distinction between slave and free Indian largely disappeared, as they were joined into one exploited class; but with the later use of debt peonage different forms of forced labor returned. Again a Maya could find himself under what amounted to slavery when orphaned, through inherited debt, or as legal punishment for nonpayment of taxes or fines. Open slavery revived with the Caste War after 1847, when both sides stopped killing prisoners and put them to work, sold them to Cuba, or held them for ransom. The average Mazehual of Chan Santa Cruz now found a servile group below him on the social scale, be it white, Mestizo, Pacífico Maya, or refugee Chinese. Slavery failed to crystallize. Younger captives and those born in captivity were considered free members of the nation.

The majority of the Maya had not suffered socially from the Spanish arrival. Whereas they had once worked for their sustenance in the cornfield for a surplus to feed the priest and nobles, and sweated in the construction of pyramids and temples, they now did the same for the foreigners, to make churches, monasteries, and roads. It was the upper class, the Almehenob ("those who had fathers and mothers"), who found themselves tumbled from high estate. A Batab who had formerly ruled over a district or province, with complete authority over his subjects, and whatever luxuries the land could provide, now found himself reduced to village chief, living in a hut no different from those of his people, allowed to judge only minor crimes, and considered lower than the lowest white man. His deputies and councilors were likewise reduced to peasants and part-time petty officials, distributing village land as Alcalde Col, or maintaining the guest house as Alcalde Mesón. A certain respect did survive for the native aristocracy, and among the Cruzob this class had room for expansion. The upper officers or Commandants were the closest equivalent to the pre-Columbian Batabob, occasionally gaining a considerable independence from Chan Santa Cruz, lording it over a number of villages, and over company commanders and the lieutenants and sergeants who were their deputies, in defiance of the authority of the Tatich and the rule that no officer could command the soldiers of another company regardless of rank. Their positions were elective rather than hereditary, although the sons of officers usually became officers. Tradition and general poverty prevented them from developing a higher living standard. They usually worked their own cornfields, and their only distinguishing mark was a gold earring worn in the left ear.

While the Batab was much reduced by the Conquest, the native priest, the Ah-kin, was destroyed. Chiefs could be used to keep order and to collect taxes, but there was no room for the preachers of Satan —for them the Spaniard had no tolerance. Temples were destroyed or taken over for the new religion, idols smashed, and hieroglyphic books burned, so that in a short time all knowledge of them was gone —an ignorance which, except for dates and a few glyphs, lasts to our

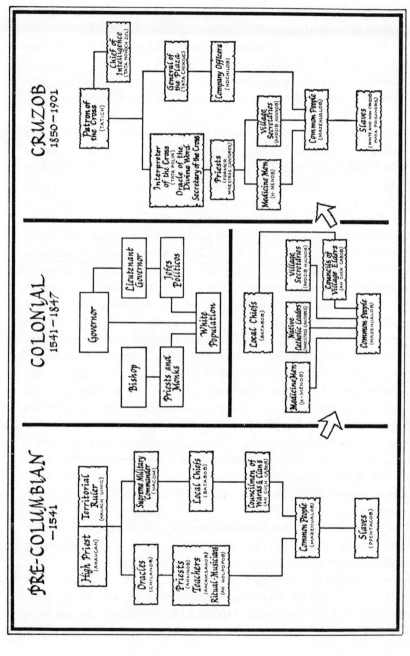

Social organization of the Maya of Yucatan in three periods.

PRE-COLUMBIAN
—1541

- High Priest (AHAUCAN)
- Territorial Ruler (HALACH UINIC)
- Supreme Military Commander (NACOM)
- Local Chiefs (BATABOB)
- Councilmen of Wards & Clans (AH CUCH CABOB)
- Oracles (CHILANOB)
- Priests (AHKINOB) Teachers (AKAMSAHOB) Ritual-Musicians (AH HOLPOPOB)
- Common People (MAZEHUALOB)
- Slaves (PPENTACOB)

COLONIAL
1541—1847

- Governor
- Lieutenant Governor
- Jefes Políticos
- Bishop
- Priests and Monks (H-MENOB)
- White Population
- Local Chiefs (BATABOB)
- Native Catholic Leaders (MAESTROS CANTORES)
- Village Secretaries (AHDZIB HUUNOB)
- Councils of Village Elders (AH CUCH CABOB)
- Medicine Men (H-MENOB)
- Common People (MAZEHUALOB)

CRUZOB
1850—1901

- Patron of the Cross (TATICH)
- Chief of Intelligence (TATA NOHOCH ZUL)
- General of the Plaza (TATA CHIKUIC)
- Company Officers (NOCHILOB)
- Interpreter of the Cross (TATA POLIN) Oracle of the Divine Word Secretary of the Cross
- Priests (FORMER MAESTROS CANTORES)
- Medicine Men (H-MENOB)
- Village Secretaries (AHDZIB HUUNOB)
- Common People (MAZEHUALOB)
- Slaves (WHITE AND NON-CRUZOB MAYA PRISONERS)

day. Efforts to celebrate the old rites were ruthlessly suppressed. Still, fragments survived. The H-men, accepted as a simple herb doctor by the whites, collected and passed down a part of the highly specialized and involved religion of the past. In his rituals were combined, on a simplified level, the generalized roles of the priest, Ah-kin; the teacher, Ah Camsah; the singer, Ah Hol pop; and the oracle or prophet, the Chilam. The H-men was a left-handed, bootlegging sort of priest, surviving through obscurity, white misunderstanding, and his vital role in the life of his people. He continued that role at Chan Santa Cruz; but with the opportunity for free expression of Maya religious ideas in the broad light of day, he lost some of his prestige to those who replaced the white priests.

In pre-Columbian times the Ah Camsah, the teacher, was a priest of great importance, transmitting to the younger generation the sacred art of literacy, the native rituals, and the legends and history of the people. His role was crucial in maintaining the ethos of the society, a fact clearly recognized by the Spaniards, who, not content with exterminating the office, replaced it with the teaching Franciscans, who used another form of writing, another history, and another religion. These monks realized that they weren't dealing with savages, and they were eager to fill the vacuum in the minds and hearts of the natives. They deciphered the hieroglyphs, learned Maya, adapted or invented letters to fit local speech, and wrote grammars, dictionaries, and prayer books in the language—all in the first decade after the Conquest. A class of Maya secretaries, or Escribanos, was quickly formed, at least one for every village. There was no intention that this office should be hereditary, but it naturally happened that father would teach son, and the family names of these scribes repeated themselves in village records. With isolation from white schools, the Escribanos became more important, particularly after the Cross lost its voice and began writing. Anastasio Caamal, who was Secretary to the Cross in 1887, signing documents in God's name, was succeeded by his son, by a second son, and then by a grandson. With no need for land grants, government orders, wills, and tax records—which had once been the major concern of the secretaries—they could dedicate themselves to the religious, the more compatible side of their knowledge, and they were treated as holy people, and ate and mingled with the higher officers. They also advised at planting and harvest time, basing their counsel on an almanac printed in Mérida, which, because of its value, always found its way across the guarded frontier.

Another function of the Ah Camsah merged with that of the Ah Hol pop, the chief singer, the master of and instructor in the all-important ritual chants. Native choirs were rapidly formed by the mission schools, singing the mass and service with great skill. From their ranks came Maya Maestros de Capilla, or choirmasters, and Maestros Cantores, lay assistants to the priests. The shortage of priests, both early and late, made the Maestro Cantor the only Catholic religious leader in many villages. Several of them attempted to take over the role of their teachers in the turbulent days of the Caste War, but they were unsuccessful until they received authority from the Speaking Cross. They then gained all powers of the priesthood: to baptize, to marry, to say mass. Appointment came from the Tatich after long years of apprenticeship and study, which sometimes included training as an H-men as well, no contradiction being recognized between the two specialties. There were supposed to be two Maestros Cantores to each military company—and every adult male served in a company. General poverty didn't allow much of a living; and if they received a considerable number of free meals as part payment for their services, not to speak of the necessary aguardiente, they were still forced to raise corn like anyone else. Prestige and religious satisfaction were their main reward. Celibacy wasn't practiced, since it was absent in their own tradition and generally lacking in white example.

The Chilam, or prophet, brings us back to the problem of the mysterious voices as an example of cultural survival or recurrence. The practice of interpreting divine voices continued at least sixty years after the Conquest; even before the Caste War, rumor claimed the existence of a speaking cross at Chan Santa Cruz; and an apparently unrelated "voice of God" figured in the Caste War of Chiapas. The verdict for survival of the pre-Columbian custom must be listed as probable but unproven. The Chilam was the obvious prototype of the Tata Polin. They both received spoken messages through artifice and passed them on to their followers. Tata Polin (literally, "Father of the Wooden Object") has been translated as "Interpreter of the Cross." The Tata Polin summoned his god with a whistle, just as the H-menob called the rain gods. There is a curious parallel here with the ringing of the bell during the elevation of the host in the Catholic mass, with which the Cruzob were familiar, and which might have helped in preserving this pagan custom. Every effort was made to add to the mystery and glamour of the service of the Speaking Cross. According to all reports, each interview with the Cross would be announced during the afternoon by the ringing of bells and a performance by the military band. All normal work came to a halt. Catholic prayers and chants sustained religious enthusiasm through the afternoon and evening, as the Cruzob gathered in and before the Temple. At midnight, with suspense at a high pitch, the whistle sounded, followed by a profound silence. God had descended.

The third official of the Speaking Cross was the "Organ of the Divine Word."* He was the man who did the actual speaking. The fact that his existence was admitted in a year when the Cross was still speaking suggests that the Cruzob didn't believe that the voice came physically from the Cross, but rather that the words of God were given sound through the medium of a possessed man. This takes us beyond tricks of ventriloquism and acoustics to a genuinely religious idea. A variation of the sound chamber and the spoken word was the use of the whistle to simulate the voice of God, which was then interpreted by the Tata Polin.

But the intentional deception, whatever the technique, still troubled some of the leaders. There are numerous firsthand reports of actual interviews with the Cross from the time of its founding in 1850 up to 1864. In 1867, Bonifacio Novelo, speaking as Tatich, was quoted as saying that the ventriloquism was the work of evil men and a thing of the past, and there are no direct accounts of the speaking rite after that date. A speaking cross was reported at Tulum in 1871, and there is other evidence that the custom was not easily given up; little more is known, since this is a matter that the present-day Maya refuse to discuss. The Cross continued to write letters, keeping up a correspondence with British Honduras, and to dictate sermons

---

* The Maya name for this office is not known; possibly it was Tata Iktan Than or Tata Kuem Than, variants of "Father of the Divine Word."

that were kept by the Secretaries. It was also said to be able to ex-
tinguish a candle placed on its altar by an unworthy supplicant.

For the Maya there was no division between the religious and the
secular aspects of life. For them, practical acts had a spiritual meaning, and religion was a practical affair. Sickness and a poor harvest
were the result of impiety; prestige was measured by piety, not
achievement, and the two elements were merged in a way that the
Western mind finds hard to grasp. In this sense it is almost an abstrac-
tion to speak of a priestly and a political hierachy in pre-Columbian
Yucatan. The Batab had many religious duties, and the Ah-kin had
political ones; the war chief lived a chaste life hedged in by ritual
laws while in office and he and his warriors fought for primarily religious reasons, collecting prisoners for human sacrifice. Then when
we reach the top of the old ruling class, the high priest or Ahuacan,
(Lord Serpent), and the temporal leader or Halach Uinic (True
Man), we find a similar blending of responsibility. The Ahuacan
could declare war. The Halach Uinic could be so holy that his subjects
were not allowed to see him, and he acted as priest in numerous matters; his title was translated first as Bishop and then as Governor in
the Motul Dictionary. These offices were replaced by the Spanish
Governor and the Spanish Bishop. Maya ambition was limited to the
village level, and there the old patterns continued. A man rose in
rank by membership in religious brotherhoods, introduced by the
foreigners but with local parallels; a Batab was expected to be devout,
aloof, unmercenary. So when the Mazehual could create his own
hierarchy he combined spiritual and political leadership in one man.
Again, this leader withdrew from his people. Bonifacio Novelo is
described as "seeking to rule in the cloister through superstitious
influence rather than openly with his colleagues in the field and the
cabinet," and similar statements have been made about his successors.
In spite of the fact that the Tatich was occasionally overthrown or
disobeyed by his military officers, it was said, "There can be no chief
greater than the Nohoch Tata [a later variant for Tatich]; his power
comes from God and not from man."

It is not only in social structure that we can find reflections of the
distant past. A hundred-odd villages and hamlets had sprung up
around the shrine at Chan Santa Cruz, wherever there was a cenote

and a stretch of decent land. Their names, as in Yucatan, referred to the water supply; there were several Chan Chens (Little Well), a Jesus Chen, and at least three called Yokdzonot (at the foot of the cenote). The saints were honored, too, with such names as Santa Rosa, San José, San Diego, and Santa Clara. The importance of these places, averaging from fifty to a thousand in population, must be emphasized, for they were the normal homes of most of the Cruzob; in the establishment of Chan Santa Cruz, another pattern was being followed, that of the pre-Columbian ceremonial center.

The ancient Maya sites of Yucatan, Chichen Itza, and Uxmal were not cities in the modern sense, and had relatively few domestic buildings. Instead, they were holy places or shrines, attracting great throngs for high holidays, but almost deserted the rest of the year. They had markets and some political functions, the priests were probably trained there, and labor gangs came to construct the temples, but all of this was on a part-time basis; the population lived in hamlets or villages spread across the land. There were two interruptions in this pattern. The first came from Mexico, where cities did exist; under Mexican domination, Mayapan was built as the capital of Yucatan. When Mayapan was overthrown by revolution and the city leveled, the Yucatecans returned to their earlier ways, dispersing throughout the countryside, to form towns of no more than five hundred houses and many smaller settlements. The second break was caused by the Spanish, who, after the Conquest, forced the Maya to abandon their hamlets and concentrate in towns, and over a period of years, the Spaniards built their cities. During the colonial period, however, economic necessity and Maya desires worked against the plans of the rulers, and hamlets were still being "abolished" in 1847. In as much as this dispersion succeeded, particularly among the Huits of the eastern frontier, it permitted the Maya to retain habits that they would enlarge upon with the coming of freedom under the Speaking Cross.

In other ways, too, Spanish desires assisted the retention of traditional custom. The Maya were excluded from the centers of the new towns and relegated to suburban villages, villages which were often miles away and largely self-governing. Because the towns had the priests and the churches, they exerted a strong attraction for the pious

Maya, and they functioned in the manner of the ceremonial centers. In evidence of this the curacy of Peto, a small provincial town, was worth 14,000 pesos a year, in comparison to the Bishop's salary of 8,000 pesos. Those pesos came from marriage, baptism, and mass fees, paid by the Maya who came into Peto from the back country. Although it is true that the priests were supposed to travel through their parishes, contemporary evidence shows that they seldom did. To a lesser extent, the custom of pilgrimages preserved the idea of a religious capital. The European background is well known, while the cult center of Chichen Itza drew the faithful from as far away as Guatemala, and the shrines of "Holy Cozumel" served pilgrims from beyond the Laguna de Términos. In 1847, pilgrimage fairs were held at Tizimin, Izamal, and Halacho. Thus the pre-Columbian settlement pattern was transmitted through the colonial period and available to the Cruzob.

The Cross reinforced the pattern. As the individual lineage crosses needed special shrine huts of their own to set them apart from daily life, so La Santísima required a holy city in which people didn't ordinarily live. The four crosses that separated each village from the wilderness were greatly elaborated upon at Chan Santa Cruz; there they were housed in thatch chapels, and these crosses marked off sacred ground. Horses, mules, and cattle were not allowed within this precinct. Chan Santa Cruz was built on the plan of a Ladino town, but not for town people, not for the town function of economic cooperation. The Tatich and a few of his functionaries were the only exceptions to the normal male work of corn farming, and in later years at least, the only permanent, as opposed to the rotating, in-habitants of the shrine city.* The others—generals, captains, Maestros Cantores and the rest—were part-time professionals, and all grew corn. Generals Aniceto Dzul, Román Pec, and Crecencio Puc ignored their stone "palace" at the shrine for the stronger attraction of their villages, except at holiday or muster time. Stone buildings were for

* A parallel might be sought between the Guardia barracks at Chan Santa Cruz, one for each village or group of villages of the Cruzob, and some of the "residential" buildings at older Maya sites. The barracks served many of the functions of the "Men's House" of Conquest times, except that they were concen-trated at the shrine rather than scattered through the villages, and this also would have been the case in the Classic Maya period.

prestige, and the Cruzob didn't really like them; they made no use of the many haciendas and the few towns in their domain. At Bacalar they erected thatch huts rather than live in perfectly good houses; they filled the church with the bodies of the former inhabitants and built a chapel of their own.

This village dispersion partially explains the many unopposed entradas to Chan Santa Cruz, entradas not to a normal capital or to a center of population, and also why the Cruzob needed time to rally after the shrine city was occupied. The village was the basic unit. It had its own chief, the captain of the local company; its own priest, the Maestro Cantor; its own church, a thatched duplication of the temple of the Speaking Cross on reduced scale, with a separate and sacred room, called La Gloria, for the village cross. The lineage cross cult had continued on pre-Caste War lines; each man had his own, as did each family and each village, and so on up to "The Most Holy" of all the Cruzob. The crosses were kept, as formerly, in Chan Iglesias or "Little Churches," the most important of them in the village churches. Some of these crosses grew to considerable holiness, challenging La Santísima itself.

An inherent function of the ceremonial center pattern is the exertion of some form of control over the dispersed population, the organization of service from the self-sufficient villages. This includes support of the priests, maintenance and construction of buildings, indoctrination of the young, and the retention of adult loyalty. Religion is the basic drive, but that drive must be focused and directed through day-by-day practice. Among the Cruzob, the company system acted against any movement of rival crosses or village independence. When members of a company lived in separate villages, it was the company that held the basic loyalty, the company that organized religious service; those who fought together prayed together. Justice was administered through the companies. Minor matters, quarreling, robbery, default of debt, wife-beating, vagrancy, lying, habitual drunkenness, lack of religious devotion, were corrected at the company level with the whip and exposure in the stocks. Refusal to work in the service of the Cross was passed up to the Commandants, whose correction was a stronger dose of the same. Capital crimes—murder, witchcraft, and association with the Dzulob—were matters for the Tatich; the condemned were hacked to death with machetes by several executioners (to make the act communal and prevent private revenge) under the sapodilla tree in the shrine plaza, the center of the Cruzob world.

We find, then, a strong family resemblance between the Cruzob and the pre-Columbian Maya worlds, in spite of the gap of four hundred years, the interposition of alien forms, and the development of a new, composite culture which La Farge has called "Recent Indian." This blurred facsimile of old patterns may be outlined as follows: (1) a speaking representation of God; (2) a social system based on divine sanction, with spiritual and political ranks merged, from supreme high priest to slave; (3) the ceremonial center settlement pattern; and (4) organization of village groups to construct and maintain the ceremonial center by rotation.

Details varied, but the basic structure was pre-Columbian. This does not prove folk memory, a Jungian theory, or racial necessity, and much less a reversion to savagery and paganism, as widely alleged by Ladino writers of the time. It was a restoration of ancient patterns of village life, in which the past was fossilized on a reduced and circumscribed level; Chan Santa Cruz was a living projection of that village mind. The Cruzob were a defensive society, their Cross making them the most successful of all the Maya who in different ways resisted the Ladino cultural attack that began in the 1830's. Conservative and reactionary, these Maya fought to preserve or regain the culture of their fathers, and in the process they brought to the surface old patterns, patterns either lost or kept hidden from the foreigner's eyes. The artistic and intellectual achievements of the ancient Maya, which had grown from such a village world, were gone beyond recall; but their religious and moral outlook, embodied in folkways that were the very fiber of their life, had endured to grow again.

As governor, judge, general, and pope, we leave Bonifacio Novelo in the fullness of power. For want of exact information, we can assume that he died naturally, at an advanced age, sometime around 1870, but definitely before 1880. The succession of the Tatich remains uncertain. As mentioned, the grandson of José María Barrera, himself Tatich, claimed it had gone directly from his grand-

father to his father Agustín Barrera. We know that this was not
the case through a number of visitors to Chan Santa Cruz; and after
Novelo's death the man most likely to have held the office, according
to documents kept by the Cruzob, was Juan de la Cruz, the original
Secretary to the Cross. Military leaders were more important in the
eyes of the outside world, and our record of them is more complete.
General Bernal Ken was replaced as Commander of the Plaza by
Crescencio Poot, victor of Tekax, his name first appearing in the correspondence of the Governor of British Honduras in 1883. The following year, Poot took the surprising step of opening treaty negotiations. There is no record of skirmishes, crop failure, or epidemic at
this time; perhaps he was simply another old soldier ready for peace.
At any event, the delegates, including Aniceto Dzul and Juan Chuc,
weren't going to sign anything more than a recognition of status quo.
The terms were as follows:

> José Crescencio Poot shall continue to be Governor of Chan
> Santa Cruz until his death.
> At the death of Poot a new Governor shall be conceded to Chan
> Santa Cruz subject to the approval of the Government of Yucatan.
> The Government of Yucatan will not send any official to govern
> Chan Santa Cruz without the consent of the inhabitants.
> Mutual extradition of criminals.
> Under the above conditions the people of Chan Santa Cruz
> acknowledge the Mexican government.

Conceived along the lines of the Chichenha treaty, this was to
formalize the existing peace, with the Cruzob trading submission for
a guarantee against invasion and retaining complete local authority.
So it was signed on January 11, 1884, by Juan Chuc and General
Teodosio Canto, Vice Governor of Yucatan, at Government House in
Belize, and afterwards the delegates sat for a joint portrait photograph. It was all very fine, a tribute to General Canto's years of
negotiations; but later there were bad words and on January 30 Poot
wrote the Crown Administrator that Canto had gotten drunk and
insulted his delegates, and that the treaty was canceled. Considering
what was to follow, this sounds like the work of Dzul, not Canto.

On August 22, 1885, Aniceto Dzul staged a coup d'état, killing
his superior, Crescencio Poot, along with Juan Bautista Chuc, two

other generals, two commandants, and sixty-seven soldiers, making himself Tata Chikiuc. It was from this slaughter that Leandro Poot fled to the vicinity of Chichén Itzá, to live out his life in the neutral forest, fearing his enemies of both races, surviving to be interviewed by E. H. Thompson some years later, and to give the quoted account of his father's wars.

And after ten years of unofficial truce, there was again fighting on the Yucatecan frontier. Désiré Charnay heard, while traveling to Valladolid, that "the savages had recommenced the war of extermination." Thompson reported that the troubles were provoked by outlaws or chicleros (the terms were synonymous in those days) who came on a Cruzob settlement and raped the women while their men were absent in the fields. On February 6, 1886, a reported four to five hundred Maya burned the village of Tixhualahtun, with the defending force of settlers retreating to Peto, seven miles to the southwest. The Cruzob went on to Tekom, another suburb, then attacked the often-destroyed outpost of Dzonotchel; but there they failed in the face of reinforced, determined settlers, and after a fire-fight of several hours with casualties on both sides, they pulled back into the forest, leaving the trail booby-trapped behind them. A sapling, armed with thorns that had been left in the decomposing body of a fox, was bent over and triggered by a cord across the trail. When released it would impale the victim in the leg, causing a small wound, which would fester for months, resisting the treatment of that day. E. H. Thompson, in reporting the use of this trap, spoke from personal experience; he was poisoned by one near Dzonotchel and almost lost his leg.

There were skirmishes along the frontier for several months, in which the white soldiers were roughly treated; and a general alarm spread throughout Yucatan, where the Caste War had been considered a matter of history. Congress authorized the purchase of 1,000 percussion rifles for the militia, who were using old flintlocks against British-supplied Lee-Enfields. Charnay was once turned out of his bed in the middle of the night by panic-stricken women at Valladolid. A signal bomb had been fired, the call to arms sounded, and with only a few hundred poorly armed elderly militia, the population expected a second massacre. A mob fled to the parish church for protection. Morning light brought the discovery that the rumor had been spread by a drunken soldier, but in such an atmosphere, Charnay gave up hope of visiting the ruins of the eastern forest. Colonel Daniel Traconis, the frontier commander for the last twenty years, had promised him an escort, but the Colonel was otherwise occupied, sending out heavy patrols for the next few months. Don Anis, as Aniceto Dzul was called, made no further moves, and the frontier returned to its normal uneasy and watchful peace.

The position of the Tatich during these events is speculation. In his sermon written two years after the coup against Poot, Juan de la Cruz speaks of the murder of his assistant, Juan Baptista Chi (probably a mistake for Chuc), but the possessive pronoun could refer either to God or to de la Cruz. If this was a question of a peace versus a war party, as seems likely, then the Tatich was definitely for war by the date of the sermon. Still, he lacked support from Don Anis; he was later reported to have said, "There are very few generals that come [here], because none of the generals believes in any of my ordinances, and the generals say that there is no truth whatever in my orders." At about the same time he said:

> Is there perhaps another God? Tell me, because I am the Owner of the sky and the earth, because, my children, maybe you can postpone the judgment over you here in the world, the last day of Final Judgment, [when] I will raise all those to whom I have given life and you can raise those that you want to judge, O creatures of the world.

The Tatich's voice, complaining and threatening, tells us of the break-up of the old authority. Don Anis had moved to his village of San Pedro, some twelve miles south of Chan Santa Cruz, and surrounded himself with his henchmen, while his second-in-command, General Román Pec, lived at Chunox. La Santísima was no longer the undisputed national symbol: another cross had appeared at Tulum. It had the unique distinction of being under the control of a woman, María Uicab, reportedly called Patron Saint and queen, who caused the cross to speak and interpreted its voice to the people. Women had always played a minor role in the Maya religion, and had been banned from all services of a pagan origin; this must have been a case of an unusually strong personality breaking through that tradition in troubled times. Tulum, three miles inland from the ruins of the same name, was a northern provincial village, set off from the center of Cruzob population; but it had a particularly holy reputation. In the Books of Chilam Balam it was called the entrance to a tunnel that led under the sea, the refuge of the Red King of Chichen Itza, and was therefore a place of pilgrimage in both ancient and modern times. The first news of the priestess came from the Traconis raid of 1871, and William Miller, on his visit to Chan Santa Cruz in 1888, heard that this cross, rather than La Santísima, had the authority to appoint military officers, and that it had ordered the execution of a missionary priest who had landed on the eastern coast. Naturally, there was more to this than María Uicab. Letters from the Governor of Belize were addressed to the Commandant of Tulum, one Luciano Pech, in which he is apparently given equal rank with Aniceto Dzul.

Aniceto Dzul had other problems. He went blind in one eye, and executed a man and a woman, saying that they were a pair of witches who had cursed him, and this seemed to help. There was another and more exotic practitioner of the black arts in Cruzob territory at this time, a Voodoo *Obeah-man*, a Negro laborer from Belize, who added the demons of Africa to the Christian devil, the Maya winds, and other unpleasant creatures of the night. Being an English subject, the witch-doctor was deported rather than killed. In replacing a theocratic government with a militaristic one, Dzul lacked divine backing. Juan de la Cruz had made the point that no one need serve the generals without pay, there having been no question of payment for service to God even if that service was directed by a general. As Crecencio Poot had turned for support to Yucatan, now Dzul asked, in 1887, unsuccessfully, for admission to the British Empire. Decay was evident in this, a loss of belief in La Santísima, the keystone of the Cruzob system, with the inevitable civil strife among petty, superstitious, tyrannical chiefs.

Perhaps geography must take the major blame for this dissolution. Maya farmers had worked the scant soil of Yucatan for at least four thousand years, adapting themselves to local conditions, succeeding in the bone-dry Chenes and in the barren north; but significantly, the ancients had left no ruins of any size in what had become Cruzob territory. The pyramids of Coba looked down on disputed forest, only fifteen miles from the white garrison at Chemax, and the other available site, walled Tulum, had been supported by fishing and trade rather than the fertility of its soil. There were a scattering of fishing villages along the east coast at the time of the Conquest, but the interior of what had been the provinces of Uaymil and southern Ecab was, with the exception of a few villages, uninhabited. Here were high rain forest and open plains of savanna grass, where the wind rustled and flamingo nested; scrub forest, with its tough grassy undergrowth; mangrove and salt swamps extending from Ascensión to Chetumal Bay; fresh water lakes from Chicancanab to Bacalar, which, lacking drainage outlets, merged with their neighbors in continuous swamp, a desolate area called "horse bones" after the animals lost there. All of this was country to hide in, not to live on. The Conquest towns of Bacalar and Chetumal near the mouth of the Rio Hondo were carriers and middlemen for the important Honduras trade. Between those places and the towns of fertile Cochuah, Chunhuhub, Kampocolche, and Tabi, the country was described as empty.

The Cruzob came from inland farming stock. They knew little of the ocean, and a dangerous lee coast was no place to learn. The white settlers on Isla Mujeres, three miles off shore, felt safe when they saw campfires on the mainland at night. A number of amphibious raids had been made against the Cruzob, and Mexican warships infrequently made cruises, so there were no coastal villages. The modern settlement of Tulum was three miles inland from the ancient ruin. There was a small amount of fishing from canoes. The village of Muyil, below Tulum, supported itself in this way on the inland lakes and waterways of that region; the more protected stretches of the three bays—Ascensión, Espíritu Santo, and Chetumal—were occasionally worked, and there was always canoe traffic on Lake Bacalar. Trade existed with Belize, but spasmodically, and controlled by the Cross, carried by soldiers, with no room for a middleman north of the Hondo, Corozal serving that need to the south.

Farming was the only means of livelihood for the Cruzob. The Mazehualob knew that the ruins of the Old Ones marked good soil, and they took the best that was available. Northern Uaymil contains a number of small ruins, one of them at the Cruzob shrine itself; and so the old settlement patterns were repeated, the villages centering on Chan Santa Cruz, spreading north to San Antonio Muyil, south to Petcacab, and west to Tabi, limited there by the enemy. This was their inheritance, their promised land, and a hard land it was. They lived at subsistence level, at the mercy of the dry year, corn fungus, hail, and hurricanes, with no reserves to fall back on, under the recurring lash of smallpox, cholera, and whooping cough.

The estimated 40,000 survivors of the Caste War were reduced to half that number fifteen years later, and in spite of peace were again halved, to approximately 10,000, by the last decade of the century. Efforts were made to halt the decline. The marriage age was reduced from sixteen to thirteen for girls, from eighteen to fifteen for boys, by order of the General; bachelors and young widows were not allowed to remain in those states very long. A close watch was kept on the Hondo to prevent the drain of refugees to Belize; raids were sent to bring them back regardless of what the English said. Militarily, this meant a sixty-man garrison now camped in the overgrown ruins of Bacalar; there were only one hundred and fifty at the shrine. The frontiers were weakly held. Theobert Maler explored Coba in 1891 without incident, and E. H. Thompson traveled to Lake Chichancanab about the same time. Socially, it meant that the Cross was failing.

Dzul's interest in joining the British Empire added to the problems of gunrunning and border disputes which stood between London and Mexico City. The British Foreign Office was on excellent terms with the Díaz regime. There were major and very profitable English investments in Mexico, and Whitehall was eager to settle what was to them an obscure border problem. But any final solution was bound to involve Mexican military action against the Cruzob, and as this could result in retaliation against English subjects in Belize, the British Colonial Office became an interested if less enthusiastic party to the negotiations. There was the further difficulty of territorial waters. Mexican ships could enter Chetumal Bay only by sailing through English waters, which the English were willing to allow as a courtesy, but not as a binding precedent. With Mexican pride, and the Colonial Office's demands for a peaceful solution, progress on the treaty was slow.

A Mexican customs cutter appeared temporarily on the river,

interfering with trade; and to Maya complaints the Governor of Belize could only reply that he was powerless to halt the legitimate action of a friendly power, and advise the Cruzob to avoid conflict with the Yucatecans. Worse was to come. On July 8, 1893, the Spencer-Mariscal treaty was signed between Mexico and Great Britain, and emissaries were sent to notify the Maya. Dzul had escaped these troubles in death (apparently of natural causes, since no one bragged of it), several years before. His successor was Román Pec, who lived in the village of Chanquec, north of Chan Santa Cruz. There was little General Pec could do. He must have realized that he was being forced into a corner, and that with English guns and bullets denied him, he would be at the mercy of the Yucatecans. But he had no intention of giving up. In the sermon written in 1887 La Santísima had warned:

I am therefore calling you one by one to punish you with fifty [lashes] because you are talking about mixing with the enemy. Although you see how the enemy exhausts me, you say that no harm will come to you through him; [but] I am advising you, my children, don't say that; it is what [the] enemy says, it is what you say because he has money, and not what my true Lord says; . . . but even so I will not abandon you into his hands, my children.

When his second-in-command, Crescencio Puc, invited a Catholic bishop to Chan Santa Cruz, Román Pec had the bishop turned back at Bacalar and executed Puc. Two of his commissioners were killed on suspicion of talking peace with Mexican authorities in Belize. With the machete he attempted to keep his people from lusting after the fleshpots of civilization, and the machete cut him down in December 1895—another coup, and Felipe Yama became General. A short period of grace kept English supplies available. The Yucatecan state government refused to accept the frontier of the Spencer-Mariscal treaty; it didn't ratify it until June of 1895, and smuggling continued. Then, on January 22, 1898, a tubby little barge was towed into the mouth of the Rio Hondo by a steamship, and at three in the afternoon it was anchored several hundred feet from the Mexican shore, off a point called Cayo Obispo. The steamer left, the barge stayed, and the Hondo was closed. And to the west, there was a stirring on the long silent frontier. Ladino soldiers occupied the ruins of Ichmul and began pushing cautious patrols through the neutral jungle.

These signs of a storm rumbling on the horizon added intensity to the great fiesta of the Holy Cross on May 3, 1900—dissension was forgotten in the common uneasiness, buried under common piety, and solidarity returned with fear. The companies assembled with their offerings and families and threw themselves into the elaborate series of interlocking rites, led by the Tatich, Pedro Pascual Barrera, in praise and thanksgiving to La Santísima. The traditional food was displayed to the double of the Cross and, thus offered, was used for the feast; then the dancing, religious and secular, the bullfights, the mass, and the novenas. On the final day, at sunset, the double of the Speaking Cross was brought out of the temple and a procession formed behind it: the Tatich, General Felipe May and his officers, the scribes, the Maestros Cantores, wives of the priests, officers, and soldiers, some 3,000 in all. From the plaza they filed to each of the four chapels that housed the boundary Crosses, and then to the fifth direction, the center of Chan Santa Cruz, the temple of the Speaking Cross, to kneel and pray. It was the last salute.

Twelve

General Bravo
1899–1912

IN MID-OCTOBER OF 1899, a seventy-year-old man of slight stature, with a drooping white mustache and a cold look in his eye, disembarked at the pier of Progreso. This was Ignacio Bravo, General in the Mexican Army and a crony of the dictator Díaz. In spite of age and appearance, he had been sent to do what so many generals had tried to do and failed: to conquer the rebel Maya and silence the Speaking Cross. He was a patient, determined, methodical man.

There had been many changes in Yucatan in the thirty-two years since Cepeda Peraza had destroyed the last of Maximilian's Empire in the shattered streets of Mérida, startling changes, all based on two causes—henequen and Díaz. Cepeda Peraza survived his victory only two years, and they were not peaceful ones; a reactionary revolt needed crushing; honest, intelligent liberals had to be found to run the government. He founded a literary institute, a teachers' college, and a library, and had many other projects for the future. But all of his wars and years had left their mark, and he died on March 3, 1869. What came after was not so heroic. A brother, Colonel José Cepeda Peraza, was interim Governor, followed by an elected liberal, Manuel Cirol, who served his two-year term but was then overthrown by the outs under Colonel Francisco Cantón. President Juárez sent an army brigade to crush this revolt. When its commander discovered that it was only a local squabble and not an attempt against the regime, he promoted Cantón to general and gave him the Eastern Brigade. The commander, General Vicente Mariscal, remained as Governor, until he could seat the surviving candidates who still wanted office. On his departure, Cantón marched again, and a second Mexican General, Guillermo Palomino, again re-established order. And so the Yucatecans played at their familiar game of politics, anarchy, and petty warfare. The year 1875 was noted as having passed without a single revolt. This was also the picture in Mexico, particularly after the death of Juárez; and the desires of an exhausted nation were met by a strongman, Don Porfirio Díaz, whose party gained Yucatan at the end of 1876. Politics of the manifesto variety were no longer tolerated, revolutionaries could expect to be shot "while attempting to escape," under the unwritten but well-understood *ley fuga*, and peace came at last.

From this time forward, Yucatecan governors succeeded one another after calm four-year terms, with decorous well-arranged elections and without bloodshed or unnecessary emotions: José María Iturralde, 1877 to 1878; Manuel Romero Ancona, 1878 to 1882; then the deserving generals, Octavio Rosado, Guillermo Palomino, 1882 to 1890; the old hero of Tihosuco, Colonel Daniel Traconis, 1890 to 1894; the intellectual, Carlos Peón, 1894 to 1898; and finally the former troublemaker, General Francisco Cantón, 1898 to 1902. If a happy country is one without history, then Yucatan was happy, and certainly the gente decente were, sitting comfortably on the right end of a future spelled henequen.

The Caste War had destroyed the sugar plantations of the south. Indio raids made reconstruction a risky business, and the hacendados were left with the barren, dry, rocky northwest of the peninsula. It was rocky, but it was ideal for henequen. New mercantile and agricultural fields were opening up abroad, international fleets were growing as fast as shipyards could launch them, and they all needed cordage. So rows of henequen were planted, rows upon rows, fields upon fields, district after district, until the state was one vast cleared plantation. Even the cornfields were gone, and a country whose economy had been primarily devoted to corn growing would be forced to import corn to feed its people. The old problems were solved. After many attempts, machines were developed to replace the primitive wooden hand raspers. The machine—whose inventors fought long and bitterly over the patents, profits, and honor—did for Yucatan what the cotton gin had done for the American South. Human arms were replaced by oxen, then by steam, and the fiber could be taken from the leaves rapidly and cheaply. The second problem had been capital, the cash to cover expenses while waiting the seven long years before the first leaves could be cut; and this was supplied by a New York bank through a Mérida agent at nine per cent. Díaz had created peace, and the industry flourished, doubling or tripling production every five years: exports rose from less than six million kilos in 1875 to forty-three million in 1885 and eighty-one million in 1900.

The market was flooded around 1880, but then another machine created a new demand. McCormick's mechanical reaper had proved a success in the United States, and further possibilities were opened up with the addition of a self-binding device, which wrapped the wheat in wire. But the wire often snagged in the machine and got into the feed, killing cattle. Sisal binder twine was the solution, and for Yucatan the horizon was unlimited. All was not sweetness and light. The original agents, following an old Yucatecan custom, had discovered a two-way profit: selling the necessary machinery to the hacendados, taking their pay in henequen (at their own price), and then reselling to the United States. There was now a hacendado of hacendados. Debt peonage had become high finance, with the real masters sitting around the conference table of Thebaud Brothers, New York bankers. Yet in this, Yucatan was luckier than the rest of Mexico, and the haciendas themselves remained in local hands. The monopoly continued with occasional resistance, but with the continuously expanding market there was profit enough for all, or at least for those who made the laws.

And a great profit it was. Over seventy-three million pesos worth of henequen were exported from 1895 to 1900, $22,616,432 in the latter year alone. Yucatan, which had been one of Mexico's poorest provinces, became one of the richest. The gente decente who had timidly gone to Havana in the 1850's could now elbow their way confidently past bowing waiters to the roulette tables of San Remo with the silver-Peruvians, the cattle-Argentines, and the steel-Americans. French lessons became popular in Mérida, according to newspaper advertisements, and a society column regularly described the gay life abroad. At this period the Bishop rode out in his new carriage, described as a delicate and exquisite work of art plated with gold, encrusted with jewels, made by a Parisian goldsmith in imitation of the carriage given by the Czar to Pope Leo XIII, at a cost of 35,000 francs. Mérida blossomed. The streets were paved with macadam, had electricity to light them at night, and were traversed by horse-drawn streetcars, numbered in the scientific way—all of this in advance of Mexico City. A row of gaudy Victorian mansions sprang up at the northern end of 69th Street, as the newly rich old families migrated away from the plaza. No more churches were constructed; instead they built for the Government. The Palacio de Gobierno was remodeled, and a Palacio Federal was erected, and as the latest word in progress, they built a scientific prison and named it after Juárez.

By the 1880's, there were 20,767 men listed as indebted servants; together with their families they numbered over 100,000, or a third of the population. The breakdown by districts of those held in peonage reflected henequen production rates—highest in the northwest, lowest along the frontier. Valladolid counted 974 "servants" and Peto 321, as opposed to 2,564 at Acanceh, and 2,036 at Hunucma, both previously unimportant villages but now in the center of the henequen zone. Three factors were involved here; henequen grew best in the west, there was a general population decline in the east, and the frontier was no place to hold a Maya against his will. Another interesting fact shown by the census rolls is the geographical redistribution of the Ladino-Maya population balance. The Maya were reduced from seventy-five to sixty per cent of the population by the Caste War, when their greatest concentration had been in the east and southeast. For economic and security reasons, this was reversed. The former Maya country around Valladolid, Peto, and Tekax now had more Ladinos than natives, while hacienda requirements in the northwest maintained the old ratio of three to one. Loss to the rebels had been less in that district, and the demand for labor drew and held refugees and prisoners of war. As the historian Baqueiro put it, "All the state is for henequen, and outside of it is nothing." "Outside" meant the frontier, where the earlier crops were still raised on land unsuitable for henequen; the state's twenty-three per cent acreage of corn and beans, the four per cent of sugar, by

1881, were worked by an eighteen per cent remnant of the population—which explains why it was necessary to import corn, and why a Mérida hotel dinner could cost the equivalent of from ten to twenty days' salary for a field hand.

Yet there were not enough hands. A number of German families settled around Santa Elena during the Empire, but they quickly moved to Mérida where the money was. A shipload of Italians was tried but failed. Puerto Ricans and Formosans came, as did immigrant Cubans. History was reversed with the arrival of rebel Yaqui Indians from Sonora, who were transported and sold to hacendados; they were still citizens of the Mexican Republic, not slaves; but their indenture was as binding and their exile from climate, language, and home more complete than the Maya had known in Cuba. Most of these people, prisoner or free, quickly learned the debt system. Men were kept in barracks and marched to work by armed and mounted guards, encouraged by mayordomos with whips, marched back, and locked in at night. The easygoing days of the past were gone. Whatever charm there had been to hacienda life was over. These places were vast agricultural factories with tens of thousands of acres under cultivation, run along scientific lines, geared for total output. One thousand henequen leaves, the harvest of a ten-hour day, were worth fifty to seventy-five centavos to the worker. A good mayordomo was one who got the greatest production at the least expense.

The lumbering, creaking oxcart was outmoded by small Decauville rails, which were laid between the rows of henequen plants; mule-drawn trolley platforms transported the cut leaves to the rasping machine, and moved bundles of extracted fiber to the drying yards, to the press, and to the local railroad. The railroads are a story in themselves. Both wide and narrow gauge, they were built after countless setbacks and bankruptcies, starting from Progreso to Mérida, down to Ticul, Tecoh, and Motul. Monopolies were granted and then revoked, the competing lines bought up by agents of International Harvester as one more whip over independent hacendados, and they eventually reached to Peto, Valladolid, and Campeche, along the old routes of the camino real. They made big production possible by providing cheap transportation of the crop to the Progreso wharf. Progreso, directly north of Mérida on the coast, was founded in 1870 as a more convenient port, replacing Sisal. Passengers were strictly second-class to the bales of henequen.

A necessary adjunct of the railroad was the telegraph, the lines following the rails; and for further ease of communication there was a telephone network in Mérida. Modern windmills were introduced, the first at Progreso, where the sea breeze caught the attention of a German, then rapidly throughout the country; multibladed sails mounted on steel towers, pumping underground water into cisterns and cattle tanks, replaced the cattle-driven water hoist and the human water-carrier. A thousand rasping machines, many of them steam-powered, rendered the henequen fiber, and improved presses reduced the bulk of the bales for shipment—all of this eliminating hand labor, releasing it for work that could not be mechanized: cultivation and cutting in the fields.

The Caste War and the Cruzob had not been completely forgotten. After the trouble of 1887, when the state legislature had bought a thousand new percussion rifles, July 30 was declared a holiday in memory of the victims of Tepich. And a society was formed, the Sociedad Patriótica Yucateca, to foment a new campaign against the Cruzob, insist on the old frontier with Belize, and ransom the prisoners.[*] Unfortunately, with all the money to be made, not many people cared, and they were always having to reorganize anew and had trouble collecting funds. The society kept a sword of Toledo steel, encased in an ornate silver sheath, donated by General Mei-jueiro in 1878; it was a sword of honor for the future conqueror of Chan Santa Cruz. Legends grew up about that nest of barbarity and superstition; the Speaking Cross itself was said to be of gold and silver studded with emeralds, a gift to the first Bishop of Yucatan from the cathedral of Toledo.

Finally, definite action was taken. In 1895 the state government voted funds to support a military force, if the federal government should decide on a campaign; and in that year General Lorenzo García occupied Dzonotchel with two regular battalions and three com-

[*] On November 15, 1878, J. Antonio Alayon, secretary of the society, published a poster to raise money to ransom prisoners of the Cruzob. Fifty-seven prisoners are listed by name, 13 male and 44 female, a proportion suggesting that women and girls had a better chance of surviving. None of the names can be associated with known military figures.

panies of National Guardsmen. There matters rested for three years, when a fresh impulse caused the occupation and fortification of the long-abandoned ruins which had been Ichmul, Tihosuco, and Sacalaca. One-hundred-and-fifty-man garrisons were maintained at these places, joined by regular patrols; but there was no aggressive action. This had been blamed on graft, inertia, and timidity, or praised as an attempt to win over the Cruzob by gradual, peaceful means. Whatever the reason or combination of reasons, supplies were accumulated, roads built, experience was gained, and a firm base for future operations was established.

To match this pressure on the west side of the rebel forest were the penetrations along the north and east coast. Concessions had been granted to two organizations, La Compañía Agrícola and La Compañía Colonizadora, to exploit the immense tract of empty forest lying to the north of Cruzob territory. The former was given the coast extending from the lonely pyramid landmark at El Cuyo east to Cape Catoche, including rich salt beds; the latter, a subsidiary of the Bank of London and Mexico, received some 4,000 square miles, from the Cape down to a short distance from Tulum. These lordly grants were made without regard to the scattered Pacífico Maya in the area, in the belief that company guards could take care of that problem. The Cruzob were another matter. In April of 1899, armed Maya warned a party from the Compañía Colonizadora against building a railroad into the interior from their base of Puerto Morelos. A small fort was constructed there, and the ancient walls of Tulum would be used for their old purpose of defense three times in the years ahead. But the promoters went on with their plans. Within a year there were 1,000 workers at Puerto Morelos—Negroes, Koreans, Mexicans, bossed by Cubans who had been displaced by the Spanish-American War—and similar numbers were engaged by La Compañía Agrícola, planting cotton, bananas, sugar cane, and collecting cocoa, chicle, and salt.

The Mexican Navy was sent to guarantee the investment, and to prepare the way for a final blow at Chan Santa Cruz. Commodore José María de la Vega, with the dual rank of Brigadier General for purposes of land operations, commanded; port facilities were prepared, and detachments were landed at Puerto Morales, at the end of a sand spit on Ascensión Bay (Campamento General Vega), and at a place called Xcalak on the deserted peninsula that formed the Bay of Chetumal, near the English frontier. It was as a part of this naval activity that orders were sent to a young officer, Othón Blanco, on a school ship in the Pacific Ocean, recalling him to General Staff headquarters at Mexico City. He was there instructed to prepare plans for the construction of a fort at the mouth of the Rio Hondo. As a naval officer, the idea of an armed barge seemed more attractive

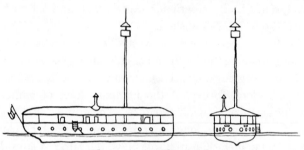

The pontoon *Chetumal*

to him, both for defense and for use against river smugglers, and this was approved. The barge, named *Chetumal* after the bay, was built in New Orleans to his specifications: sixty-six feet long, twenty-four feet wide, two and one-half feet in draft, with a ninety-ton displacement—a fat, tubby thing, with a single mast supporting an armored crows nest and the deck lined with a protective bulwark, gun ports, and a machine gun. The *Chetumal* was towed to Campeche, commissioned as a ship of the Mexican Navy, and, with Blanco in command, towed around the peninsula to Belize; the crew of thirteen was completed during a stop at Isla Mujeres. While the *Chetumal* was given dry-dock repairs at the English colonial capital, Blanco tried his hand at diplomacy, explaining his role as customs official and the arms inspection he would maintain on the river which the lumbermen and merchants had long considered their personal artery of trade, but which was now once more an international boundary. It was not a popular mission, but Blanco seems to have managed well, and he secured an English steamer to haul the *Chetumal* on the last lap of its one-way voyage. At three-thirty in the afternoon of January 22, 1898, the anchor was dropped three hundred yards from the Mexican bank of the Rio Hondo, near where the river met the bay. The *Chetumal* would stay there until her task was done, and she is there today, the ribs of her wreck showing above the water at low tide.

Besides checking for more than a normal amount of guns and ammunition in the canoes headed upstream, and counting the rafts of mahogany logs drifting down (most of which he knew had been stolen from Mexican territory), Blanco had been ordered to collect all the information he could on the various tribes. He took advantage of an offer by the English Governor to join in an inspection tour up the Hondo, remaining in his cabin until they had passed the Cruzob lookouts at Chac and Santa Lucia. The Governor's itinerary ended at the head of navigation, Agua Blanca, but the Mexican officer, against good advice, decided to continue overland for a visit to the Pacífico village of Icaiche. Together with a guide, he followed a small-gauge track used to move mahogany logs and then a foot trail through the roughest country he had ever seen, where the only source of water was scummy, weed-choked swamps. He realized that this was the only way in or out and that he would never be able to find his way back alone. Pacíficos or no, the Maya gave him a bad time until the arrival of their chief, General Tamay. In conference, Blanco was able to satisfy them that the troop movements to the north weren't directed against Icaiche, and heard their side of the English complaints about raids—that they were simply defending their own land. The commandant rode back to the river with an escort, free of the anxiety he felt coming in, and with a promise by Tamay to visit the barge, which would lead to a new treaty and a guarantee of peace in the future.

Hearing repeated threats of an attack by the Cruzob on his barge, Blanco decided on a second and more dangerous reconnaissance. Posing as a merchant, he took his quartermaster as interpreter and paddled up to the village of Santa Rosa in a canoe filled with merchandise. The local garrison accepted them at face value and passed them on, first to Chac, then up that marshy stream to the lake and across to what had once been the city of Bacalar. Not wishing to press his luck or seem overcurious, Blanco stayed with the canoe, while his interpreter wandered through the ruins, returning to report that

most of the inhabitants were gone, called north to Chan Santa Cruz
to reinforce the companies under attack from Yucatan. They quickly
disposed of their goods and headed home. Blanco, with his light skin
and blue eyes, was passed off as an Englishman, which explained his
inability to speak Maya. He sketched a map of what he saw, noting
the three cannons emplaced at Chac, and other fortifications. He also
did what he could through the interpreter to reassure the Cruzob
that the barge wasn't hostile and that the river was open to free passage, following Commodore Vega's policy of peaceful persuasion.
His superior had reason to be well pleased with the work of Commandant Blanco, who would one day become an admiral himself.

The crew of the *Chetumal* had meanwhile been clearing the bank
close to their anchorage, erecting a defensive log rampart near the
water's edge. After a time they were given leave to visit the nearby
English town of Corozal, to meet their long-exiled countrymen and
court the girls of that place. On the encouragement of Blanco, some
of these ex-Yucatecans settled in the clearing on the north side of the
Hondo, under the protection of the barge's guns. The settlement was
called Cayo Obispo, and it eventually grew to become the capital of
a new territory under its present name of Chetumal.

This, then, was the military background with which General Bravo
was presented: the Cruzob had been gradually and more or less
peacefully encircled by sea, isolated from English supplies, and put
under pressure from the west. The plan was for a double thrust: the
occupation of Bacalar by forces under the direct control of Rear Admiral Angel Ortiz Monasterio, and a central drive to Chan Santa
Cruz under Bravo. About six months after his arrival in Yucatan,
Bravo was at the forward camp of Okop, inspecting and preparing
his first move. This place had been the focus of Cruzob attack, but
now there was a lull, a period of negotiation from June to October
of 1900. Bravo hoped to make a peaceful settlement; the Maya attempted to ransom prisoners. There were other reasons for waiting.
On September 15, the Governor of Yucatan, Francisco Cantón, and
various notables got up early to take the first train from Mérida to
Peto, ninety-five miles of track, twenty years in construction. After
the officials had arrived at Peto, inaugurated the new station, and
driven the last spike, General Bravo took the sledge hammer and

drove the first spike of the projected Ferrocarriles Sudorientales de Yucatán, to be driven straight through the Cruzob jungle to Ascensión Bay. The truce period was also the rainy season, bad for fighting and impossible for road-building.

There had been considerable talk of corruption under General García—complaints of rancid lard, polluted grain supplied with kickbacks for those in charge, inefficiency, and preventable sickness—and if most of these conditions would continue under Bravo, the inefficiency at least was at an end. Taking over the camps of his predecessor, he built up supplies at Saban; and around October of 1900, as the rains slackened and the ground began to dry up, he jumped off from Okop, heading southeast. This was not to be like any entrada of the past, a five-day march by a guerrilla of riflemen and pack mules, with a battle, a burning, and a return. Bravo was going to stay. Invasion was almost secondary to the construction of what was intended to become a right-of-way for the railroad. There were four federal battalions (the First, Sixth, Twenty-Second, and Twenty-Eighth), Yucatecan National Guard units, and five breech-loading cannons; but rather than acting in a tactical sense, they formed an elaborate bodyguard for the engineers, the surveyors, and the 400 laborers. Through October and November these men pushed southeast, cutting and burning trees, clearing the bush, leveling the ground, moving at about ten miles per month. The soldiers were in almost permanent camp, living behind regular defenses, patrolling the road, in contact with base camp through the telegraph line that followed their advance. This mass of power offered no weak point to the Cruzob, who sniped and awaited their chance, traditionally avoiding open battle. A diversion was tried. The Cruzob of San Antonio Muyil enlisted the aid of one of the unallied Pacífico tribes of the north, from the village of Yokdzonot, and began killing and burning around Tizimin. It was a small and unsuccessful effort, easily crushed by local National Guardsmen.

Through December, January, and February the road continued. Santa María to Hobompich, five miles, two barricades easily taken; Hobompich to Tabi, ten miles, three barricades; modern repeating rifles against muzzle-loaders, the crack of their fusillade beating down a stuttering defensive fire. To the Cruzob there was a horror in this new type of war, a power they couldn't face: the slow, deliberate movement, the cleared road pointing at the shrine city, straight and wide through forest untouched for forty years. Between Tabi and Nohpop, a distance of ten miles, they defended twenty-two barricades, fighting in the only way they knew, with the weapons they had; there the fieldpieces were unlimbered for the first time against them, shrapnel ripped through barricades and flesh, and the end had come. They dragged their wounded and their dead back into the bush and scattered. Their numbers had been estimated at from 3,000 to 1,500 at the beginning of the campaign; now it was said that no more than 800 obeyed the generals Pat, May, and Ek, 200 men having been lost in combat and the rest by desertion. Prisoners were starving. An epidemic of measles was the final blow, and the Cruzob ceased to resist. General Bravo continued to act the engineer, ignoring the lack of resistance as he had ignored the attacks. The last skirmish was on March 23, and though he knew himself to be within fifteen miles of Chan Santa Cruz, he made no immediate move to take possession of the place. Patiently he continued his road, on through the villages of Nohpop, Sabacche, and Chankik. On April 17 an *arriero* went looking for a lost mule, which reveals the confidence felt by this time, and stumbled onto some houses in the forest, gradually realizing, as he walked along a deserted street into a plaza, that this was the legendary shrine. He reported to his commander, but Bravo was not a man to hurry; he made his formal entrance some two weeks later, on the fourth or fifth of May 1901. May 5 was a national holiday; May 3, the Day of the Holy Cross.

About the time Bravo was leaving Saban, a fleet of four steamships had sailed from Veracruz with several battalions of infantry, which, together with elements out of Progreso, joined the forces of General and Rear Admiral Angel Ortiz Monasterio. Supported by the various east coast bases, these units landed at the mouth of the Hondo on March 10, ending Blanco's lonely vigil; when they got their shore legs, they arranged for canoes and headed upstream. The colonial cannons taken from the walls of Bacalar to defend Chac were not used against them, the Cruzob having heard about machine guns, and that garrison was taken under fire as it fled to the south side of the river. Monasterio sent his forces on up the Chaak to the lake and across to Bacalar on March 21. The soldiers found a single native, guarding a Santo in a thatched hut. The twin objectives of generations of generals were taken, and the Caste War was ended.

When the telegrapher in Mérida decoded the good news with the unbelievable date line that spelled victory on the fifth of May, a grateful state congress voted the erection of a statue of President Díaz in thanks for his assistance; honorary citizenship was bestowed upon General Bravo, and they renamed the shrine Santa Cruz de Bravo. Bacalar became Bacalar de Cetina. The Sociedad Patriótica Yucateca, with a longer memory than most, waited four years to see if the conquest would stick before awarding the long-guarded honorary sword to the General. Governor Cantón took the train to Peto, then went by horseback along the new road with a one-hundred-man escort, to offer personal congratulations at Santa Cruz. The troops were marched in review for him, and a photographer climbed to the roof of the temple to record that scene: the platoons, companies, and battalions, field artillery with mule trains, the band, the soldiers in dark uniforms with full field equipment, the officers in dress white. Off to one side stands a contingent of Maya laborers. In another shot, members of Bravo's staff posed before the Balam Na; on that day, the two old men, both generals and both past the age of military vanity, were dressed in civilian suits and panama hats. This group of pictures, the first ever taken of the shrine, reveals details that had never been described: the neglect and decay, the overgrown ruins on the plaza, the forest returning, trees and vines growing on the Temple of the Cross. They also show that Bravo's soldiers had been busy in their single month of occupation: a roofless building being rethatched, and trees for shade and adornment planted in the plaza, signs that the heathen shrine would soon become a city worthy of the new century. All of this should have convinced the skeptics that civilization had come to stay. Heavy patrols scoured the back trails, looking for the enemy, seldom finding any but the sick, the starving, the dying. They made contact with the units at Campamento General Vega on Ascensíon Bay, with Monasterio's forces at Bacalar, and strung a telegraph line to the southern camp. By November, Bravo felt confident enough to leave his army and return to Mexico.

Disaster had fallen on the Cruzob. Their number reduced by

casualties, epidemics, and now starvation, cut off from English weapons and munitions, unable to resist Dzul power, they had fallen back before the advance in helpless rage. The villages along the line of Bravo's advance—Tabi, Nohpop, Sabacche, Chan Santa Cruz itself —were evacuated, the refugees fleeing north or south, only to flee again when the patrols followed, many heading for the safety of the British Crown. Felipe May, apparently General of the Plaza, was one last victim of the war party, assassinated in April by his militant subordinates. The surviving Generals Pat and Ek led only small bands and had no central authority; their morale was shattered, their hope gone. A machete could be used against the single-shot muzzle-loader if losses were accepted, but it was suicide against repeating rifles. They couldn't fight but wouldn't surrender, and so they hid in the most inaccessible places, in the swamps, with no tracks leading to their settlements, killing roosters so that the cock's crow would not betray them. Cornered and desperate, but still dangerous, they prayed to God and their refugee Cross.

Bravo's trip to Mexico had not been made for social reasons. On November 4, 1901, President Díaz had sent a proposal to the Federal Congress suggesting the creation of a Federal Territory in the eastern part of Yucatan, to be called Quintana Roo. A mighty howl went up in Yucatan, where citizens remembered the more than a half million pesos and countless lives spent in recovering the area, the lost cities and towns, and above all, their humiliation at the hands of the eastern Maya. General Bravo was needed in the capital, and Admiral de la Vega passed through Mérida on November 11 enroute to Santa Cruz as his replacement. There was anguished negotiation to stop creation of the new Territory. Governor Cantón wrote Díaz a series of letters begging for the coast north of Tulum if nothing more, but he was finally constrained to say, "The resolution of General Díaz is taken, and it is impossible to contest it." Yucatecan Senators at the Federal Congress, and the representatives of the State Congress, gave their unanimous rubber-stamp approval after expressing a few face-saving regrets, and on November 24, 1902, the resolution became law. Criticism was notably absent from a number of prominent Yucatecans, the names Peón, Molina, and Sierra Méndez appearing on the list of those who received huge grants of eastern forest. The principle invoked in support of the separation was that Yucatan lacked sufficient means to develop and pacify the area; the real objective was closer Federal control over expected profits. Vega's two years of command at Santa Cruz de Bravo were spent in the construction of a canal, the "Zaragoza," between the Caribbean and the Bay of Chetumal, to shorten the sea lanes to the bay and eliminate the necessity of sailing through English territorial waters; in the development of the nearby port of Xcalak; and in an effort to win the still hostile Cruzob by peaceful means. Bravo returned in December of 1903, and these projects were dropped for the time being, the focus of activity shifting to the north. The General had plans for his new territory, and there was much work to be done. No one in his right mind would have gone to Quintana Roo without a big share in the profits, which had already been divided by the cronies of Díaz in Mexico and Mérida; but General Bravo had the army to use for the necessary labor, and he arranged to have convicts and political dissidents sent to help. The latter category was always large under the Díaz regime, and, for that matter, military service was used as an alternative to prison. These men didn't provide the best type of colonists, but discipline would cure the incurables who survived, and Bravo knew all there was to know about discipline.

His first problem was one of communications, finding a means of getting forest products to the market. He hadn't forgotten his railroad, the Ferrocarriles Sudorientales de Yucatán. Since this was no longer Yucatan, it would be a new company, the Ferrocarriles Norte de Quintana Roo, and since Santa Cruz was only thirty-six miles from the sea, as opposed to ninety miles to the rail head at Peto, he decided to ignore his cleared road and start the eastern branch first. A new site was picked on Ascensión Bay and called Vigía Chico; it was to serve as a port, some ten miles up the bay from Campamento General Vega, which was abandoned as too exposed to the hurricanes of that coast. Vigía Chico was a collection of barracks, whorehouses, a clapboard hotel with a veranda, and miserable pens of convict labor scattered along the beach, all centering on a pier of considerable dimensions. In spite of the railroad and telegraph line to Santa Cruz, and visits from occasional ships, it was an isolated, hated place. The principal sight was the rusting hulk of the wrecked gunboat *Independencia.* The quality of life there is suggested by the presence of glass floors in several of the buildings, floors made by pushing rum bottles upside down into the sand.

The railroad was started from Vigía Chico, under Colonel Aureliano Blanquet, who had come out with Bravo as a captain; he was destined to become a general, a counter-revolutionary, and briefly President of Mexico, and to be remembered by his countrymen as "the jackal." He was a pistol-waver, but efficient; the line progressed rapidly west and then southwest, swinging around the swamp, mule-drawn platforms and steam locomotives hauling narrow-gauge tracks from the port, the line building on itself. There were bitter memories of that work by ex-colonels, ex-politicians, ex-journalists, and ex-businessmen; unused to the bad food and manual labor under a tropical sun, dreading the snakes, the prospect of malaria without medicine, and the savages, they were humiliated by vicious foremen, whipped, and shot "while attempting to escape." Dynamite, used to blast the roadbed, sounded a warning to the beaten Cruzob: the nails were being hammered into their coffin; and having recovered a bit, thanks to the misunderstood pacifism of Vega, they returned to military activity. A guards barracks was added to the repair shop at the halfway point called Central; a tree near there is known as "El Indio Triste," The Sad Indian, for a sniper who repeatedly scored on members of the garrison from long range until he was discovered and treated in the same fashion by a marksman sergeant whose Mauser had telescopic sights. The attacks continued after the line was completed and a second major expenditure of sweat cleared the jungle for several hundred feet on either side to prevent ambush. Defense was organized around a boxcar, coupled ahead of an engine, which had cast-iron sides, a corrugated roof, and could hold a squad of soldiers and a machine gun. But the patient Mazehualob took what they could—small work parties, handcars, and the mule-drawn platforms. Kilometer twenty-nine marked one such engagement; the first volley killed three of six men on the exposed handcar and wounded two, the survivors holding out under their machine until help arrived.

A second Decauville railroad was driven inland from Puerto Morelos to Santa María, headquarters of La Compañía Colonizadora,

1. *The Well at Bolonchen,* by Frederick Catherwood (ca. 1843).

2. *Two officers on the day of Corpus Christi,* by Gabriel Gahona (ca. 1850).

3. *Those officers on the day of battle,* by Gabriel Gahona (ca. 1850).

4. *Song of Discord*, by Gabriel Gahona (ca. 1850).

5. Yucatecan battle scene, detail of a primitive painting (ca. 1850).

6. The church at Tituc, destroyed early in the Caste War.

   Left: View of the ruins. *Right:* An image with face and hands chopped off.

7. The half-ruined monastery and church at Ticul.

8. (*Left*) The cenote in Chan Kiuic, where the Speaking Cross first appeared.

9. (*Right*) Pedro Pascual Barrera, Nohoch Tata (on left), and Lieutenant Sulub.

0. Huts in a Maya village near Chankom.

1. Juan Bautista Poot, a minor chief at X-Cacal.

12. Review of General Bravo's army at Chan Santa Cruz, 1901

13. The Balam Na at Chan Santa Cruz, 1901.

14. Don Norberto Yeh, patrón of Chancah, in 1959.

which boasted an ambitious two-story clapboard house for the fore-
man and a collection of shabby huts for the loggers and chicleros.
Chicle, the basis for chewing gum, was developing into a valuable
commodity. The Compañía Agrícola also began railroads, from El
Cuyo and Solferino, hauling their products to the sea for transship-
ment. Both companies were examples of tropical exploitation at its
worst: fortunes for the distant stockholders and directors, and for
silent partner General Bravo, and sickness, hardship, poverty, and
death for the workmen. The settlement of Cayo Obispo barely survived after most of its settlers followed the troops to Bacalar, where a
start was made at clearing out the ruins and repairing some of the
better houses. The original Twenty-First Federal Battalion was sent
home in October of 1902, replaced by the Seventh; the Twenty-Second, which had served under García, Bravo, and Vega, for four hard
years in the jungle, was also transferred to Mexico, with the Sixteenth
Battalion taking its place at Santa Cruz. Work was taken up again
on the Zaragoza canal after several years. An estimated thirty million pesos were spent on that project, much of it absorbed by dis-
honest contractors and corrupt officials, and, of course, by General
Bravo. It was never finished. Rusty machinery and an abandoned
dredge are its monuments.

The nerve center of all these enterprises and capital of Quintana
Roo, Santa Cruz de Bravo, was a changed and bustling town. To
the one-story stone buildings of the Cruzob, the new inhabitants had
added second stories of frame construction, with corrugated iron
roofs and balconies. Bravo moved his headquarters and home from
the residence of the Tatich to a large building on the northeast
corner of the plaza which took up an entire block, with a balcony
running the length of the outside walls; the Tatich's residence became a hospital. The schools that flanked the church were converted
into barracks, with parade grounds enclosed by thatched buildings
to the rear; stores and shops lined the plaza, which was planted with
orange trees and boasted a fence, walks, benches, and a stone fountain. A generator was installed for the telegraph and for electric
lights; a pump carried water from the cenote to a concrete reservoir;
warehouses and workshops were built. Through indifference, or because of evil memories, the church was not used as such. Instead,

the main entrance was walled shut and it was turned into a prison for convict labor, male and female, who were locked in together for nights of fornication and murder. It could not have been desecrated more effectively. Civilization had indeed arrived. There were around 4,000 people living at Santa Cruz de Bravo, few of them because they wanted to.

General Bravo has been accused of many things. It was said that he slaughtered the Cruzob after Vega had attempted friendly persuasion, that he condemned his own soldiers to death by making them march with the breeches of their rifles open, that he punished those who shot natives; it was said that he had a secret pact whereby the Maya would never attack when he was personally commanding, in return for which he offered treaties, gifts, and free passage to Belize, and that he intentionally prolonged the fighting to keep himself in power. The stories of his personal graft, at least, were true; he himself bragged about it, claiming to be the silent partner of every merchant in the state. A large sum of money was assigned to the hospital of Santa Cruz, but it never had medicine or bandages. He took his cut from the canal fiasco, from chicle and lumber contractors for protection and licenses, from the shopkeepers that supplied them, from the railroad that carried their goods, from port fees, and he even had an interest in the shipping lines. He had complete coverage. Living in small, isolated forest camps, the lumbermen and chicleros, mostly convicts and political prisoners, together with Negroes from Belize, were most exposed to Cruzob vengeance. And their dead joined the mail carriers, road workers, telegraph linemen, and the uncautious patrols of soldiers, on the expense side of the General's ledger. Political offenders, vagrants, and thieves cost the concessionaires twenty-five pesos, f.o.b. Veracruz. The killings continued in their vicious tradition; Indios were burned alive, white men castrated and tortured to death. Contemporary rumors, doubtless greatly exaggerated, said that thousands died in those years; at any rate, the fear of attack was such that when the Seventh Federal Battalion was withdrawn from Bacalar in 1907, the inhabitants abandoned the city and moved down to Cayo Obispo, where the sanctuary of British Honduras was just across the river.

In February of 1906, the General traveled up to Mérida to attend a reception for the President of the Republic, Don Porfirio Díaz. Yucatan had seen nothing like it since the visit of the Empress Carlota. Bravo welcomed his patron, together with Justo Sierra Méndez, Mexico's first Minister of Education, who had himself just returned to his native land to prepare the way for the President and to unveil a statue of his father, Justo Sierra O'Reilly. Special trains carried the party to the outskirts of Mérida, where a carriage and a cavalry escort was waiting; and a triumphal entry was made down the flag-draped streets, beneath a series of elaborate arches, to the general applause of a populace that had now forgotten the theft of Quintana Roo. For the next four days there was a succession of banquets "at the champagne hour," some with two hundred places set; torchlight parades, and a parade with floats representing scenes of provincial history and ending with a bust of Díaz being crowned with a laurel wreath by a local beauty; balls, fireworks, dedications, visits to public works; and a party set in a formal English garden that contained a replica of the Parthenon, an imitation ruin in a land of ruins. And there was a visit to the Hacienda Chunchucmil, where Don Porfirio could see the source of all this wealth. He toured the henequen fields, the rasping plant, the drying room, the machine shop and power plant, the hospital, the store and eight workers' huts, finding happy, contented natives, well-washed, dressed in spotless clothes, owning such luxuries as sewing machines. At the inevitable banquet he gave his impressions:

> Some writers who do not know the country, who have not seen as I have, the laborers, have declared Yucatan to be disgraced with slavery. Their statements are the grossest calumny, as is proved by the very faces of the laborers, by their tranquil happiness. He who is a slave necessarily looks very different from these laborers I have seen in Yucatan.

Potemkin could have learned from the henequen hacendados. This presidential visit cost millions of pesos, the individual banquets running to fifty and sixty thousand each. It was the golden age of the gente decente.

General Bravo returned to duty. As the first decade of the new century drew to a close, there were signs of trouble in the wind. The Díaz regime couldn't last forever. Re-election was denounced in

Mérida, feeling ran high against Governor Muñoz, and after some thirty years of civil peace Yucatecans again turned to armed rebellion. Valladolid was the center of the revolt; civilians there killed the jefe político and captured the city. A federal battalion was rushed from Veracruz, Bravo marched up from Quintana Roo, and the 1,500 rebels were crushed in a brief but vicious battle; the captured leaders were shot, and the men sentenced to forced labor and military service under Bravo. But there was no peace. Riots erupted in Peto, Temax, and Yaxcaba, all symptoms of the Madero revolution that was sweeping Mexico, and they ended only with the news that Porfirio Díaz had fled the country.

These distant events were reflected in Santa Cruz de Bravo, when, in September of 1912, General Bravo learned that a representative of the new President, Francisco Madero, had landed at Vigía Chico. This was General Manuel Sánchez Rivera with fifty men. Bravo had two battalions, but he was past eighty, and he bowed to the inevitable, giving his word of honor that he would report to the authorities in Mexico City. The political prisoners were called into Santa Cruz from the various camps, and on Independence Day, September 16, given their passports, passage, and money. A banquet was held in the plaza that night, a celebration by the ex-convicts who had suffered every humiliation and survived the cruelty of General Bravo; and in their joy they remembered what they had been through, and thought of revenge. Sánchez Rivera had given his word, and he stopped the lynching party, guarding the aged General until he could ship him off to Vigía Chico the next day, and from there to Veracruz. Thus the conqueror, Ignacio Bravo, by a defeat not of his own making, was taken from the capital of his petty kingdom—in fear of his life, ruined, with only a few years left to live. Even for him, the country of the Cruzob wasn't lucky.

The first duty set before the new Governor of Quintana Roo was to make peace with the Maya. Sánchez Rivera succeeded in negotiating with the Maya General Maximo Cauich, but this could not dispel the generations of hatred or the suffering of the last eleven years. A truce was established, but that was all. The Cruzob simply kept to themselves, avoided their former shrine city, and refused to integrate with the Dzul. The territory was assigned a new governor, General

Arturo Garcilazo, who was ordered to see that his troops were self-supporting and productive. He brought with him workers from Mexico, fifty tailors, groups of carpenters, and mechanics to repair and maintain the railroad that had fallen into disrepair. He completed the public market at Santa Cruz started by his predecessor, constructed a new pier at Vigía Chico, and bought two small boats to regularize coastal traffic. General Garcilazo had little time for these good works. Taking the wrong side, or at best remaining neutral in the face of a Yucatecan counter-revolution, he trusted in the reputed generosity of the Federal victor, General Salvador Alvarado, and obeyed his command to report at Mérida in May of 1915. This decision led him to imprisonment, torture, attempted suicide, and the firing squad, strapped to a chair because he was too weak to stand. His executioner, a revolutionary of stern idealism, said that the revolution was made for the oppressed—and this included the ex-rebels of Quintana Roo. Since the Maya had not accepted white presence, he had decided that the whites must leave; besides, he didn't care to leave potentially hostile battalions so far from his control.

And so Santa Cruz de Bravo once more became Chan Santa Cruz. The city was formally, if hastily, deeded to Generals Lupe Tun and Sil May, together with the surrounding forest; the workers, merchants, concessionaires, and soldiers packed up, took the train to Vigía Chico, and sailed away. Stunned by this sudden and fantastic turnabout, the Cruzob ventured uneasily into the Dzul town that had once been their shrine, and fell on their knees to give thanks for this final victory of the Speaking Cross.

Thirteen

The Cross Sleeps

THE CRUZOB DIDN'T RETURN to Chan Santa Cruz. The Dzul was gone, but his evil winds remained. They stared for a time at his transformations, then set to work with the purifying torch, ax, and dynamite. The locomotives, coaches, and platforms were burned, the railroad tracks torn up in several places and thrown into the jungle, telegraph lines cut; the new market, the pump, and the reservoir were dynamited, and the former school buildings flanking the temple, which had been used as barracks, were burned. Acts of childish vengeance, yes; but also a guarantee that the enemy wouldn't change his mind. The temple itself, the mysterious center of tribal faith, the Holy of Holies, was beyond purification. The stabling of animals there, the fornication and defecation of convicts, the knifings in the house of God, these were things that could never be forgotten, and the Cross could not go home. So after the destruction, the Cruzob returned to their villages.

If God hated the Dzul and had driven him off, he still had a score to settle with his children for allowing such things to occur, and the scourge of smallpox was laid upon them. The leaders and the older men, those who had negotiated with the enemy, were the first to drop, to be followed by children, whole families, entire villages. Neighboring villagers came to bury the dead, and caught the disease in turn. People died of thirst and starvation with no one to tend them; dogs foraged at will, and vultures entered the houses to feed on the victims, as was written in the Books of Chilam Balam. Many escaped into insanity, and disappeared screaming into the forest.

That fatal susceptibility of the American Indian to European diseases, which from the time of Cortés and Captain John Smith has outkilled bullets one hundred to one, was still in effect. From an estimated eight to ten thousand, smallpox reduced the Cruzob to an estimated five thousand. There was no defense against the silent killer except a bath and a drink of corn juice, and prayers; it traveled faster than a man could flee, crushed the strongest, made cowards of the brave. Silently it came, and then at last silently it left the forest.

Cautiously the survivors gained hope, established contact, village by village, counting the living and incorporating the orphans into foster families. Generals Cauich, Tun, and May were dead; and new leaders came forward. Sergeant Francisco May, a stepson of General Felipe Yama, with whatever prestige that gave and with his own aggressive nature, promoted himself to General. Juan Bautista Vega, a Ladino of Cozumel by birth and captured as a child when his father was killed by Cruzob, one of the tribal agents in 1915 and later Secretary to the Cross, also claimed authority as a General. As Chan Santa Cruz ceased to exist within their religious framework, centrifugal forces took over and divided the Cruzob into two groups: Francisco May and his people had headquarters at Yokdzonot, and Vega established himself at what had become the holy village of Chunpom, in the northern area including Tulum. Both resumed their organization by companies, maintaining Guardia at their separate shrines; both had crosses. But May's people, by far the largest, continued to worship the true, the Speaking Cross. Hidden during the persecution of Bravo's soldiers, carried from place to place in a wooden chest, it now graced the altar of the thatched church at Yokdzonot, a church with an inner Gloria and an outer public room, in humble imitation of the great temple, and similar to the cult's earliest shrine. And in legitimate apostolic succession, the Tatich, now commonly called Nohoch Tata or Great Father, was Pedro Pascual Barrera, grandson of the founder. There was no friction between the two groups; they maintained correspondence, but preferred to live apart, giving their loyalty to their respective leaders with separate shrines.

Chicle, the resin of the sapodilla tree, had been burned as incense by the ancient Maya along with copal and rubber; possibly they also chewed it, as the Aztecs did. By the twentieth century the world, particularly and traditionally the North Americans, had learned this habit, and the taste for chewing gum created a demand that sent white men back into the Cruzob forest. At first, the foreign chicleros (chicle-collectors) were killed by the Maya or hustled off minus their mules and equipment; but in 1917, a Dzul named Julio Martín appeared in deserted Chan Santa Cruz and made contact with General May. Gifts of aguardiente and guns were offered, and possibilities were discussed. Francisco May realized that a good thing had come his way, and the firm of Martín y Martínez was given approval to set up shop. General Octaviano Solís, once a political prisoner at Santa Cruz and now Governor of Quintana Roo at the new capital of Cayo Obispo, was involved in this, and he arranged that May should travel to Mexico City to meet the President as a step toward the incorporation of the Maya into national life. So off went Pancho May, the first of the Cruzob to willingly leave his forest. The President, Don Venustiano Carranza, tall and white-bearded, was the perfect great white father and he acted the part, recognizing Pancho as a General with the gift of sword and uniform, and impressing him with a review of the nascent Mexican Air Force. But the humble native got what he came for: authority over twenty thousand hectares of forest tax-free, plus money and the right to use the railroad, the property of the defunct Ferrocarriles Norte de Quintana Roo. There were other attractions in the capital. The General found himself a lady beyond all his backwoods dreams (in a house where there were other equally friendly ladies), and, not content with a brief affair, he decided to bring her home. She got as far as Vigía Chico, where the General's subjects gave her a less than friendly welcome; and in spite of Pancho's demands to the Governor for troops to put down this revolt against properly constituted authority, the Cruzob meant it, and the General had to let her go. The great adventure was over for Pancho. He unbuckled his ceremonial sword, took off his General's uniform, and, with machete in hand, set about weeding his cornfield.

The Martín y Martínez company set up chicle collecting points at Santa Cruz and Central, using the repaired railroad and mule-drawn platforms to haul it to the port for shipment. Chicle is a latex and harvested much like rubber. A series of diagonal cuts are made in the trunk of the sapodilla, each connected and at right angles to the one above so that the sap will flow down to be collected in a canvas bag. The chiclero climbs thirty or forty feet to make these cuts, with a rope around the trunk and behind his back, bracing himself with his bare feet. The sap is then boiled in a kettle, cooled somewhat, and cast in wooden molds into blocks for convenient transport. The sap ran in the rainy season, from July to January. It was a lonely, unhealthy, and dangerous life, but the pay was good, and once the way had been cleared, chicleros poured into the forest and scattered out in small camps; almost 6,000 of them came in a single year. Chicle had been of no interest to the Cruzob, and its exploitation robbed them of nothing; so they accepted the new invasion and quickly learned the simple techniques to become chicleros themselves. General May, knowing better than to tax his own people, contented himself with the rent paid by the various concessionaires. It was a very nice rent. In 1925 he made 40,000 pesos, all his personal property, plus income from the aguardiente monopoly and other sidelines. This kind of thing stimulated imitation; General Vega began renting his forest, and May's own nominal subordinates, Captain Cituk of X-Maben and Lieutenant Sulub of Dzula, followed suit, causing friction, double taxation, and raids.

Production multiplied, from 45,000 kilograms in 1917 to over one million by 1925, reaching a peak of roughly two million in 1929. During this period, a Cruzob worker could earn more than three hundred pesos a month for the seven-month season; furthermore, he did not live a hard life of exile like the foreign chicleros, but simply worked the trees in his neighborhood in time left over from the cornfield. His had been a moneyless barter society, practically speaking; there were no pockets in his baggy white pants, his people had no tradition of saving, and the money was not long in his hands. By word of mouth the good news spread, and those ubiquitous merchants to Latin America, the Lebanese and the Chinese, loaded their pack mules and headed into the forest. At first they offered traditional goods, including shotguns, pistols, and ammunition; then luxuries, like whiskey, canned goods, cigarettes, silk shirts, and jewelry; and then novelties of the new age—sewing machines, flashlights, phonographs, anything that would catch the native imagination, at any price. If the flashlights went dead, the records broke, and the sewing machines rusted beyond repair, no matter; there were always more where they came from. It was the millennium. Foreigners were welcome and could travel safely through the jungle. The Wrigley Company of the United States had done what generations of Ladino soldiers had failed to achieve.

After 1929, the peak year of chicle production and wealth in Quintana Roo, a boom year world-wide, came the crash. In 1929 a bale of cured chicle had sold for fifty pesos; in 1930 the buyers offered thirty pesos, and in 1932, seventeen and a half pesos. The Maya were outraged. Not understanding economic theories, but remembering Dzul betrayal, they stopped collecting, so that production was cut in half and then in half again. Added to this, there was a second, more serious cause for alarm. In August of 1929, fearing hostile Cruzob action and determined to protect the lucrative chicle industry, the Mexican Secretary of War ordered the Thirty-Sixth Federal Battalion to Quintana Roo. It was shipped to Cozumel, where it broke up into small detachments, occuping Cayo Obispo, Santa Cruz, Puerto Morelos, Vigía Chico, Santa María, and Kantunil-Kin. The concessions to General May were ended, his taxing was stopped, and law, order, and graft were to be administered by white politicians and enforced by white soldiers. Cruzob independence was gone forever. In previous years the reaction would have been a bloody one, but even the more defiant now realized their weakness; they expressed their hostility by deposing, but not killing, General May. The more conservative companies withdrew from the central group, which held Guardia at Chancah, to a new site northwest of Santa Cruz called X-Cacal. La Santísima went with these people under the care of the Tatich, Pedro Pascual Barrera, and the military command of Major Eulalio Can and Captain Cituk. There were about seven hundred of them, and they called themselves "Los Separados," the Separate Ones, looking down on the other groups as irreligious, aware that only they maintained the complete and the legitimate traditions of the past.

Sóstenes Méndez, originally of Peto, orphaned and captured by the Cruzob as a child, had been a sergeant in the fight against Bravo, and he now continued the tradition of Mestizo leadership by becoming the general of the Chancah majority. Purely Maya in his outlook, he never considered returning to his family now that this was possible, and he shared the common hatred for the white race. But that hatred was much reduced. Constant contact with the Dzul at nearby Santa Cruz and dependence on the chicle market had brought the Maya more or less into the Mexican nation. When young schoolteachers, eager to carry the message and fruits of the revolution to the most backward members of the Republic, began fanning out from Santa Cruz, they met little resistance from Méndez; and once Vega had been bribed with a pension, he also accepted the schools. Only the separatists at X-Cacal held out.

In April of 1933, Lieutenant Evaristo Sulub of Dzula, a village of the Chancah group, was accused of planning the death of a certain Maya, a man under his authority as village chief; hearing this, the government decided to make a show of force, to demonstrate that such practices were no longer allowed. Patrols of the Thirty-Sixth and Forty-Second Battalions, sent to arrest Sulub, met resistance, and in the skirmish five Maya were killed, some wounded, and two soldiers were lost. Dzula was then looted and burned. A wave of fear swept the native zone; rifles were brought out and ammuniton collected; but there was no further action. Sulub and the former villagers of Dzula settled at the shrine of X-Cacal, joining the Separate Ones, and reinforcing their hatred and fear of Dzul soldiers. The soldiers were identified with the Jews that had persecuted Christ. It was said, "They are like hogs. They do not have crosses, and they do not go to Mass." It was thought that they left evil winds behind them, causing epidemics; and as active resistance was impossible, these Maya adopted passive techniques, refusing to answer questions or to sell food to any white man.

It was in this hostile atmosphere that a young Dzul merchant traveled through the X-Cacal villages attempting to break down suspicion and make contact with the natives. American archeologists had been active in nearby Chichen Itza, and responding to their friendly treatment, the Cruzob regarded them as allies and possible sources of weapons for further rebellion. Using this friendship, the merchant, a sometime schoolteacher and a full-time student of the Maya named Alfonso Villa Rojas, was able to settle at Tusik, the home of Captain Cituk, and conduct an intensive study of their culture. His efforts helped the tribe to adjust more easily to the inevitable, and to accept schools and government assistance.

The Second World War brought a slight increase in chicle prices, putting an extra pig and a few more chickens into the family diet, if not the boom delight of the twenties. A new influence entered the territory in 1942: the American Maryknoll Fathers established missions at Bacalar, Santa Cruz, Tihosuco, and Cozumel, and worked with the nominally Catholic Ladinos of those places in attempting to win the Cruzob back to a more orthodox form of Christianity. The fact that they were North Americans gave them a certain prestige with both groups, for they had an impartial attitude toward Maya-Ladino conflicts. Soon various American Protestant sects also began to proselytize among the villages, to the annoyance of both Catholic and Cruzob leaders. But the biggest change was the real arrival of the twentieth century, heralded by bulldozers, tractors, and grading machines: the highway through Peto, Santa Cruz, Bacalar, and Chetumal, completed in 1958. The new road swings south of the old entrada route, touching the southern end of Lake Chichancanab at the hamlet of Esmeralda, linking reoccupied Polyuc and a dozen colonies and workers' camps with civilization. Chicle and mahogany travel the road, along with foodstuffs, at a cost that makes their exploitation economical; buses run twice daily from Mérida and Chetumal, with Santa Cruz as their halfway stop. The road has encouraged an eastward migration, which had already begun at Tihosuco and Ichmul; Quintana Roo is becoming part of the Mexican nation, and there are rumors that it will be reabsorbed by Yucatan.

There is a strange familiarity about post-revolutionary events in Yucatan, as if they were a retelling in modern dress of actions a century old, a play with new characters in old roles. As with Independence from Spain, the Mexican revolution came with a minimum of disorder to the peninsula; as before, this calm beginning was only a postponement of revolution, a powder train lit to explode when the implications of the new era were understood. Pino Suárez, the first Governor of Yucatan under the new Republic, was said to be honest and idealistic. He decreed a minimum wage of seventy-five cents for twelve hours' labor in the sun; he felt compassion for the Maya, but left debt peonage untouched; and he was elected Vice President of the Republic, to be murdered with Madero by the generals of reaction. After the counter-revolution was crushed by Venustiano Carranza, Major Eleuterio Avila was sent to tidy up Yucatan, and he did it with an army that met no resistance but was intensely disliked by the Yucatecans. And after Avila read a proclamation ending debt labor, he was disliked even more by the "decent people." That document sent a jolt of horror through the hacendado class; there were anguished meetings of the henequeneros and discussions with the agents of International Harvester; delegations were sent to the Governor and pressures of various sorts applied, including the purchase of guns abroad. The Governor was reminded that Yucatan was the most prosperous of Mexico's states; that the counter-revolutionary Huerta had taken two million pesos from the state treasury, and that Carranza had been able to take eight million to fight his battles; and that it would be stupid to destroy this source of wealth, which of course depended on making the lazy natives work. Preoccupied with intrigue, Avila saw sense in these arguments and failed to enforce the decree. The hacendados breathed again, not forgetting that the decree, although a dead letter, was still law.

Carranza, uneasy about provincial obedience, ordered that the Cepeda Peraza, a state militia battalion, be sent to Veracruz and replaced by a federal unit, and that its ex-Díaz commander, Colonel Patricio Mendoza, be dismissed. Avila tried to soften the blow, but Mendoza refused to be mollified and sent his battalion against the government camp in full rebellion. His troops were routed by loyal soldiers, police, militia, and railroad workers, and he fled east. Yucatecan battalions were Yucatecan first and Mexican second, even if, as in this case, they were recruited mainly among deported Yaquis; and as Santa Anna had learned long before, they could not be ordered about with impunity. Carranza's suspicion extended to Governor Avila, who obligingly resigned and returned to Mexico, leaving General Toribio de los Santos in his place. This general, wishing to remove the military commander of Mérida, Ortiz Argumedo, sent him with a detachment to pursue the survivors of the Cepeda Peraza Battalion, who had gone to the old nest of defeated revolutionaries, the northeast bush beyond Temax. Instead of fighting, Ortiz Argumedo joined Colonel Mendoza, turned back, and took Mérida. Toribio de los Santos fled, while the population cheered their local boy made good.

As there had been Yucatecan reaction during the Huerta regime, there was now reaction with a vengeance. The forced loans of the central government, the insults of Mexican troops, the planned overseas use of Yucatecan soldiers, anticlericism, and above all the threat of an end to debt labor—these were the reasons for the cheers of the Meridanos. Ortiz Argumedo wired the government of Campeche that he was not against the present Mexican government, but that his movement was intended simply to throw out those elements that offended the society of Yucatan. At the same time he sent a commission to the United States, declaring the sovereignty of Yucatan without claiming independence from Mexico. These familiar Yucatecan contradictions were carried even further by popular rumor; as in the days of Méndez and Barbachano, there was talk of annexation by the United States.

Mexico's answer to this revival of regionalism was General Salvador Alvarado, the military commander of the southwest, with headquarters at Carmen. The General immediately sailed for Campeche, adding his 6,000 troops to a 900-man brigade led by Colonel Joaquín Mucel, who was also the Governor of Campeche. This army started up the railroad, smashing the rebels at a hacienda called Blanca Flor and cutting them off at Halacho, where the fight lasted all day, house-to-house, with detachments holding out until annihilated. Entering what they thought was an abandoned church, the victors were met with a last fusillade; and after they captured these holdouts, they stood about 100 prisoners against the church wall and organized firing squads. Colonel Mucel and General Alvarado arrived after the executions had started, and it was necessary for the General to put himself in the line of fire to stop his enraged troops. In other parts of the town there was burning, shooting, and hanging. That was the end of the revolution. Ortiz Argumedo boarded a Cuban schooner after looting the Banco Peninsular Mexicano of one million one hundred thousand pesos, five million from the Henequen Trust, and all he could find in the state treasury. Two days later, on March 19, 1915,

Alvarado entered a frightened, shuttered Mérida, without resistance.

Everyone had heard of revolutionary atrocities in Mexico, of mass executions and the miles of railroad along which each telegraph pole was a gallows, and the Yucatecans had a guilty conscience; but all was quiet and orderly in Mérida under the new regime. There were

General Salvador Alvarado

no lootings, burnings, or reprisals, and the only executions were those of convicted soldiers of the invading force. Gradually the wealthy returned from the haciendas to which they had fled, to meet the mild-looking General; they found him intelligent, not a bad sort, in fact an excellent man, and they laughed at their fears of anarchy and Bolshevism. It was true that General Garcilazo, the military commander of Quintana Roo, who surrendered at this time of general amnesty, was imprisoned and later shot for his involvement with Argumedo; still, that was the way of politics, and no one else had suffered. Throughout the spring and summer of 1915, Alvarado restored order, appointed new judges and jefes políticos, studied the local situation through his rimless glasses, and appointed a commission to recommend reforms. Henequen production was off slightly, owing to the troubles, and more serious, the price had fallen; yet this had happened before, and the hacendados were glad to be able to worry about such familiar matters. Then, on September 15, came a decree: all churches were to be closed. This was a reflection of revolutionary anticlericism and an answer to the "Cristero" bands, who had been fighting the government in the name of the Church, although neither group had ever been strong in Yucatan. A week later a mob of railroad men and Mexican agitators invaded the cathedral, burning the organ and high altar and destroying many famous images. The cathedral was only a few steps across the plaza from the Government Palace and the central police station, but the vandals were not disturbed in their work. Fear for established order and doubts about the new Governor returned. Worse was to come. With his reports in and his information gathered, General Alvarado was ready to act.

In late September the decrees came, one after another. The ignored law canceling debt labor was to be enforced, sixty thousand Maya and their families to be set free; the slavery of three hundred and fifty years was over. This applied equally to the servants in the towns, who had worked for board and keep through the generations, and to slaves of a different kind, who were counseled to find honest work as seamstresses or maids. Alvarado's inflexible morality intended to sweep all before it, to reform a culture as well as an economy, for he believed that the two were inseparably linked; and so along with prostitution went raffles, lotteries, cockfights, bullfights, and alcohol. In their place he would establish a thousand schools, a hundred libraries. The Revolution had arrived.

It was obvious where the wealth of Yucatan came from, and where it went, and for a socialist the solution was equally obvious. Alvarado's tool had already been made for him: the Regulating Commission of the Henequen Market. We must go back to the turn of the century to understand how such an organization could exist among that most individualistic race, the hacendados. It was at that time that a group of exporting companies began negotiating with the various American consumers, advancing money to the hacendados for current and development expenses, and taking futures of henequen at their own price as security. In 1903 Pierpont Morgan led McCormick, Deering, and several other harvesting machine manufacturers into a trust, The International Harvester Company, whose need for binder twine would absorb four-fifths of the Yucatecan crop. Whereas previously there had been a number of henequen customers bidding against one another, now there was basically only one, and Morgan had a way with the dollar. His agents selected one of the Mérida exporters, O. Molina and Company, and signed a secret contract with them, the explicit purpose being to drive the price of henequen down to the lowest possible level. Ten thousand bales were to be dumped on the market by Molina and the loss made good by International, which in the future would deal exclusively through Molina, guaranteeing that no other buyer would pay higher prices.* The plot worked according to plan. In 1902 henequen had sold for almost ten American cents per pound; in 1903 it was down to eight cents and by 1911 to a bottom of three, past which even Morgan couldn't push without forcing the haciendas out of business. It has been said in defense of Molina that he wanted volume production at a low figure to prevent foreign competition and broaden the market; but production did not materially increase, and foreign competition with transplanted henequen was still many years in the future. Why the Meridanos didn't lynch the man is a mystery.

In 1906 an association called the Cámara Agricultura was formed to combat Molina's successor, Avelino Montes. It won permission to borrow from the National Bank of Yucatan using henequen as security, and with those sums to keep the hacendados going, it collected bales of the fiber to hold off the market until a decent price was offered. All went well until they had cornered a sixth of the annual crop, when they were told that the bank had orders to sell its security at the prevailing lower price. The outraged businessmen pointed the finger of blame at the State Secretary of the Treasury, who in a public letter denied that he had anything to do with the bank under his control. The Secretary was Olegario Molina. Several private firms sprang up, but they were pygmies against Morgan, and realizing their weakness they pressed for a government agency; they were obliged with the Regulating Commission of the Henequen Market, which they would later call the wooden horse of socialism.

Founded in 1912, the Commission took over the henequen stock of the private ventures and filled its warehouses with 100,000 bales, which it held while the world demand grew. Again Morgan's trust operated through its lackeys at the National Bank, which held paper

---

* Some years later, *La Revista de Yucatán* carried an article exposing the contract, which it said began as follows: "It is understood that Molina & Company will use all forces in their power to lower the price of fiber of sisal, and that they will pay only those prices which from time to time are dictated by the International Harvester Company."

on one of the private agencies that had contributed to the Commission's stock; and so when the price rose to seven cents, there was another forced sale, this time not only of the part held as security but of the entire amount, with the Commission withdrawing from the market. Again there were cries of scandal and bribe, and demands for an honest director of the Commission, a man independent of the Governor who could not be bought with Morgan money. A tax had been imposed on henequen for the benefit of the Commission, to be used as a war chest. Instead it was used as a slop-barrel by the politicians in charge: Huerta took two million pesos for his counter-revolution, Carranza disposed of over six million for pacification, and Argumedo stole five million outright.

This was the history of the Commission when General Alvarado took it in hand. The hacendados had asked for a director who could not be bought; now they got one. First the General arranged a meeting with them and spoke of a cooperative, which was well received, but their ideas about the nature of a cooperative were quite different from his. Henceforth, he decreed, all henequen would be bought by the Commission and sold by it as sole agent. The firms of Montes and Peabody were expelled from the state. Hacendados who couldn't be persuaded by logic needed only to consider the fate of various enemies of the Revolution to assist them in making the correct decision. Not that they had anything to complain about. The First World War had created a rising and imperious demand for henequen, and American buyers, considering Mexican political instability, decided to stockpile. These favorable conditions enabled the Commission to parlay prices from below six cents per pound in 1915 to more than 23 cents in 1918. In spite of a reduced crop, earnings more than doubled in those three years, reaching ninety-one million pesos in 1918.

With such profits, Alvarado's wildest dreams became possible. Henequen paid for those hundred libraries, those thousand schools; it provided capital for a development company that revived and modernized a fiber plant and reinstituted the Peninsular-Mexico railroad project; it bought a fleet of five steamers to transport the harvest in those ship-scarce times; and it financed a futile attempt to find oil beneath the limestone of Yucatan. Alvarado even considered digging a canal that would make a seaport of Mérida. Perhaps his most durable achievement was creating a new constitution for the state. Promulgated in 1918 as a foundation for his various new laws, it was the most advanced of its day in matters of social justice. Accepting social welfare as a direct responsibility of the state, it provided for compulsory education, government pensions, the regulation of working conditions, age limitations, accident insurance, and standard work contracts. Another monument to the man was that even his enemies never accused him of dishonesty or of dipping into what was the greatest treasury the state had ever known.

And then came the fall. Reluctantly obedient to a constitution that allowed no self-succession, the General relinquished his position to Carlos Castro Morales, a party man and former railroad worker. This was 1918, and with the end of the World War the henequen market collapsed. From his unofficial position Alvarado urged a lowering of prices and a belt-tightening in government expenses to prepare for and soften the blow, but his successor was unable to take such unpopular steps and thus lost all. Unsold henequen piled up in the Commission accounts as the price fell to six and a half cents; money was borrowed from American banks to keep the haciendas running, and when that failed, the failure of payment caused heavy devaluation of the paper money in circulation. Public gatherings and riots spelled the end. The monopoly of the Commission was revoked and an open market revived, but it wasn't enough. There were still 800,000 bales to be paid for, and not with worthless money. In October of 1919 the Commission was suppressed and its goods liquidated. The fleet, machinery, railroad equipment, and all its assets went in an effort to meet the debt.

As with a captured tiger, it was easier to grab than to release the tail. The American banks were still to be satisfied, and they satisfied themselves by taking their collateral of henequen at $8.33 per bale, arranging that in the future Yucatan and Campeche would be forced to sell all the harvest to their agents, and further that production should be restricted until the surplus could be absorbed. The banks were paid off and they forced the price to four and a half cents, Morgan's old price of 1912. These matters could only be negotiated through a single body, so the Commission was reorganized as the Export Commission of Yucatan, which was replaced temporarily by a cooperative and then revived once more as Henequeneros of Yucatan. The wealthy hacendados were always against the organization whatever its form, but the smaller henequen growers supported it as their only source of credit, and the organization survived. Inheriting the policy of maintaining the highest possible prices, Henequeneros followed through with a logical restriction of production—logical, that is, if Yucatan was the sole producer. In fact, this course simply encouraged the growth of foreign plantations in Java and in British Africa, and their yield passed that of Yucatan by 1930, destroying the monopoly forever. Furthermore, the henequen plant, grown under scientific management in richer alien soils, was altered to produce longer fibers of greater tensile strength. Unfortunately, when these plants were reimported and planted in their rocky natural habitat, they reverted to their natural, less valuable state. Low quality, mismanagement, and the world-wide depression cut henequen acreage in half, and the price fell to an all-time low of 1.9 cents per pound. Yucatan, once the most prosperous of Mexican states, faced bankruptcy.

The old books of the Maya, the almanacs from which the H-menob prophesied, were pessimistic, filled with bad omens, bad days, and bad years. With slash-and-burn corn farming, man had achieved a precarious balance on that barren peninsula, a small surplus when the rain was good, catastrophe when it failed. But henequen had replaced corn, which was now imported, and henequen faced dangers far more formidable than rain, locusts, and rot—man-made threats unknown to the Balamob, difficulties that could not yield to the Cha-Chaak. Henequen had not replaced corn in the heart of the Maya. Although he had lost his land to the plantations, there was always a little patch he could work on and fulfill his religious duties, but it was not enough for survival. He was a part of a money economy now, and he needed a minimum salary from the hacendado in order to buy what he couldn't raise; and with henequen under two cents a pound and the producing fields cut in half, the hacendado had no jobs to offer. The years between 1930 and 1934 were black ones for the Maya —the kind of starvation years that had once been cyclic but had been unknown since henequen prosperity. As in the old days, pathetic columns of men toured the haciendas and towns and shuffled through Mérida, begging for work and food. Before, they had sold their communal land and even themselves. Now the land was gone, debt servitude was illegal, and there was no demand for servants at any event. This was the freedom of the Revolution.

But the Revolution was far from over. All of Mexico suffered through the depression, and popular demand for the fulfillment of old promises began to assume a militant note. To meet this, the official party gave the presidency to General Lázaro Cárdenas, a former Governor of Michoacan with a record of personal honesty and an interest in social welfare. He began his regime by refusing to occupy the presidential palace built by Maximilian on Chapultepec Hill, and the work of his first years was often referred to as "the revolution of today." Of all his promises, the most important concerned land. The land reform program, law for a number of years, had barely scratched Mexico or Yucatan. Cárdenas ordered the program to become a reality, and, impatient with Yucatecan excuses that the land was organized for henequen rather than corn, he replied that the peons would grow henequen themselves. The traditional form of *ejido* or village communal land, typical of all colonial Mexico and before, the institution that Barbachano, Méndez, Juárez and Díaz, with different motives, had worked to suppress, was revived. Surveyors invaded the haciendas, drawing up new property lines; a special bank was organized to extend credit to the new groups; and twenty-five per cent of the henequen land was divided among the Maya.

The hacendados were reluctant to accept this dispossession passively. They made much of the real and imagined mistakes of the program, and of course they had a great deal to work with. The government had assigned some ejidos consisting only of young or old plants, which could not be self-sufficient for years to come, while others were given stands of productive plants that had an unfairly high immediate value but would face a difficult period as their fields aged. The haciendas had developed as economic units, keeping a proper balance between the number of new, producing, and aging plants, thus preserving a continuity of production. They had also grouped naturally around a central rasping plant from which radiated the Decauville tram rails, but this organization was lost with partition. Further trouble grew from the fact that the Mexican government didn't distinguish between the farmer and the townsman or villager; tradesmen and artisans who had never worked the land were given grants equally with others, to the bitter resentment of the farmers. Using their traditional authority to mobilize this discontent, the hacendados were able to recruit peons to their cause, and they armed them in the struggle against the ejido and unionized labor. Their possession of the rasping machinery was another weapon, and they could refuse to process henequen from the ejidos or overcharge for the service.

Revolutionaries had come to Yucatan before, and there were traditional ways of handling them. First, the socialist party leaders were bought out. When the Governor couldn't be bought, he was removed through fomented strikes; his successor, an even more determined agrarian reformer, was likewise driven out by the scandal of a strike, which the infusion of reactionary money and alcohol had made into a massacre in the plaza of Mérida. Class was set against class, interest against interest, and amid the general discontent of depression, committee after committee traveled to Mexico City with new studies and plans of reform to meet the special conditions of Yucatan. The hacendados had logic on their side. Ejido, they said, was conceived for corn farmers, but corn grew poorly in a dry and barren Yucatan and was worth a fraction of the value of henequen. But the Maya wanted their cornfields. Well, there was better land, plenty of it, they said, out of the henequen zone. But the Maya was bound to his village in a way the cosmopolite couldn't understand. So the henequeneros argued while they used the army to put down disturbances and their peons to slaughter strikers.

Finally President Cárdenas had had enough. With a boatload of engineers, surveyors, agricultural experts, and bureaucrats, he traveled to Mérida in August of 1937. His technique with Mexican landowners and capitalists had been to start with negotiations, and, if he met with much resistance to right thinking, to expropriate. This approach was used on the henequeneros. All hacienda lands, with the exception of a 150-hectare nucleus including the buildings of each, were to be seized and turned over to the people as ejidos, beginning with the largest. For once, the hacendados had nothing to say. Along with this, the central government was to supply money for development, reasearch, industrialization, improved transportation, and hospitals and schools, an echo of Alvarado. Unfortunately, little came of this part of the plan. With matters thus arranged, Cárdenas returned to Mexico, and the dispossessed landowners set to work to see what they could retrieve from the ruins. Among other things, they developed a late-blooming social conscience: they deplored the fact that the ejidos were unfairly distributed and that the landholder or *ejidatario*, theoretically his own boss, was no longer protected by the labor laws, could no longer strike, and was simply a peon of the Banco Ejidal—all of which was true. And they continued to use their rasping mills to maintain control. Two of these problems were solved by the new Governor, Canto Echeverría, who like his predecessors strongly resented the tremendous control of patronage and opportunities for graft available to the directors of the Banco Ejidal. All 272 ejidos, he decreed, should be equalized by merging them into one Gran Ejido (under his control), and the rasping plants should be seized under the same authority. This left the former rulers of Yucatan the option of joining the bureaucracy or driving taxicabs in Havana.

Everything that could be done on paper had been done. The Maya owned his own land, could raise corn or henequen as he pleased, and had fair use of the processing equipment and the selling agency. The Revolution was complete. Yet still he starved. He had traded one master for many, and the new masters, lacking the interest of a landholder in the future of his estate, cared only about lining their own pockets during a tenure in office. Local inspectors lied about the number of henequen plants under cultivation, and withheld pay; their superiors, who connived in this, took their share, and sold government medicine to the public. Jefes políticos licensed cantinas and sold alcohol against the principles of the Revolution. The Auditor of the Ejido said, "To rob the ejidatarios isn't robbery because they are also thieves"; from relative poverty, this man quickly became a leading property owner in Mérida, and because he built a church he was known as "the good thief." The hierarchy of corruption was dominated by the governors, whose tricks ranged from insurance fees and holding companies to simple seizure of haciendas and henequen warehouses. Even those governors whose reputations were otherwise relatively clean accepted commissions on the sale of the Ejido's harvest—commissions for the difficult arrangements between a single producer and a single consumer.

Gradually the hacendado class came to an accommodation with

the new age; as one of its leaders said, "The Revolution has given me more than it has taken from me." They infiltrated all ranks of the Ejido bureaucracy, including its executive level, for which they were qualified by their superior knowledge of the industry; and when, in 1942, they regained their seized rasping plants, they were well content. And with reason: freed from the expenses and concern of raising henequen, they granted themselves fifty-two per cent of the price of fiber for the service of processing it. The ejidatarios, who theoretically owned seventy per cent of the land, were in the familiar condition of their fathers and grandfathers. According to the figures of Miguel Angel Ménendez, the approximate division of henequen profits in 1942 was as follows: hacendados (500 families), 31 per cent; bureaucrats, 25 per cent; ejidatarios, 24 per cent; taxes, 19 per cent.

The Second World War increased demand, stopped competition from the Far East and Africa, and brought sufficient earnings to keep the workers from starving. If they were being robbed on a grand scale, that was nothing new, and at least times were better than during the depression years. Production increased fifty per cent during the war, reaching half of the all-time high of 1916. Prices climbed to nine cents per pound from a bottom of two; and those in charge, avoiding the error of the First World War period, did not alienate the market by demanding excessive prices in a time of scarcity.

If Cárdenas sustained a period of revolution, his successors leaned toward readjustment or reaction (depending upon one's view), a lessened hostility to foreign capital, and all-out industrial expansion. The graft that went along with this was naturally enormous, and the candidacy of Ruiz Cortines was presented to the people as a reform calculated to bring honest administration. With this motive, the burden of parasitic officialdom was removed from the back of the Maya farmer. On February 9, 1955, the Gran Ejido was dissolved, and the ejidos returned to local control. It is indicative that the Gran Ejido, attacked by the hacendados as communistic seventeen years before, was now ardently defended by that same class, which claimed allegiance to the ideals of agrarian reform and to the old principle of state sovereignty. They resisted this loss of easy profit just as their fathers had done, by refusing to process the henequen of the free ejidos. This attitude, and the confusion of change, caused a decline in the shipments of 1955; but by the following year production was up again, and the transfer is now accepted. The future depends on reasonable contracts between the ejidos and the owners of the rasping machinery, or by ejido ownership of the machinery. There is a free market today, but the individual ejido is still a weak organization. The upper class has shown its ability to adapt to all Revolutionary organizations and come out on top. The struggle of the Maya is far from final victory.

Henequen has dominated life in twentieth-century Yucatan, but there have been other changes. Peninsular population surpassed the old high of 1847 during the 1940's, and has grown at an accelerating rate. By 1960 there were 622,500 in Yucatan, 160,700 in Campeche, and 41,000 in Quintana Roo, representing percentage increases in the last decade of 20.8, 32.2, and 52.0, respectively. This may bring real problems in the future; over half of these people can speak Maya, and for some fifty thousand of them it is the only language. The peninsula is no longer isolated from the rest of the Republic. At great expense, Alvarado's dream has been fulfilled. Railroad tracks have broken through the jungle and swamp of the Isthmus of Tehuantepec and have now been joined by a highway. Paved roads connect Mérida with Campeche, Valladolid, and Peto; gravel roads continue on to Chan Santa Cruz, Bacalar, and Chetumal, while a new road extends past Valladolid to a new town, Puerto Juárez, on the east coast opposite Isla Mujeres. International flights land daily at Mérida, and local airlines link that city with Campeche, Chetumal, and Cozumel. Much of this travel is based on a new industry, tourism, drawn by beach resorts and by the excavated and restored ruins of the ancient Maya at Chichen Itza and Uxmal. Predominant in the tourist trade is the Barbachano firm, run by the grandson and great-grandson of the governor. There are other familiar names in Mérida today, Rosado, Gutiérrez, Ruz; the same cluster of colonial mansions still surrounds the plaza, and there is still the Casa Montejo and the cathedral. Only the fortress of San Benito is gone, its loss balanced by the addition of several skyscrapers. The past is very near the surface in Mérida.

Fourteen

Postscript

1959

THE BUS EMERGED from the forest, passed a few huts, rattled down a street, turned into the plaza, and stopped. The driver announced the noon break for lunch, and then I realized that this was Felipe Carrillo Puerto, formerly Santa Cruz de Bravo and Chan Santa Cruz. As I climbed down from the bus and looked around at the typically Yucatecan but strangely familiar plaza, I was seven hours from Mérida, three days from the snow of my home in Saint Louis, and nearing the end of three years of study which had centered largely on this little town. Food was the first requirement, since we had arrived late, and over chicken *mole* and beer I tried to explain my interest in this place to two European fellow travelers. They had doubtless encountered cranks before and were quite polite, but they were relieved, I think, to get back on board and ride on to Chetumal and Belize. Vendors of oranges, tamales, tortillas, and soda made last assaults on the passengers, and the chauffeur leaned on his horn for the second driver, who was courting a barmaid. Late passengers came running, and new luggage was lashed on top, along with a crate of chickens and three turkeys. There was a false start, the bus stopped by cries from friends who were saying goodbye and wanted out; then a second start, backfiring, more horn-blowing, and dust; and then peace returned to the plaza.

I made my arrangements at the only hotel—formerly the chicle house of Martín y Martínez and before that the barracks of a Guardia company—which stood on a corner facing the church. Since I hadn't brought my own hammock, I was forced to use a native one made of sisal, with sharp fibers guaranteed to prevent sleep. These were the dead hours of the afternoon, so I arranged my gear on the floor near the hammock, brought my notes up to date, and stretched out. Later, the sound of children playing woke me, and from the balcony I saw that the little plaza with the fountain was now a soccer field, and that the building flanking the Balam Na was still serving the children as a boarding school to accommodate distant, inaccessible villages. The town was coming to life, so I began my inquiries by a visit to the civil authorities in the Palace of the Patrón, which they shared with the town garrison. A sergeant ushered me in to the official in charge. I explained my interest, asked a few questions, and got nowhere at all. The man was new to the territory, and his concern was exclusively with the town's Ladino population and with the new road stretching back to Peto and down to Bacalar and Chetumal. My map of the villages in the area was better than any available to him. He would confirm village chiefs in their authority as sub-delegados, send out schoolteachers, and keep the peace; as far as the Maya were concerned, that was that. There had been no census, not even of the town, which was guessed to have a population of three thousand. The man was pleasant, and wishing to make up for his inability to answer my questions, he insisted that I visit his last post, Isla Mujeres, which had ruins, all very old, very beautiful, and very interesting.

A small boy was assigned to guide me to the house of the Maryknoll missionary, Father Frank Collins of Philadelphia. I had previously imposed myself on the kindness of his colleagues, particularly Father Norbert Verhagen, formerly at Bacalar and now at Tihosuco; I had always found them kind and helpful, and found no exception here. Father Collins's parish was the ex-Cruzob territory, and his church was the Balam Na, which, he said, had been successively a store, a motion-picture theater, and a Masonic building before it was deeded to the Maryknoll Fathers in 1942. He was well aware of the past, and had a copy of Alfonso Villa's book—to keep track of what was, in fact, his competition. He implied that the other faith was still a going concern.

The work had not been easy. One missionary arrived in a village to discover that the old stone church was the "Indian" church, while the Catholic one was a small thatched hut. When he rebuked the

Maya for not giving him feed for his mule, they replied, "But Father, we did not ask you to come." Another priest refused to celebrate a fiesta during Lent, only to find himself barred from his own church. These new priests, although free from the racial prejudice of their Ladino predecessors, lack tolerance for native customs, and they are attempting to suppress not only Cruzob rites but also the pagan agricultural ceremonies that had been ignored throughout the colonial period. In an effort to stop the Chaak ceremonies of the cornfields, and realizing that he could not possibly visit them all, one priest has his parishioners bring him a little earth from each field, to be blessed at a special ceremony. This seems to have supplemented rather than replaced the older ritual.

I asked Father Collins about the reported existence of an earlier church in Chan Santa Cruz, and, changing into heavier shoes, he led me on a walk out of town and through the woods to Chan Kiuic, the original home of the Speaking Cross. The little valley is now a backyard to an outlying hut, whose inhabitants use the holy cenote for domestic purposes; there seemed to be no recollection or knowledge of its former sanctity. It was only after checking historical descriptions and comparing the layout of this cenote with the other one— where the remains of a pumphouse, pipe, and reservoir, all destroyed by General May's dynamite, had been patched together in a haphazard fashion—that identification could be made. The shrine, an open, vaulted structure, stood up on the hill, on the other side of a rubble stone wall, neglected and overgrown. A large blue cross had been painted on the inner wall and two smaller ones on the outer, flanking walls. A mound of rubble spilled down from the platform, the work of a Yucatecan merchant who, with secret information, dug here one night and left before morning with the treasure of the Cruzob—or so the story goes. Beyond this, I was on a cold trail; the priest could tell me nothing more about the enigmatic structure. We then went on to a hut in the vicinity, where Father Collins knew a man who could serve me as a guide and interpreter.

Raimundo Canul, called Mundo, about thirty-five and a native of Tulum, said he would be glad to take the job, and I told him to hire mules for the next day. Sitting in the plaza that evening, watching children playing around the bandstand, a squad of soldiers at drill, listening to a loudspeaker advertising a movie with a cha-cha tune (thus competing with the evening mass), I seemed a long way from Chan Santa Cruz; I could be in any small Central American town, without local color or local costume. I bought a beer in the combination restaurant-bar, heard conversations about high prices in New Orleans and about how much *gringa* women drink, and wandered out to find that the advertised movie was for the next night. There was one redeeming sight: a Maya, standing outside the church, wearing the huit, the loincloth I had only read about and had never seen in Yucatan. Then Mundo came up out of the dark to say that the mules had been hired, and that we should leave very early. To make conversation, but not expecting much, I asked him if he knew anything about the Nohoch Tata.

"He died one hundred years ago, patrón. If you want to know about those things you should ask General May."

"He's still alive?"

"Yes. He is one hundred perhaps." (Everyone old, I discovered, was either fifty or one hundred.)

"Where does he live?"

"Near here. I'll take you there if you wish. He used to live there," Mundo said, pointing at the Palace, "in the Chikinik, but now he lives in a little house like everyone else."

The idea of meeting the General, a man I had assumed long dead, a historical figure, stunned me. At last, I thought, Ladino ignorance and lack of interest in the Cruzob past would be replaced by information from the very source, historical guesswork would be replaced by real facts; and I wondered where to begin my questions, how to break through the suspicion I had come to expect. But this was not to be. We walked a block and a half to the edge of town, brilliant moonlight replacing the electric light of the plaza, to a lane of detached huts, where we were told that the old man was at his cornfield some thirty-six miles away. I called again the next day, and several times on my return to Carrillo Puerto, but without luck. All I can add to his biography is that he still has his government pension, a small one, is respected by the Maya, and is considered a rich man, owning thirty mules.

My departure for Chancah was less than dignified. The Yucatecan mule is diminutive, but mine was all male and determined to mount the jenny that Mundo had reserved for himself; in the excitement I managed to keep my seat until the rotten girth broke and both the animal and I went down on the slippery pavement, much to the amusement of the early morning loungers and school children. I was relegated to the *burracita*, a change I didn't resist; because if there wasn't far to fall, there were always rocks to fall on; and I spent the rest of the day matching wits with that amorous he-burro, maneuvering to keep him in front.

Our way led past the airstrip and down the Chetumal highway. It is hard to describe what the road means to Quintana Roo. On the bus coming down from Mérida the dust and bad roadbed made it seem nothing but a necessary evil, a sad deterioration from the paved roads of Yucatan. But the fact that you can take a bus to Felipe Carrillo Puerto at all, and make the journey in a few hours instead of five days, that a sick man can be driven to a doctor in Peto instead of dying, that food can be brought in during a bad year for the corn, that the starving farmer can move one hundred miles in search of work—these things tell part of the story. Physically, the road is alien to the jungle. It runs straight and flat as far as the eye can see, with the undergrowth cut and burned back a hundred feet on either side; beyond is the endless forest, with its twisting, narrow, rocky trails, where you can seldom see more than thirty feet in any direction, are always submerged under foliage, and must pick your way carefully around fallen trees and ravines. Re-emerging on that road, you can share the awe of the villagers you see waiting for the bus, squatting on their haunches at the edge of the road, distrustful and uneasy about this faster and louder civilization.

As we rode along the highway, and then turned off at the Chancah trail, I questioned Mundo. We started with a discussion of the animals of these parts, and I asked after that siren of the woods, X-tabai. "No," he said, "not in the territory; they have them in Yucatan."

"And the Aluxob?"

"Yes, we have them. I have heard them many times. They whistle to frighten the deer, they beat with sticks against trees, thump, thump, to frighten the deer, when you are hunting. You give them corn, meat, water, and they don't bother you." With the ice broken, I plunged ahead. "Balamob?" "Yes, but those you never see." The first-fruit and the rain-making ceremonies are still practiced in the villages. As Mundo was from Tulum, I asked him about Bautista Vega, of nearby Chunpom, and he told me that the old leader is still alive:

"Don Bautista is a very intelligent man. He has a book, a very big book, written in Maya, which tells everything. Don Bautista can read! In this book it tells of the coming of the airplanes, of the road. People were frightened at these things, but he knew. Are your people the same as the English?"

"Yes," I said, not wishing to distract him.

"The book says that one day the English will give us arms and the people will go to war to throw out the Yucatecans. The sign will be when money disappears from the hands, Mexican money; that will be the balance of the year, the end of the world."

"When will this happen, Mundo?"

"Who knows if it will be this year or in a thousand years. It will be the balance of the year. There is writing on old stone walls in a place to the south of here. None of the white men can read it. One day I will copy it, draw it, and take it to Don Bautista. Perhaps it will say when the end of the world will be."

He told me other things. There were three books, or bibles, which had been kept by the secretaries of the Holy Cross, just as there were three crosses and three villages—Chancah, Chunpom, and X-Cacal. Lorenzo Be, the former secretary at X-Cacal, has succeeded to the position of Nohoch Tata, but the other groups don't recognize him as superior to their own priests; Paulino Yama is the Commandant there, Bautista Vega holds both civil and religious authority at Chunpom, while at Chancah the Patrón is Norberto Yeh and the Commandant is Román Cruz. I couldn't get accurate population figures on the surviving Cruzob; the local estimate was one thousand to fifteen hundred for each of the three subtribes, with two hundred or less living in the three shrine villages.

It was a beautiful morning, cool among the trees in the filtered sunlight, and noisy with parrots, orioles, canaries, and blackbirds. We shouted back and forth as we rode along, Mundo correcting my Maya pronunciation, which was lacking in precision and harshness. The trees weren't the giants of Petén, but they were impressive enough compared with the low bush of western Yucatan—each fork crowded with bursts of airplants, orchids, birds of paradise, and parasitic lianas, all embracing the trunks in a tentacled grip. Heavier rainfall explains this rank growth, for the soil is equally thin throughout the peninsula. Roots spread far and wide above the surface, over the rock, looking for nourishment; when a tree falls you can see by the absence of taproots how shallow was the penetration. In this jungle it was easy to visualize ambush, undetected concealment, and the impossibility of pursuit. I had come twenty-five hundred miles in two days; now I would travel fifteen miles a day, the same as the missionary, the merchant, and the government official in this area. The forest begins a few yards from Felipe Carrillo Puerto. Once in it, you make your way through an ocean of trees stretching for thousands of square miles, empty of man except for the occasional island-like village clearing. The jungle is a barrier isolating those villagers, allowing them to live apart and to live in the past, a past I was discovering still alive in Mundo. My discouragement of the previous day was gone. If the home of the Cruzob looked like a shabby Yucatecan village, with the bush visible in all directions from the plaza, its unique quality lay just below the surface. Mundo had said, "There are many old men in Carrillo Puerto who could tell the old stories, but they will never speak because of white insults, maybe punishment." The minds of these people had created the Speaking Cross and given it voice. It was in their minds that I would find the answers I sought.

Three leagues of trail had been the promise, and surprisingly, at the end of three hours we came out of the jungle to a thatched shrine, and beyond lay the village. We rode past three small, pre-Columbian altars (unmentioned in the literature, but possibly an explanation for the name Chancah or "little town") and tied our animals, safely apart, in a cluster of orange trees. Mundo asked after the Patrón and we were led to his hut; learning that he was still at his cornfield but would return shortly, we made a quick tour of the village. A stone church with a thatched roof stood on an outcropping of rock in the middle of a large irregular clearing, surrounded by four Guardia huts, each on its own hillock, their fence-like paling walls only four feet high, leaving an open space beneath the thatch. Three of the Guardia huts belonged to Chancah, Kopchen, and Chasil, the fourth being shared by the other villages. Only one man was on duty in the Kopchen building, stretched out in his hammock. A hollow formed by hillocks to the east of the church was being used as a plaza, and had a post to which the bull is tied for the local style of bullfighting during fiestas. A number of huts scattered at the edge of the forest completed the village. The Patrón was still out when we returned to his house, and we were given lunch, a gourd of water and a *macal*, a tuberous plant something like a potato, baked in the ashes of the breakfast fire. Then at around two-thirty he returned, an old man and his adult son, both carrying heavy baskets of corn, strung on tumplines across their foreheads. He asked if I was a missionary or from the government, and Mundo explained who I was in a long introduction of which I could only understand the words "San Luis." We shook hands and Don Norberto Yeh said he would be very glad to talk to me after he had washed and dressed more fittingly.

I began by asking after the crops and the weather, which he said had been bad, and inquiring his age, which he said was about fifty; he looked older, though, with his patient, heavy-lidded eyes, grizzled mustache and beard, and wrinkled face, and there was dignity in his bearing in spite of the dogs, chickens, baby pigs, and children, who, together with curious adults, had crowded into the hut. He spoke in a low, soft voice, looking at me rather than at Mundo, as if hoping I could understand him by his eyes and expression. He sat in a hammock, Mundo and I on three-legged stools. My next question, Did he remember the time of General Bravo, brought a long, explosive diatribe (and Maya can be very explosive) which was translated, "The Señor says Yes." In his youth Don Norberto had fled from a village to the west of Santa Cruz before the advance of the General's troops, wandering in the woods with his parents, weak from hunger and thirst, while many fell victim to exposure and disease. He went on to say that he was very glad to talk to me, and with a shy smile, as if we shared a secret, explained that the old books had prophesied that a *Chachac-mac* would come to ask questions and to inspect the villages. Was I going to all the other villages of the people; and did the chief of San Luis send me? "We are no longer able to go to Belize," he added, "so we can't buy the things we need."

It is one thing to read of cults and prophecies in books, to accept the fact that they are still believed by people in a remote country, to accept what is out of our own experience as we accept so much that is printed; it is another matter to find yourself playing a role in such a belief. Don Norberto believed me to be the emissary promised in the Books of Chilam Balam; one of the Chachac-macob, or Red Men, now living in North America, who once built the ancient cities and who will return someday to aid the Maya. He was making the common error of confusing Americans with the old benefactors of his people, the English south of the Hondo, and I asked what sort of goods he wanted to buy in Belize.

"Carbines," he said, and the word needed no translation. The interview was going his way, not mine, and I shifted back to safer ground, asking about the old days. Nohoch Santa Cruz Balam Na is the full name of the shrine city today, "Nohoch" having replaced "Chan" as little had grown to big, differentiating the town from Santa Cruz Chico at the head of Lake Bacalar. Don Norberto talked of the services, the shrines, the barracks, and said "What you see there today, we built, the Dzulob didn't build; it is our town." In discussing the Guardia barracks, he mentioned the Protestant missionary in Santa Cruz and the Yucatecan laymen who traveled through the villages converting the Maya, dissuading them from doing their Guardia service in Chancah. "Why do they come to us?" he asked. "We don't go to the cities to tell them how to worship God. This is our country, and we know it better than they do." I inquired after the Chan Kiuic, asking if it was the valley where the Cross first appeared, but he said he didn't know. Was it certain that the Cross had the power of speech? Again he said he didn't know: "the Dzul tells many lies about our people and the Cross." I replied, "That is why I want to know the truth, the Maya truth, so it can be told," but it was no use. Further knowledge was closed to me in spite of my status as a Chachac-mac. A Polaroid camera providing immediate pictures is the best way I know of making friends across the language barrier, and I gave Don Norberto a photograph of himself. His wife, who had shyly accepted a cigarette but shyly refused to smoke it in front of me, now shyly but firmly wanted a picture of herself; and after much giggling and hesitation this was accomplished, and we left to allow the Patrón to eat his long-delayed meal.

Don Román Cruz, the Commandant and sub-delegado of Chancah, forewarned, was waiting for us in clean white pants and shirt. Also "about fifty," he was much more urbane and sophisticated. Having fled to Corozal as a small boy before Bravo's patrols, he remembered how the forest had been tall and the tree trunks huge at that time, and how much they had shrunk on his return as a young man. Made Commandant in the time of Cárdenas, he had traveled to Mexico City with the other native leaders, returning by airplane. Did he like the city? It was beautiful, he said, but he had no place there and everything was very expensive. Mundo told me Don Román was wealthy, owning twenty head of cattle. He also had a growth in his chest and needed an operation, for which he would go to a Ladino doctor. Neither he nor Mundo seemed to have much faith in the H-menob and laughed at how their predictions had failed to come true, but they both believed in the prophecies of the Holy Books. Don Román's last name indicates that he has white blood, although he appeared to be purely Maya. He remembered Sóstenes Méndez, the former Commandant of Chancah, who had died some years ago in another village, but the line of succession wasn't direct or clear.

As we left Don Román's house and returned to our mules, the Patrón crossed the plaza to intercept us. He was stripped to the waist, wearing white pants of the old style, cut in a half moon below the drawstring belt on either hip, as shown in Catherwood's drawings; holding a thin stick, more a wand than a cane, he was followed by a retinue of men and boys—the image of Maya priesthood going back thousands of years. He had more to say to me. We all followed his example and seated ourselves on some rocks in the shade of the trees to which the mules were tethered. He looked older and smaller without his shirt, more Maya. Mundo translated:

"The book promised that your people would come and give aid to the Mazehual."

"What kind of aid does he need?"

"Rifles and men to help drive the Mexicans out. When will this be done? Shall I send a delegation to San Luis to arrange these matters?"

This is what I had avoided earlier, what I knew he was expecting, put bluntly so that no evasion was possible. I had gone looking for recollections of the Caste War, and now I was invited to enlist.

Appendixes and Index

Glossary

Listing Spanish and Maya words used in the text.
(M) indicates a Maya word.

Adelantado. Archaic title for governor of a province.
Aguada. Water hole, small swamp.
Aguardiente. Liquor, usually rum.
Ah-kin (M). Maya priest.
Ahuacan (M). Maya high priest.
Alcalde. Mayor, justice of the peace.
Alcalde Col. Official in charge of village land.
Alcalde Mesón. Official in charge of village rest house.
Almehenob (M). Maya aristocracy, literally, "those who have fathers and mothers."
Alux (M). Maya forest spirit.
Amparo. Provision for judicial protection of the citizen against acts of the government.
Arriero. Muleteer.
Atole (M). Corn gruel.
Audiencia. Court or town hall.

Balamob (M). Class of Maya gods.
Balam Na (M). House of God; a church, particularly the church of the Speaking Cross at Chan Santa Cruz.
Barbachanista. Follower of Governor Barbachano.
Barrio. A district or suburb of a town.
Batab (M). Leader, chief.

Cacao. Chocolate-nut.
Cacique. Chief, boss.
Camino real. Royal road, main road.
Campechano. Citizen of Campeche.
Canche (M). Three-legged stool.
Cantina. Bar, saloon, rum shop.
Cargador. Porter; official of a religious brotherhood.
Carga. Load of 100 pounds.
Caudillo. Leader.
Ceiba. Cottonsilk tree, the Yaxche or holy tree of the Maya.
Cenote. Sinkhole or cave well, the most common source of water in northern Yucatan.
Chaak (M). Maya rain god; a small river originating in Lake Bacalar.

Cha-Chaak (M). Maya rain ceremony.

Chachac-mac (M). Red man, the Maya name for a North American; in the plural, a legendary people who will one day return to help the Maya.

Chan (M). Little; used with various Spanish words, as in Chan Iglesia (Little Church) and Chan Santa Cruz (Little Holy Cross).

Chan Kiuic (M). Little Plaza; the small valley several hundred yards west of Chan Santa Cruz where the Speaking Cross was first displayed.

Chen (M). Well.

Chicle. Sap of the sapodilla tree, used to make chewing gum.

Chiclero. Chicle collector.

Chikinik (M). West wind; palace of the Tatich at Chan Santa Cruz.

Chilam Balam (M). Prophet of God; legendary author of the Books of Chilam Balam.

Chilam (M). Prophet.

Choza. Thatched hut.

Cocomes (M). Area in west central Yucatan and its inhabitants, named for the Cocom family of pre-Conquest rulers.

Cofradía. Religious brotherhood.

Comandante. Commanding officer or major.

Costumbre. Custom.

Cruzob (M). The rebel Maya group ruled by the Tatich and the Speaking Cross.

Degüello. Bugle call meaning "attack without quarter."

Diana. Reveille.

Dzul (M). Foreigner, white man.

Ejido. Common land.

Ejidatario. Worker on an ejido.

Entrada. Long military raid.

Escribano. Secretary, clerk.

Escudo. Shield, coat of arms.

Fagina. Period of work required of citizens every year.

Fuero militar. Spanish colonial status giving special privileges.

Gente decente. "Decent people," leaders of Ladino society.

La Gloria. Sanctuary of a church.

Guardia. Military duty at Chan Santa Cruz.

Guerrilla. Detached raiding party, a commando unit.

Hacendado. Landowner.

Halach Uinic (M). True Man; the ruling office among the pre-Conquest Maya.

Hidalgo. Nobleman; also used for loyal Maya who fought on the Yucatecan side against the Maya rebels.
H-men (M). Maya herb doctor.
Huipil (M). Maya woman's dress.
Huits (M). The primitive Maya living beyond white influence in Yucatan before 1847; literally, "loincloths."

Indígena. Native, a polite word for "Indio."
Indios Bravos. The rebel Maya.
Itza (M). An important group of pre-Conquest Maya.

Jefe político. District political official.

Kampocolche Cah (M). Kampocolche Village, name given to a small valley west of Chan Santa Cruz; also called Chan Kiuic.
Kaz-Dzul (M). Half-foreigner; hence a Mestizo or half-breed.
Kuilob Kaaxob (M). Maya spirits who protected the forest.

Ladino. A Yucatecan belonging to "white," as opposed to Maya, society.
Ley fuga. Law of flight, a justification for shooting prisoners "while attempting to escape."

Maestro Cantor. Lay religious leader.
Mayordomo. Superintendent, overseer.
Mazehual (M). An average Maya, his word for himself.
Mendecista. Follower of Governor Méndez.
Meridano. Citizen of Mérida.
Mestizo. Person of mixed Spanish and Indian ancestry.
Monte. Forest, jungle.
Monte del Rey. The King's Forest, common land during the colonial period in Yucatan.
Mordidas. Bribes; literally, "bites."
Muchachos. "Boys."

Nohoch (M). Great, as in Nohoch Tata (Great Father, another name for the Tatich).
Norte. Seasonal storm from the north.

Oración. Taps.
Oratorio. Small chapel.

Pacíficos del Sur. "Peaceful Indians of the South," the southern Maya who submitted to Yucatan.
Palacio Federal. Federal Building.
Palacio Municipal. Town hall.

Pardo. Person of mixed Indian and Negro ancestry.
Partido. District.
Patria chica. "Little homeland," one's native region.
Patrón. Boss.
Picota. Whipping post.
Plaza mayor. Main plaza.
Plazuela. Small fortress, any small plaza.
Pozole. Corn gruel with beans.
Presidio. Fortress or penitentiary.

Rebozo. Woman's shawl.
Retablo. Altarpiece.

La Santísima. The Most Holy, title of the Speaking Cross.
Santo. Saint, representation of a saint, a cross that stands for a saint.
Sapodilla. Tree from which chicle is gathered.
Soldado. Soldier; name for the average male Cruzob as opposed to one with a high rank.

Tamen (M). State of harmony existing between a Maya and his gods.
Tata Nohoch Zul (M). Cruzob intelligence officer; literally, "Great Father Spy."
Tata Polin (M). Interpreter of the Speaking Cross.
Tatich (M). Religious leader of the Cruzob.
Tata Chikiuc (M). Military commander of the Cruzob.
Terreno baldío. Uncultivated land.
Tunkul (M). Wooden, drum-like gong.

U-Hanli-Col (M). Maya first-fruit ceremony.

Xoc-kin (M). "Count of days," Maya technique of telling the future, of Spanish origin.
X-Tol (M). Maya dance of the "conquest" type.

Maya Leaders

ORIGINAL CONSPIRATORS

Manuel Antonio Ay: Executed at Valladolid, July 26, 1847.

Cecilio Chi: Northern chief; victor at Valladolid and Izamal; murdered by his secretary, May 1849.

Jacinto Pat: Southern chief; victor at Peto, Tekax, and Ticul; assassinated by rivals, September 1849.

SUCCESSORS TO CECILIO CHI

Venancio Pec: Northern chief; killed in battle, late 1852.

Florentino Chan: Southern chief; died 1852.

CRUZOB

José María Barrera: Mestizo and original conspirator; creator of the Speaking Cross; died 1852.

Manuel Nahuat: Ventriloquist of the Cross; killed in battle, March 23, 1851.

Agustín Barrera: Son of José María; Tatich; murdered in 1863, probably by Venancio Puc.

Leandro Santos: Mestizo and General; member of a peace party; probably assassinated in 1863, along with Barrera, by Puc.

Dionisio Zapata: Mestizo and General; member of a peace party; probably assassinated in 1863, along with Barrera, by Puc.

Venancio Puc: General; captor of Bacalar; overthrown and killed by Crescencio Poot in 1864.

Crescencio Poot: General; captor of Tekax; overthrown and killed by Aniceto Dzul in 1886.

Juan de la Cruz Puc: Secretary of the Cross; Tatich; active from 1851 to at least 1887.

Bonifacio Novelo: Original conspirator and fighter; Tatich in 1867.

Aniceto Dzul: General; military commander from 1886 to about 1890.

Román Pec: General; successor to Dzul; assassinated in 1895 or 1896.

Felipe Yama: General; successor to Pec; died in January 1899.

Felipe May: General; successor to Yama; assassinated in April 1901.

POST-BRAVO CRUZOB

Francisco May: General at Dzonot Guardia and Chan Santa Cruz; still living in 1959.

Juan Vega: General at Chunpom; still living in 1959.

Sóstenes Méndez: General at Chancah; died about 1935.

Román Cruz: Sub-delgado at Chancah; still living in 1959.

Norberto Yeh: Patrón of Chancah; still living in 1959.

Pedro Pascual Barrera: Grandson of José María; Tatich.

Eulalio Can: Major at X-Cacal.

Concepción Cituk: Captain at X-Cacal.

Paulino Yama: Comandante; chief at X-Cacal in 1959.

Lorenzo Be: Tatich at X-Cacal in 1959.

PACIFICOS OF CHICHENHA

José María Tzuc: Chief in 1852–64.

Marcos Canul: General; chief, 1864–72; moved to Icaiche in 1866.

Rafael Chan: General; chief, 1872–79.

Santiago Pech: General; successor to Chan.

Gabriel Tamay: General; chief in 1894.

PACIFICOS OF IXCANHA AND MESAPICH

General Arana: Suppressed by Yucatecan forces in 1869.

General Eugenio Arana: A brother; still holding command in 1894.

SUB-TRIBE OF LOCHA

Pedro Encalada: A Caste War fighter; chief until at least 1861.

Chronology

1519–1846

1519–46: Conquest of Yucatan by the Spaniards. **1697:** Conquest of the Itza at Tayasal. **1761:** Revolt by Jacinto Canek at Quisteil. **1821:** Mexican Independence from Spain. **1838:** Iman revolt against Mexican centralism. **1840:** Yucatecan separation from Mexico. **1842:** Abortive Mexican invasion of Yucatan. **1843:** Re-unification of Yucatan with Mexico. **1845:** Second separation of Yucatan from Mexico. **1846:** Mexican-American War; Campeche revolt for neutrality.

1847

January: Massacre by the Maya at Valladolid; neutralist revolt succeeds. **February:** Mérida revolt fails, Barbachano exiled. **July 18:** First report of planned Maya rebellion. **July 26:** Execution of Manuel Antonio Ay; Colonel Cetina begins a revolt. **July 30:** Tepich attacked by the Maya, the official beginning of the Caste War. **October:** Cetina takes Mérida, drawing Méndez troops from the frontier and allowing rebels to strengthen their position by capturing Tihosuco and various villages. **December:** A Ladino counterattack fails, Ichmul falls to the Maya.

1848

January: The Cocomes Maya revolt; Peto and Valladolid are besieged. **February:** Ladinos abandon Peto and Yaxcaba. **March:** Fall of Valladolid and Sotuta; Méndez offers the sovereignty of Yucatan to three powers, then retires in favor of Barbachano. **April:** Ladinos conclude a treaty with Jacinto Pat, but it is nullified by Cecilio Chi; Ladinos abandon Tekax. **May:** Ticul, Izamal, and Bacalar fall to the Maya. **June:** Ladino counterattack; the Maya army leaves the field for spring planting; Izamal is recovered. **July–September:** Tekax is recovered; deep Ladino patrols in the north, heavy fighting in the center. **November:** The Peto offensive. **December:** Valladolid, Ichmul, and Tihosuco are recovered and the Maya are driven into the forest; Chi is murdered.

1849

April: The Maya besiege Tihosuco and Saban. **May:** Bacalar is taken by a Ladino expeditionary force; the slave trade is begun, but is stopped by Mexican authorities. **September:** Pat is assassinated; Ladino patrols probe deep into rebel territory. **October:** Superintendent Fancourt of Belize meets with Maya leaders at Ascensión Bay.

1850

General Micheltorena replaces López de Llego in February; deep entradas are made through the spring months, culminating in O'Horan's march across country to Bacalar in July. Fighting continues through the rainy season, with many prisoners taken. The refugee settlement of Chan Santa Cruz becomes important toward the end of the year, with the first appearance of the Speaking Cross.

1851

The Cruzob make their first attack at Kampocolche, and the new cult is discovered by the Ladinos in January. The Shrine is raided by Colonel Novelo in March and by Colonel González in May, but it continues to grow. Micheltorena is replaced by Díaz de la Vega in May, and the army is reduced, with most soldiers put on inactive reserve. A treaty is made with the rebels of Chichenha, who are then attacked by the Cruzob.

1852

Ladino reserves are recalled and columns sent to Bacalar and to Chan Santa Cruz in February and in May. In spite of famine, the Cruzob make reprisal raids on the frontier. José María Barrera dies in December.

1853

Barbachano cedes the state government to General Díaz de la Vega in response to the centralist victory in Mexico of Santa Anna. The Molas-Cepeda revolt in September is crushed. Cholera breaks out, and the Cruzob make a massive and successful raid into the Cocomes. A pursuing Ladino column goes to Chan Santa Cruz. The slave trade is revived.

1854

An entrada is made to the shrine in April; another in May, which is hit by cholera and ends in a massacre by the Maya; and another in November, when Ladinos discover the new church. Two Ladino bases are maintained in Cruzob territory through the end of the year.

1855

After heavy fighting the bases are evacuated in February, and one of the returning garrisons is massacred. Santa Anna falls and Méndez is elected governor of Yucatan. Official end of the Caste War.

1857

Barrera succeeds Méndez as governor. Several revolts occur in Campeche, and these serve as a cover for the Cruzob massacre and sack of Tekax in September. The Cruzob attack Chichenha, whose inhabitants move to a new site called Icaiche. Peraza replaces Barrera as governor.

1858

Campeche and Yucatan separate, and García is made governor of Campeche, but fighting continues between various forces in the rival states. Bacalar falls to the Cruzob. Irigoyen becomes governor. The Balam Na is begun at Chan Santa Cruz.

1859-61

1859: Irigoyen cedes the governorship to Castellanos, who is overthrown by Agustín Acereto. **1860:** An expedition to Chan Santa Cruz is made by an army under Pedro Acereto, but it ends in failure with heavy losses. The elder Acereto is overthrown and succeded by Vargas, and then by Cano. **1861:** Acereto recovers the government, loses it to Irigoyen, then is caught and shot. The Cruzob capture and sack Tunkas.

1863-65

1863: Navarrete is elected governor. Civil war is fought by Yucatan and Campeche, which is under blockade by the French navy. The Imperial cause is triumphant in Yucatan. **1864:** Campeche and Yucatan are reunited, and Navarrete is replaced by the Imperial Commissioner Ilarregui. Venancio Puc is overthrown by Crecencio Poot. **1865:** An attack against the Cruzob is launched by General Gálvez, with little success and heavy losses. Gálvez is replaced by Colonel Traconis. Empress Carlota visits Yucatan.

1866-70

1866: A second campaign is fought on the frontier, with a long siege of Tihosuco; that town holds out, but it is abandoned as being too exposed. Republican forces become active in Yucatan. **1867:** The Empire falls and there is a bitter and successful siege of Mérida by Cepeda Peraza, who becomes governor of the Yucatecan part of the re-divided peninsula. The Icaiche Maya invade western Belize. **1870:** On the death of Cepeda, his brother succeeds for an interim term, and is replaced by Manuel Cirol.

1871-73

1871: Traconis makes an expedition to Tulum and the northern Cruzob area. **1872:** Colonel Cantón revolts and seizes Mérida. A Federal army is sent from Mexico under General Mariscal, who, after peaceful negotiations becomes governor, leaving Cantón in command of the eastern forces. **1873:** General Alatorre replaces Mariscal and presides over a bitter election in which Castellanos is the victor. Cantón stages another revolt.

1874-76

1874: Anarchy; Eligio Ancona is named governor. **1875:** The year without a single revolution. **1876:** Victory of the Porfirio Díaz party in Yucatan brings an end to the decades of anarchy.

1884–86

1884: The Poot-Cantón treaty is signed but never put into effect. **1886:** Poot is overthrown and killed by Aniceto Dzul, with general skirmishing the following year after ten years of quiet.

1893–99

1893: The Spencer-Mariscal treaty is signed. **1897:** The barge *Chetumal* closes the Rio Hondo. **1899:** Ichmul is re-occupied, and commercial exploitation of the north and east coast begins.

1901–12

1901: General Bravo conquers Chan Santa Cruz and Bacalar is occupied by Ladino troops. The Cruzob area is detached from Yucatan and made the Federal Territory of Quintana Roo. **1912:** The Madero party is victorious in Mexico, and General Bravo is recalled.

1915–37

1915: Civil war breaks out; General Alvarado arrives in Yucatan; the Ladinos evacuate Chan Santa Cruz. **1929:** Height of the chicle boom, reestablishment of military authority in Quintana Roo. **1937:** Cárdenas applies land reforms in Yucatan.

Bibliography

This is a selected bibliography, listing only the sources I found most valuable in my research; for other sources on the Caste War, the reader is referred to Howard F. Cline's work of 1945. In the following preliminary remarks, works referred to by author and date are described in full in the alphabetical list.

My general background material on Yucatan before the Caste War is based on the works of Baqueiro (1878), Ancona, Molina Solís, Acereto (1904), and Aznar Pérez. Cline's various studies were extremely helpful for their explanation of social and economic trends in the decades preceding the war.

For details of military history, particularly betwen 1847 and 1853, I have drawn heavily on Baqueiro (1878). Although he was an anticlerical liberal of the Mérida faction, Baqueiro's bias was slight. He undoubtedly wrote with official reports before him, for he often lists weekly losses in killed and wounded and specifies how many prisoners and rifles were captured by the Ladino forces. He wrote at a time when many Caste War veterans were still living, and I have found no contradiction of his facts.

Although Baqueiro's knowledge of the Ladino part in the Caste War was extensive, he is much less reliable on the Maya side. Many of his facts and figures on the Maya were given by Ladino officers eager to excuse their defeats and magnify their victories. Nevertheless, from his reports of the tens of thousands of Maya that were captured, of the Ladino prisoners that were rescued, and of the messages that were intercepted, it is possible to reconstruct a general picture of rebel moves. A similar source is Ancona (1889), which draws largely on Baqueiro but gives additional facts and carries the story forward in time. Both of these works contain a wealth of documentation, including numerous letters, orders, and treaties translated from the Maya.

Another important source (and one not available to contemporary Yucatecans) is the Archives of British Honduras, which has been presented, in edited form, by Burdon (1935). The actual documents in Belize were bound, but Burdon's classification scheme was not clear to me, so I have cited the names and dates as I found them. Although useful for the war years, the Archives are most valuable for later periods, and particularly for information on Chan Santa Cruz between 1853 and 1901. Among the documents are reports on visits to the shrine, including a number of interviews with the Cross; letters written by the Cross to the governors of Belize and British Honduras, in the original Maya or Spanish with English translations; and letters to and from the various Cruzob leaders, which shed light on the succession of the Tatich and many other interesting details. The existence of the Archives today is in doubt. Government House in Belize, the wooden building in which they were kept, was destroyed by a hurricane in 1960, with heavy loss of life. According to newspaper accounts, it is planned to move the city of Belize to a new and safer location.

The most valuable source on the origin and nature of Cruzob society is *The Maya of East Central Quintana Roo*, by Villa R. (1945). It deals with such important questions as the organization of the Guardia companies and the blending of pagan and Catholic rites; presents information on Cruzob society in this century; and contains the valuable text of the Sermon of the Talking Cross. *Chan Kom*, by Redfield and Villa R. (1934), helps define the traits common to all Maya before the Caste War and to isolate the innovations of the Cruzob. Points of Maya ethnology are based chiefly on these two works.

Acereto (1947) provides a general outline of post–Caste War politics in Yucatan and Mexico, and is particularly useful for its quantity of names and dates. Acereto's writing becomes more partisan in the post-Díaz years, and so I have tried to balance his interpretations by consulting the works of liberals and critics of the regime, notably Carlos R. Menéndez, Molina, and Benítez. Many important facts and some interesting political propaganda, chiefly from the twentieth century, may be found in the files of the newspaper *Diario de Yucatán*, which have been organized by its editor, Carlos R. Menéndez, and in the Librería Cepeda Peraza, both in Mérida. A great deal of information on the state of Quintana Roo, with useful photographs and maps, can also be found in Gabriel Menéndez (1936).

Because many towns and villages referred to in contemporary reports of the Caste War have ceased to exist, and because in the late nineteenth century many Maya settlements disappeared or changed locations (often keeping the same name), considerable research was necessary to construct the maps presented in the text. Details on names and locations were taken primarily from Stephens (1841 and 1843), Norman (1843), Aznar Pérez, Berendt (1867), Sapper (1904), Miller (1889), Villa R. (1945), Pacheco Cruz (1934), and Menéndez (1936). The plan and sketch of Chan Santa Cruz are my own, and based on personal observation; the streets and stone buildings could be located with certainty, but no effort was made to determine the location of thatched huts and back lots, since these had changed many times since the Caste War period.

A.B.H.
Archives of British Honduras.

Acereto, Albino
1904 Evolución histórica de las relaciones políticas entre México y Yucatán. México.

1947 "Historia política desde el descubrimiento Europeo hasta 1920," Enciclopedia Yucatanense, Vol. III. México.

Aldherre, F.
1869 "Los Indios de Yucatán," Sociedad de Geografía y Estadística de
la República Mexicana, *Boletín,* Ep. II, t. 1, 73–78. México.

Ancona, Eligio
1889–1905 Historia de Yucatán desde la época más remota hasta nuestros días. 5 vols. Mérida (vols. 1–4) and Barcelona, Spain (vol. 5).

Arnold, Channing, and Frederick J. T. Frost
1909 The American Egypt: A Record of Travel in Yucatan. New York.

Aznar Mendoza, Enrique
1947 "Historia de la industria henequenera desde 1919 hasta nuestros
días," Enciclopedia Yucatanense, Vol. III. México.

Aznar Pérez, Alonzo, and Rafael Pedrera
1849 Colección de leyes, decretos, y órdenes o acuerdos de tenencia
general del poder legislativo del estado libre y soberano de Yucatán.
3 vols. México.

Baqueiro, Serapio
1878 Ensayo histórico sobre las revoluciones de Yucatán desde el año
1840 hasta 1864. Mérida.

1907 Reseña geográfico histórica y estadística del estado de Yucatán.
México.

Baranda, Joaquín
1907 Recordaciones históricas. 2 vols. México.

Barrera Vásquez, Alfredo
1948 El libro de los Libros de Chilam Balam . . . con introducciones
y notas. México.

1961 "Contrato de un Maya de Yucatán, escrito en su lengua materna,
para servir en Cuba, en 1849," *Estudios de Cultura Maya,* pp. 199–211.
México.

Benítez, Fernando
1956 Ki, el drama de un pueblo y de una planta. México.

Berendt, Carl H.
1867 "Report of Exploration in Central America," in Smithsonian Institution, Annual Report for 1867, pp. 420–26. Washington, D.C.

Berkeley, [?]
1864 Report to the Governor of British Honduras, February 10, in
A.B.H.

Berzunza Pinto, Ramón
1949   Desde el fondo de los siglos, exégesis histórica de la Guerra de Castas. México.

Blake, William
1858   Various reports to the Governor of British Honduras, in A.B.H.

Burdon, John
1935   Archives of British Honduras. 3 vols. London.

Calcott, W. H.
1936   Santa Anna. Norman, Oklahoma.

Cámara Zavala, Felipe de la
1871   "Memorias de Don Felipe de la Cámara Zavala," Sunday editions of Diario de Yucatán for August and September 1928. Mérida.

Cámara Zavala, Gonzalo
1944   "Historia de la industria henequenera hasta 1919," in Enciclopedia Yucatanense, Vol. III. México.

Campos, Domingo
1849   "Relación que hace el doctor Don Domingo Campos de su viaje a Yucatán, y cuenta que dá al público de su piadosa comisión. México.

Canto López, Antonio
1954   El Territorio de Quintana Roo y Yucatán. Mérida.

Canto, Gregorio
1885   "Report on affairs at Chan Santa Cruz," in Ancona, Vol. IV, 432–34.

Chamberlain, Robert S.
1948   The Conquest and Colonization of Yucatan, 1517–1550. Carnegie Institution of Washington Publication 582. Washington, D.C.

Charnay, Désiré
1885   Les anciennes villes du Nouveau Monde: voyages d'exploration au Mexique et dans L'Amerique Centrale, 1857–1882. Paris.

1887   Ma dernière expédition au Yucatan. Paris. Translated into Spanish under the title "Viaje a Yucatán," by Francisco Cantón Rosado, Mérida, 1933.

Clegern, Wayne M.
1962 "British Honduras and the Pacification of Yucatan," *The Americas*, No. 18, 243–54.

Cline, Howard F.
1945 "Remarks on a Selected Bibliography of the Caste War and Allied Topics," Appendix C in Villa R. (1945).

1947 "The 'Aurora Yucateca' and the Spirit of Enterprise in Yucatan, 1821–1847," *Hispanic American Historical Review*, Vol. XXVII, No. 1.

1948 "The Sugar Episode in Yucatan, 1825–1850," *Inter-American Economic Affairs*, Vol. I, No. 4, pp. 79–100.

1950 Related Studies in Early Nineteenth Century Yucatecan Social History, in the Microfilm Collection of Manuscripts on Middle American Cultural Anthropology, No. XXXII, University of Chicago Library: "War of the Castes and the Independent Indian States of Yucatan" (1941); "War of the Castes and its Consequences" (1945); "Regionalism and Society in Yucatan, 1825–1847" (1947).

Diario de Yucatán
1907–10 Archives of C. R. Menéndez, Mérida.

Echánove Trujillo, Carlos
1944 "Manuel Crescencio Rejón," Enciclopedia Yucatanense, Vol. VII. México.

Ferrer de Mendiolea, Gabriel
1944 "Justo Sierra O'Reilly," Enciclopedia Yucatanense, Vol. VII. México.

1944 "Justo Sierra Méndez," Enciclopedia Yucatanense, Vol. VII. México.

1944 "Historia de las comunicaciones," Enciclopedia Yucatanense, Vol. III. México.

Foster, George M.
1960 Culture and Conquest, America's Spanish Heritage, Viking Fund Publications in Anthropology, No. 27. New York.

Fowler, Henry
1879 "A Narrative of a journey across the unexplored portion of British Honduras, with a short sketch of the history and resources of the colony." Belize.

Gann, Thomas W. F.
1918 "The Maya of Southern Yucatan and Northern British Honduras," Bureau of American Ethnology Bulletin 64. Washington, D.C.

1924 In an Unknown Land. New York.

García Guiot, Silvano
1944 "Pedro Sáinz de Baranda," Enciclopedia Yucatanense, Vol. VII. México.

García Preciat, José
1944 "Historia de la Arquitectura," Enciclopedia Yucatanense, Vol. IV. México.

Heller, Carl B.
1853 Reisen in Mexiko in den Jahren 1845–48. Leipzig.

Hernández, Juan José
1846 "Costumbres de los Indios de Yucatán," Registro Yucateco, 3: 290–98.

Hernández Fajardo, José
1944 "Historia de las artes minores," Enciclopedia Yucatanense, Vol. IV. México.

La Farge, Oliver, and Douglas S. Beyers
1931 "The Yearbearer's People," Middle American Research Series, No. 3, New Orleans.

1940 "Maya Ethnology: the Sequence of Cultures," in The Maya and Their Neighbors. Salt Lake City.

Lothrop, Samuel K.
1924 Tulum, an Archaeological Study of the East Coast of Yucatan. Carnegie Institution Publication 355. Washington, D.C.

Madariaga, Salvador de
1947 The Fall of the Spanish Empire. London.

Manzanilla, Yanuario
1888 Recuerdos de la campaña de los republicanos contra el Imperio en el Estado de Yucatán. Mérida.

Mason, Gregory
1927 Silver Cities of Yucatan. New York.

Méndez, Santiago
1861 "The Maya Indians of Yucatan in 1861," in Saville (1921).

Menéndez, Carlos R.
1923 Historia de infame y vergonzoso comercio de Indios vendidos a los esclavistas de Cuba por los políticos yucatecos desde 1848 hasta 1861,

justificación de la revolución indígena de 1847, documentos irrefutables que lo comprueban. Mérida.
1937   90 años de historia de Yucatán. Mérida.

Menéndez, Gabriel Antonio
1936   Quintana Roo, Album monográfico. México.

Miller, William
1889   "The Indians of Santa Cruz," Proceedings of the Royal Geographic Society, N.S. II, pp. 23–28. London.

Molina Font, Gustavo
1941   La Tragedia de Yucatán. México.

Molina Solís, Juan Francisco
1921–27   Historia de Yucatán desde la Independencia de España hasta la época actual. 2 vols. Mérida.

Norman, B. H.
1843   Rambles in Yucatan, or notes of travel through the Peninsula including a visit to the remarkable ruins of Chichen, Kabah, Zayi, and Uxmal. New York.

Pacheco Cruz, Santiago
1934   Estudio etnográfico de los Mayas del ex territorio Quintana Roo. Mérida.
1953   Diccionario de etimologías toponímicas Maya. Chetumal.

Palma Cámara, Fernando
1944   "Historia de la legislación desde la Conquista Europea," Enciclopedia Yucatanense, Vol. III. México.

Pérez, Gregorio
1906   El Ahorcado de 1848. Mérida.

Pineda, Vicente
1888   Historia de los Sublevaciones Indígenas habidas en el Estado de Chiapas. Chiapas.

Plumridge, [Lieutenant]
1861   Report of a visit to Chan Santa Cruz, April 12, in A.B.H.

Redfield, Robert
1941   The Folk Culture of Yucatan. Chicago.

———, and Alfonso Villa R.[ojas]
1934   Chan Kom, A Maya Village. Carnegie Institution of Washington Publication 488. Washington, D.C.

Regil, José María, and Alonzo Manuel Peón
1853   "Estadística de Yucatán," Sociedad Mexicana de Geografía y Estadística, *Boletín* 3: 237–40.

Rosado, José Hilario
1889   "Report on Affairs at Chan Santa Cruz," *Diario de Yucatán*, January 11. Mérida.

Roys, Ralph L.
1933   The Book of Chilam Balam of Chumayel. Carnegie Institution of Washington Publication 438. Washington, D.C.

1939   The Titles of Ebtun. Carnegie Institution of Washington Publication 505. Washington, D.C.

1943   The Indian Background of Colonial Yucatan. Carnegie Institution of Washington Publication 548. Washington, D.C.

1957   Political Geography of the Yucatecan Maya. Carnegie Institution of Washington Publication 613. Washington, D.C.

Sapper, Karl
1904   "Independent Indian States of Yucatan," translated from the German in Bureau of American Ethnology Bulletin 28, 623–24. Washington, D.C.

Saville, Marshall H.
1921   "Reports on the Maya Indians of Yucatan," Museum of the American Indian, Heye Foundation, Indian Notes and Monographs, 9: 143–95. New York.

Severo de Castillo, [?]
1869   Cecilio Chi. Mérida.

Seymour, [?]
1858   Report of November 17, in A.B.H.

Shaffer, Ernesto
1951   "El Corregidor del Petén, Cnel. Modesto Méndez," *Antropología e Historia de Guatemala,* Vol. III, No. 1.

Sierra O'Reilly, Justo
1847–48   Diario de nuestro viaje a los Estados Unidos. Published in 1938 with preface and notes by Hector Pérez Martínez, ed., México.

1861   "Informe sobre rentas eclesiásticas en el Estado de Yucatán," in Suárez Navarro (1861).

Soza, José María
1957   Pequeña Monografía del Petén. Guatemala.

Stephens, John L., and Frederick Catherwood
1841 Incidents of Travel in Central America, Chiapas, and Yucatan. 2 vols. New York.
1843 Incidents of Travel in Yucatan. 2 vols. New York.

Stevenson, William
1856 Various reports in A.B.H.

Suárez Navarrete, Pablo
1850 Letter of June 1 from New Orleans, in Menéndez (1923).

Suárez Navarro, Juan
1861 Informe sobre los cambios políticos de Yucatán. México.

Thompson, Edward H.
1905 "A Page of American History," American Antiquarian Society, Proceedings, N.S. 17: 239–52.
1932 People of the Serpent. New York.

Tozzer, Alfred
1907 "A Comparative Study of the Mayas and the Lacandones," Archeological Institute of America, Report of Fellow in American Archeology, 1902–5. New York.
1921 A Maya Grammar. Peabody Museum Papers, 9. Cambridge, Massachusetts.
1941 Landa's Relación de los Cosas de Yucatán. Peabody Museum Papers, Vol. XVIII. Cambridge, Massachusetts.

Traconis, Daniel
1871 "Diario de las operaciones de la Expedición militar contra los indios rebeldes, al oriente de la peninsula," Diario de Yucatán, April 28, May 5 and 12, 1935. Mérida.

Trejo, José María
1861 Report of a trip to Chan Santa Cruz, April 12, in A.B.H.

Trujillo, Narcisa
1944 "Las primeras máquinas desfibradoras de henequén," Enciclopedia Yucatanense, Vol. III. México.

United States Senate
1847–48 Executive Documents, 30th Congress, 1st session, Vols. 5 and 6, Documents 40, 42, 43, 45, and 49. Washington, D.C.

Valadés, José C.
1944 "José María Gutiérrez de Estrada," Enciclopedia Yucatanense, Vol. VII. México.

Villa R.[ojas], Alfonso
   1945   The Maya of East Central Quintana Roo. Carnegie Institution of
   of Washington Publication 559. Washington, D.C.

Vogt, Evon Z.
   1961   "Some Aspects of Zinacantan Settlement Patterns and Ceremonial
   Organization," *Estudios de Cultura Maya*, II, 131–47. México.

Waldeck, Jean Frederick
   1835   Voyage Pittoresque et Archéologique dans la Province de Yucatan. Paris.

Wallace, Edward S.
   1957   Destiny and Glory. New York.

Williams, Mary Wilhelmine
   1929   "The Secessionist Diplomacy of Yucatan," *Hispanic American
   Historical Review*, IX, 132–43.

Index

Acereto, Agustín, 177, 179
Acereto, Pedro, 176ff
Alvarado, Salvador, 249, 258–60, 262–63
Alayon, J. Antonio, 234
Amalia, María Carlota, 191–92, 198
American Indians, 133
American volunteers in Caste War, 110–14 *passim*, 123
Ampudia, Pedro de, 163
Ancona, Eligio, 155
Ancona, Manuel Romero, 230
Anderson, Captain, 171
Avila, Eleuterio, 257
Ay, Manuel Antonio, 48, 55f, 57, 59, 151

Bacelis, Onofre, 166, 169
Balam Na, 173–74, 245–46, 271
Baqueiro, Civilo, 140, 143f, 165
Baqueiro, Serapio, 137, 155, 232
Barbachano, Miguel: early political career, 28, 32ff, 46; and Mérida revolt of 1847, 54, 61, 64; alliance with Méndez, 75f; negotiates treaty with Pat, 86; becomes governor, 87; renews Méndez's offer of sovereignty, 103; declares reunification with Mexico, 104; tries to isolate Belize from the Maya, 115–16; begins slave trade, 128–29; succeeds Méndez as governor, 148f; death of, 163–64
Barrera, Agustín, 161, 221
Barrera, José María, 69, 143, 149, 151; as Pat's field commander, 76, 87, 93, 106, 108, 112; captures Tituc, 123–24; and peace negotiations of 1850, 126–27; establishes cult of the Speaking Cross, 135–41; attacks Chichenha, 141; successors to, 160–61
Barrera, Pantaleón, 164f, 176
Barrera, Pedro Pascual, 161, 228, 251, 254

Barret, Domingo, 33, 53f, 61
Be, Lorenzo, 275
Beitia, Captain, 56, 59f
Belize: colonization of, 18; trade and gunrunning, 68, 85, 124–25, 131; Cruzob relations with, 170–73, 181–84, 189, 191, 201–5, 226–28; closed to trade with the Maya, 227–28, 236–38
Bello, Carmen, 94–95, 98
Blake, William, 170–71
Blanco, Othón, 236–38
Blanquet, Aurelio, 244
Books of Chilam Balam. *See* Chilam Balam
Bolio, Miguel, 65, 67, 80ff
Bravo, Ignacio, 229, 238–41, 245f, 248
British Honduras. *See* Belize
Bureau, Domingo, 193

Caamal, Anastasio, 213
Cádenas, José, 129, 141, 163
Cámara Zavala, Felipe de la, 144
Can, Eulalio, 254
Canek, Hyacinth, 48
Canek, Jacinto, 43, 46, 109, 190
Canto Echeverría, 267
Canto, Teodosio, 221
Cantón, Gregorio, 149–50
Cantón, Francisco: 190f, 230, 238, 241f; and siege of Tihosuco in 1866, 193; and overthrow of the Empire, 196, 198; revolts of, 229–30
Canul, Marcos, 201–4 *passim*
Canul, Raimundo, 272–80 *passim*
Canuto Vela, José, 76, 87f, 125–26, 127, 151
Cárdenas, Lázaro, 265–67
Cargo Cult, 132–33
Carmen Bello, José del, 94–95, 98
Carmichael, John, 200–201, 203f
Carranza, Venustiano, 252, 257, 262
Casanova, Francisco, 193